LOUIS PASTEUR

Ten Frenchmen *of the* Nineteenth Century

BY

F. M. WARREN, Ph.D., L.H.D.

PROFESSOR OF MODERN LANGUAGES IN
YALE UNIVERSITY

Author of

"A Primer of French Literature," "A History of the
Novel previous to the Seventeenth Century," etc.

The Chautauqua Press

CHAUTAUQUA, N. Y.

MCMIV

CONTENTS

CHAPTER   PAGE

I. INTRODUCTION - - - - - I

II. GUIZOT AND THE CAUSE OF CONSTITUTIONAL MONARCHY - - - - - 16

III. FOURIER AND SOCIALISM - - - - 43

IV. THIERS AND THE GROWTH OF REPUBLICAN PRINCIPLES - - - - - 70

V. GAMBETTA AND THE THIRD REPUBLIC - - 96

VI. VICTOR HUGO - - - - - 117

VII. BALZAC AND REALISM IN LITERATURE - - 147

VIII. ZOLA - - - - - - 176

IX. RENAN AND BIBLICAL CRITICISM - - 202

X. PASTEUR AND THE GERM THEORY - - 229

XI. DE LESSEPS AND INTER-OCEANIC CANALS - 249

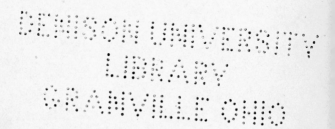

LIST OF ILLUSTRATIONS

PAGE

Louis Pasteur - - - - Frontispiece

François Pierre Guillaume Guizot - - - 16

François Marie Charles Fourier - - 43

Louis Adolphe Thiers - - - - - 70

Léon Michel Gambetta - - - - 96

Victor Marie Hugo - - - - - 117

Honoré de Balzac - - - - - 147

Émile Édouard Charles Antoine Zola - - 176

Joseph Ernest Renan - - - - 202

Ferdinand Marie de Lesseps - - - - 249

TEN FRENCHMEN OF THE NINETEENTH CENTURY

CHAPTER I

INTRODUCTION

The achievements of the nineteenth century were the carrying out of the ideas of the eighteenth. Before the French Revolution men theorized; after it they employed themselves in turning the theories into facts. Science left the study for the shop; steam and electricity were put to practical uses; chemistry became a handmaid to industry; while physiology created medicine anew. Likewise in public affairs. The application of the social views of philosophers and essayists transformed governments, changed constitutions, created states.

THE FRENCH REVOLUTION AND FRANCE

In no country of Christendom were these results so evident as in France. By the temperament of its people France is subject to violent changes. Other nations yield to the invasion of new ideas gradually, peacefully. In France devotion to tradition and custom is so strong in all matters of private or public import that the forms of the past continue to stand after their content is exhausted. They must be broken by the impact of other forms of new and vigorous content. Hence revolutions in politics and literature, violent antagonisms, strifes between the living present and the dead past. The French Revolution is an instance of the way changes in politics are made. By their attacks on religious and civil authority, which went hand in hand in old France, Voltaire and his allies destroyed respect for creed and statute. Their influence was wholly towards pulling down. With his dreams of the primitive happiness of man, a golden age which civilization had corroded and tarnished, Rousseau showed how justice and truth would be found only in a return to nature and a purely democratic state. He would destroy, but in order to create anew. The skepticism of Voltaire and the faith of Rousseau met in the French Revolution. Faith won, as always, and from the chaos of the Reign of Terror a new France emerged.

THE WORK OF NAPOLEON

This new France was a land of passion. It believed it had a mission: to proclaim liberty, equality, and fraternity to all mankind, and free from injustice and oppression the peoples of the world. To direct this enthusiasm Providence raised up a leader. Bonaparte was a great administrator. Modern times have not seen his equal in this respect. His foreign wars may not have been an unmixed blessing to Europe, and were quite certainly an evil to France; but they carried abroad the principles of liberty, and made Germany and Italy nations. His work at home, however, was beneficial. It fashioned the France of the present day. The results of the Revolution were accepted, and incorporated into the common law of the land. Peasant proprietorship was sanctioned, and primogeniture abolished. To recompense the Church for the loss of its revenues appropriations were granted direct from the public treasury. Public improvements were planned, set on foot, and carried out in many instances. The internal administration of the country was systematized, and concentrated in the central authority. Art and science were fostered. Whatever the political vicissitudes which have followed, France has remained in all essential particulars the France of the Empire.

THE RESTORATION

With Napoleon finally at St. Helena, Louis XVIII on the throne, and the emigrant nobles back after a twenty years' exile, during which little notion of the great changes at home had entered their minds, France seemed in fair way to return to the ideas of the eighteenth century. The great bulwark against this ebb in the social tide was the peasant proprietorship, sanctioned by the Napoleonic Code. Country and city, though weary of war, joined in successful resistance to a political reaction. Fifteen years after Waterloo the Bourbons fled, never to return.

But the Restoration did more than hold the ground gained by the Revolution. Its era of peace fostered learning and literature. Science became more and more experimental. Literature, which had been antagonized in its development by the pagan ideals of the Revolution, renewed its connection with the nature-worship of Rousseau, who had rejected classical models. Its votaries were divided into two camps. One party became deeply religious. Turning away from antiquity it found new and Christian sources of inspiration in the writings and art of the Middle Ages. Chateaubriand headed this group, and many of its members wrote under the influence of English and Ger-

man romanticists. In politics this faction was conservative, reactionary. The other camp held the liberals, the
advocates of democracy and equality of sex. In matters
of religion it sided with Voltaire, though its leaders,
Mme. de Staël, and later, George Sand, were the especial
disciples of Rousseau. This group was much less numerous than the other. Perhaps also the division between
the two is more apparent than real. It is strongly marked
only in religious belief and in politics, and towards 1830
both factions found themselves united in the French
Romantic School. This school included poets like Hugo
and Lamartine, and historians like Thierry and Guizot.
Beside them stood the romanticists of art, Boulanger and
David d'Angers.

THE REIGN OF LOUIS PHILIPPE

Liberalism in politics triumphed in the July Revolution
of 1830. The aristocracy of birth, which strenuously
held to the ways of old France, was supplanted by the
caste of bankers and merchants, the Third Estate, which
had made the French Revolution, and was now demanding
the fruits of its labors. The new monarch, Louis Philippe,
of the House of Orleans, a man of simple and democratic
ways, received his throne at the hands of Parliament.
Napoleon had recognized the democratic principle. His
generals had risen from the ranks and had become the
dukes and princes of a new nobility. The year 1830,
therefore, in many ways joined on to 1815. A significant sign of this close connection was the substitution of
the tri-colored flag of the Empire for the royal white
banner and golden lilies of the Restoration. But the July
monarchy was in favor of peace. It was a business man's

government. The only war it was called upon to undertake was one of territorial aggrandizement, by which Algeria was added to the possessions of France.

Still the inevitable evolution of the principles of the French Revolution—liberty, equality, fraternity—went on under this rule of the *bourgeoisie.* The constitution of the country was patterned on the constitution of England. A property qualification underlay tenure of office and the suffrage. In the eyes of the masses this was not equality. Democratic ideas flourished. Socialism found advocates in theory and practice. The government did not understand how to trim its sails to ride out the growing storm, and the Revolution of 1848, supported by the mechanics and day laborers, drove it from power.

During this period of eighteen years many men of letters had played at politics. Thiers and Guizot, both historians by vocation, had in turn guided the destinies of the nation. The glory of the Empire, now seen in retrospect, had thrown its suffering into the shade. The so-called Napoleonic legend had daily been gaining strength. The triumphal recovery of the remains of the emperor, in 1840, and their interment at the Invalides had aroused an enthusiasm which disturbed the monarchy and cost Thiers his office. Guizot's failure to comprehend the times and their demands forced the crisis of 1848. Other writers who took part in public affairs, as Lamartine and Hugo, attained no more lasting success. As republicans they survived 1848, but only to lose place and power in the stormy years that followed.

Their contributions to the literature of their country were, however, more beneficial and more lasting. Around Hugo the second generation of romanticists had gathered,

Alfred de Musset, Théophile Gautier, Sainte-Beuve. In sympathy with them, but not in such close touch, were the other great writers of the Romantic School, Alexandre Dumas and George Sand. Inspired by them and inspiring them in turn were the artists Horace Vernet and Delacroix; the musicians Chopin, Meyerbeer, and Rossini. On the other hand, opponents of romantic views, while partly imbued with them, included the first and the best of the realists, Stendhal and Balzac. They did not care for art, they gave little heed to style. Observation directed their pen, not imagination; what they saw, rather than what they felt. They left emotion and sentiment to the romanticists. Skeptics in religion, conceiving life to be a struggle for material enjoyment, in which the strongest and shrewdest succeeds, taking their model from Napoleon, the great *parvenu*, and possessed with the spirit of the exact sciences, they substituted in their works descriptions for emotions, the careful narrative of physical man and his surroundings for a picture of the human soul, and the heroes of the shop and professions for the knights of the Middle Ages and the musketeers of Louis XIII. The Third Estate had seized the political power. Why should it not be eulogized in more lasting annals? Some of the realists went farther. Eugene Sue laid the plots of his romances in the resorts of the revolutionists of 1848.

THE SECOND EMPIRE

The Republic of 1848 proved to be lacking in vitality. Its leading men were theorists or Jacobins, and France was not yet ready for representative government pure and simple. The Republic established universal suffrage, and fell at once into the hands of Louis Napoleon, whom uni-

versal suffrage first elected president, then president for
ten years, and finally emperor. The attempt to return
to the political ideas of 1793 had failed. Public opinion
forced on the country a despotism, for fear of a lapse
recurring to the anarchy of the Reign of Terror, and
socialistic views of ownership.

The main strength of Napoleon III was derived from
the Napoleonic legend, which had grown until it had quite
crowded out all other political sentiment. But he possessed also a keen appreciation of the desires of the French
people, knew foreign countries, was inclined towards
idealism. He declared at once for peace and industry,
and in public affairs leaned towards the establishment of
a constitutional monarchy. His internal administration
was excellent. Important works of improvement were
undertaken in the larger towns. Paris was made over,
given parks and public buildings. Universal expositions
in 1855 and 1867 fostered national industry and art.
And all the while the absolute autocracy of the earlier
years was yielding little by little to the increasing demand
for liberty of thought and action. But in foreign affairs
his rule was singularly unfortunate. Intent on making
France the center of European diplomacy, and on cheaply
purchasing a large amount of military glory, Napoleon III
engaged in alliances and expeditions more and more unfortunate. The Crimean War, in which he opposed Russia,
the natural ally of France, and assisted in perpetuating
the power of the Turk in Europe, the Italian War of
1859, which ended in a way unsatisfactory to the Italians,
the Roman Catholics, and Europe generally, his unfortunate attempt to found a Latin state in Mexico were each
recognized at the time or later to have constituted a series

of political mistakes, from which France had gained nothing but enmity and distrust. The final blunder of the Franco-Prussian War proved fatal to the Empire.

In the domain of ideas the Second Empire did not show the robustness of either the Bourbon or the Orleanist monarchy. Its pretense of religion and morality was regarded in many quarters as a sham, a cloak to cover irreligion and wrongdoing. However this may have been, the popular philosophy among the scientists was Comte's positivism, which formulated agnosticism. The effect of this creed on literature was striking. With 1848 romanticism had ceased to rule, and the best of realism had departed. Chateaubriand had died in that year, and Balzac in 1850. Lamartine had turned hack-writer, De Musset's muse was silent. George Sand had retired to the country, and the *coup d'état* of 1851 had driven Hugo into exile. · Yet experimental science grew, favoring mental doubt until results have been attained, while criticism and research occupied the greater talents, who looked to Germany and England for guidance. These include Renan, the historian; Littré, a disciple of Comte, the linguist and essayist; and Taine, of the same school, the critic.

Of works of the imagination there are few, apart from Hugo's novels and poetry; for realism in literature had degenerated into a bastard naturalism. Man passed more and more for a mere animal, an animal endowed with evil instincts to the exclusion of the good. The novelist of the day, Flaubert, is a chronicler of human imbecility and physical decay. Baudelaire gave these ideas expression in verse, while a new school of poets, the Parnassians, were devoting their energies to the perfection of technique and form. The drama, in its representatives, the younger Dumas and Augier, portrays the unwholesome traits of contemporaneous manners or argues for reform in social conditions. It is realistic, like Balzac.

Art also left the domain of the imagination for the field of observation. Studies of nature, landscapes, attained unwonted excellence in the paintings of the Barbizon School. The Empire also had its eulogists, who delineated with extreme care and attention to detail the battles of the Grand Army and the military experiences of Napoleon III. Towards the end of the period a revolt in the direction of naturalism becomes manifest. More freedom, a broader treatment, a rejection of conventional themes and color, point the way to greater originality of thought and expression. But official influence was ever on the side of conservatism in either literature or art. Censorship was often exercised.

THE THIRD REPUBLIC

The battle of Sedan brought the opposition to imperialism to the front, and the republicans of Paris, unrestrained by the presence of the regular army, captive or besieged, proclaimed the Third Republic. The numeral is significant. It preserves the memory of the French Revolution and the Republic of 1848. There is no question but that the nation as a whole was taken by surprise by this action of the Parisians. For when, after the war and the Commune, deputies were elected to the National Assembly, it was found that the republicans were in a minority. But the majority was made up of such antagonistic factions— Bonapartists from the north, Bourbons from the west, and Orleanists from many districts controlled by the *bourgeoisie*—

that no agreement among them was possible, and the
Republic continued by sufferance. For nearly twenty
years this peculiar state of affairs lasted. The existence
of the government was often menaced. It often seemed
on the verge of destruction. But it was not destroyed,
and since 1890 its stability has not been seriously doubted.
From a strife between partisans of a monarchy or empire
and partisans of representative government, the political
contest within the country has passed to the usual struggle
between liberals and conservatives. Religious opinion
forms much of the party difference. The liberals, who
include the moderate socialists, are on the whole against
Church influence in public affairs. The conservatives are
quite generally stanch churchmen.

The Republic has shown itself fairly competent in the
management of internal affairs. The centralized system
of administration, established by Napoleon, remains in
full force, though many of the more enlightened citizens
favor greater local autonomy, and some steps have been
taken toward increasing the attractions of other towns
than Paris. This is especially noticeable in the matter of
education. Shortly before the fall of the Second Empire,
the minister of public instruction, Victor Duruy, the historian, brought forward a measure for the extension of
common schools under governmental direction. Primary
education had been almost entirely in the control of the
Church. The Republic, with its leanings away from
clericalism, succeeded to Duruy's idea and pushed it forward until the youth of France of both sexes enjoy practically the same educational privileges that are enjoyed in
Germany. Hand in hand with this movement has gone
the development and improvement of the more advanced

schools of learning. Universities in the provinces, at
Grenoble, Montpellier, Toulouse, or Lyons, have enlarged
their resources quite as much as the University of Paris.
Scientific privileges formerly concentrated in the capital
are now available in the more remote districts also.

In the matter of public works the present government
has continued the plans of the Empire. The buildings in
Paris ruined by the Commune have been in part replaced,
and with greater magnificence. Broad avenues have taken
the place of city alleys, bridges have been constructed,
while the expositions of 1878, 1889, and 1900 have fairly
outdone the fairs of the Second Empire. The policy of
fostering art has been continued, museums have been
multiplied, and private individuals have vied with the state
in increasing the collections open to the public. A notable
instance is the gift of the old Condé estate at Chantilly by
one of the Orleanist princes, the Duc d'Aumale, to the
Institute of France. No previous era has seen so much
done for the enlightenment and comfort of the people.
At the present time the chief obstacle to the success of
the existing régime in France is the burden of taxation
which its military budget lays upon the people. Neither
monarchy nor empire had to contend with expenditures
for war when there was no war.

In foreign affairs the Republic has followed the vacil-
lating policy of its predecessor. It has in turn estranged
and reconciled Italy, has shown its sympathy with Spain,
during the Spanish-American War, and its distrust of
England. But no complications have ensued because of
its feelings—other than those of a tariff war with Italy.
And to its great credit can be placed the alliance with
Russia, the utility of which had appealed to Bonaparte,

but had escaped his nephew, Napoleon III. The wars it has waged have been small, if unfruitful, prompted by the spirit of colonization. Algeria has always been commercially unprofitable. Now Tunis has been added to it under the guise of a French protectorate. Expeditions to the eastern seas have also been undertaken. Tonquin was wrested from China, and Madagascar from its native rulers. All these petty campaigns have involved some expenditure of blood and still occasion considerable expenditure of money. It is a question whether the resources thus applied might not have been employed at home to better advantage. The French do not colonize. They wisely prefer to dwell in their own fair land.

The progress of ideas under the Third Republic has kept pace with the evolution of western thought. Inventions and discoveries—notably those of Pasteur in the line of chemistry—have contributed their share to the advancement of mankind. In all departments of science there are many workers, some of whom have attained eminence. Literature has suffered, as it has everywhere else. Its springs of inspiration, imaginative or realistic, seem to have dried up. Hugo, the great genius, who had labored in all the epochs of the century since Waterloo, worked on in this also in full possession of his powers; but there was no one to bear him company. In fiction the better writers are realists or naturalists, like Daudet and Zola. In poetry the Parnassians, who counted among their number two men of note, Coppée and Sully-Prudhomme, were soon opposed by the symbolists, who tried to carry poetry back to its origin in music, appealing to the ear and not the eye. The dramatists of the Empire have had no successors. The stage has been occupied with theatrical experiments, more or less realistic in their bent, and is now freed of all conventional restraints. Rules of construction have given way to complete liberty. Throughout the whole period the influence of Russian and Scandinavian writers has been plain, affecting now fiction, now drama. But on the whole the various branches of literature, having exhausted the impetus born of the social changes which produced the French Revolution, are waiting for new sources of emotion to reveal themselves.

THE PRESENT OUTLOOK

The future of France may be judged to some extent from her past. In government she may have reached her goal. No other form of administration since the French Revolution has lasted so long as the Third Republic. Its existence has at times been precarious, but it has survived the revival of Cæsarism in Boulanger, the financial scandal of the Panama Canal, the injustice and party spirit of the Dreyfus affair. There is every likelihood that its strength of resistance will grow. In the thirty-four years since Sedan a whole generation has come to maturity, a generation which neither ties of sentiment nor of self-interest attach to a dynasty. The common-school system, spread throughout the land, is in itself a great protection against reaction to a monarchy, where clerical instructors and parochial education would be supreme. Pretenders to the throne are too far removed in blood from the old sovereigns to create any serious diversion in their favor. In foreign affairs the Republic has attained a position of dignity.

Among the French people there is a visible drift towards socialism, as in all other countries. But in

France this drift is opposed even more resolutely than elsewhere by the peasant proprietors and the steady, self-centered *bourgeoisie*. Legislation in behalf of the artisans and non-property-holding classes may be expected, forced as elsewhere by the broadening of the democratic principle and the growth of altruism. But revolutions should be less and less feared as the people learn the art of self-government, and acquire the habit of making the ballot-box the arbiter of disputes. Some decentralization will undoubtedly be carried through, as much as the genius of the nation, which demands order and unity, will allow. In short, the Republic will continue to be, but it will continue to be French, not Germanic nor Anglo-Saxon. Offering, as it does, full play to the expression of individual thought and opinion, it should be more completely representative of French genius than any despotic or restricted kind of administration.

As a military power the France of the future will be of less consequence than the France of the past. And the France of the future will also be a less important factor in the industrial world. Individual selfishness and the selfishness of family feeling combine to restrict that growth in population which is a necessary foundation of enterprise and power. If children only avail to fill the places vacated by their parents, invention will decline and the power of initiative will be dwarfed for lack of exercise. But France will continue to lead the nations in taste and art. She is the Greece of the modern world. To an unusual degree receptive of ideas, from whatever quarter they may come, she assimilates these ideas, recasts them, and presents them again to their originators clad in her own inimitable form. This process has been repeated at every stage of her existence, since the battle of Hastings and the crusade of Peter the Hermit, ever since France has felt herself a nation. It will continue until she ceases to be a nation. For her supremacy does not rest on the might of armies, but on the charm of thought.

BIBLIOGRAPHY

The French People. Arthur Hassall.
Modern France, 1789–1895. André Lebon.

CHAPTER II

GUIZOT AND THE CAUSE OF CONSTITUTIONAL MONARCHY

[FRANÇOIS PIERRE GUILLAUME GUIZOT, born at Nîmes, October 4, 1787; Adjunct Professor of Modern History in the University of Paris, 1812; Secretary-General in the Ministry of the Interior under Louis XVIII, 1814; Counselor of State, 1816–1820; deputy from Lisieux and Minister of the Interior, 1830; Minister of Public Instruction, 1832–1836; member of the French Academy, 1836; Ambassador to England, 1840; Minister of Foreign Affairs and Prime Minister, 1840–1848; Died at Val Richer, in Normandy, September 12, 1874. Principal works: "History of Civilization in Europe," 1828; "History of Civilization in France," 1830.]

The fall of Napoleon was brought about quite as much by the exhaustion of France as by the uprising of Europe. For two decades the French people had lived in a state of almost constant alarm. Campaign had succeeded campaign with but short intervals of intermission. To defend the existence of the Republic at first and afterwards to maintain the glories of the Empire, the mask under which Bonaparte concealed his personal ambition, the land had been fairly drained of able-bodied men, and disease and death had seated themselves in the corner of every hearth. Through these privations the nation as a whole had wearied of war. The return of Napoleon from Elba met with only moderate enthusiasm. Few save his restless veterans gathered around his standard. The country longed for peace. For peace it was ready to sacrifice its

FRANÇOIS PIERRE GUILLAUME GUIZOT

ambition and much of its pride, and Waterloo occasioned
at the time but slight regrets.

Still the task which devolved on the monarchy of Louis
XVIII was not an easy one.   The sympathies of the king
were naturally with the old order of things.   His court,
composed in large part of the nobility which had fled from
France during the Revolution, and whose estates had been
confiscated by the government in consequence, was moved
by every private interest to help undo the work of the
administrations which had remade France during its
absence.   But almost at the other end of the social scale
was the large body of newly created proprietors, peasants,
and small tradesmen, who had held by law these confiscated estates for twenty years and more.   Whether their
title was based on right or not, they constituted so numerous an element of the population, perhaps even the majority, that it was out of the question to dispossess them.
And in the center was the great French *bourgeoisie*, which
had carried on the Revolution in order to secure its natural
rights, and had increased its wealth gained by manufacturing and commerce to a degree that made it the equal
of the nobility in all material things.   This class aimed at
social equality, and possessed the means requisite to reach
that goal.   Over against the nobles its interests lay with
the peasant proprietors.   The alliance was formidable,
preponderant.   The advisers of the restored monarchy
were forced to heed it.   All but the most narrow of the
émigrés at once realized that the *ancien régime* was gone
beyond recall.   The age of special privilege bestowed by
birth had passed.   It was probable that the influence of
the former privileged class would wane.   The rising tide
of democracy, which had swept the state from its moor-

ings during the Reign of Terror, had found a ruler to be
sure in Bonaparte, but a ruler who increased its volume
while curbing its current.   His check removed, if it was
not to engulf anew the whole social fabric, a dike was
necessary.   This dike could only be found in a union of
the nobility with the upper *bourgeoisie.*   Such was the
political problem of France from 1815 to 1848.

Foreigners think of Guizot as a great historian; and
in truth, his historical work constitutes the lasting basis of
his fame.   But he himself desired to be regarded as a
statesman, and the years of his most vigorous manhood
were given over to politics.   Born in Nîmes, the old
Roman town in the south of France, in 1787, but two
years before the beginning of the French Revolution, his
career was both made and marred by that great event.
It was made because he was a child of Protestant parents,
and Protestants of the *bourgeois* grade could hope for little
favor in royal France.   It was marred because Guizot's
father, a zealous advocate of liberty, was revolted by the
horrors of the Reign of Terror, and answered for his
defection with his head, in 1794.   The mother remained,
a woman of unusual endowments of mind and firmness of
character.   Under her steady hand the young François
grew to manhood.   She had fled to Geneva with her
family, and there, under the protection of a republican
form of government, and perhaps subjected to the leveling
theories of Rousseau, a native of Geneva, the son began
his education and learned the carpenter's trade.   In 1805
he went to Paris to study law, and at once showed his
aptitude for a literary calling.   Journal articles, reviews,
essays, books even, followed one another in rapid succession, for Guizot ever possessed the capacity for hard labor.

Finally an annotated translation of Gibbon's "History" gave evidence of his real talent, and brought about, in 1812, his nomination to the chair of history at the university. With his opening lecture his conception of historical investigation was formulated, the school of philosophical history was founded.

The abdication of Napoleon called Guizot into political life as an officer in the Interior Department. But he soon found that the royalists had much to learn, and provoked by their arrogant demands, he resigned his post on the eve of Napoleon's return from Elba. During the Hundred Days, however, the group of liberals who wished a constitutional monarchy, shaped according to the English pattern, perfected a tentative organization. Guizot was their chosen spokesman, and before Waterloo was fought had already carried to Louis XVIII, who had taken refuge in Ghent, their advice to accept the work of the Revolution without reservation, and dismiss all reactionary councilors. This embassy to the exiled king, at a time when France was again engaged in foreign wars, was never forgiven by the Bonapartists. In the days of Guizot's unpopularity it was the great reproach that his enemies cast upon him, so that even the urchins in the streets of Paris were familiar with "that rascal of a Guizot who went to Ghent," without knowing in the least what the phrase meant.

The Second Restoration called him back into the administration. Again his moderation, his middle course, opposed at once to the extreme reaction towards the old rule and to the claims of unrestrained popular sovereignty, ruined his political prospects. He and his friends, men of patriotism and learning, wished a government which should recognize the existing material and social status of the country, and should rule through a sovereign held in check by a constitution and by a parliament, elected from such limited number of citizens as possessed the requisite property qualifications. This program satisfied neither the people nor the nobles. It seems to have been neither reactionary nor progressive. It tried to hold things as they were. The members of this group were maliciously termed "Doctrinaires," and their downfall in 1820 was rejoiced in by both liberals and conservatives. This catastrophe, however, restored Guizot to his professor's chair, and marks the beginning of his professional reputation.

Lectures, political pamphlets against the government, and historical publications succeeded or accompanied one another during the next decade. Because of his attitude as an opponent the government took the extreme measure of suspending his courses from 1825 to 1828. But this punishment only allowed the student greater opportunity to prosecute his private work. It was also a great factor in increasing his popularity with all classes of society. When, in 1828, he was allowed to resume the duties of his chair, he was greeted with an enthusiasm that quickened his natural genius to an unwonted degree, and made the next two years the brilliant ones in the annals of historical science. For Guizot's fame rests on his professional writings of this period. They are numerous and weighty. In their preparation he received a very considerable help from his talented wife, particularly in the great collection of "Memoirs Relating to Mediæval French History" and the "Memoirs Relating to the English Revolution" (under Cromwell), both of which seem to

have been planned by her.   From Guizot's own pen came
the "Essays on the History of France in the Fifth Century," the "History of the English Revolution," and
finally the fundamental treatises of the "History of Civilization in Europe" and the "History of Civilization in
France."   In the field of pure literature he gave his name
to a revision of a translation of Shakespeare, made by
Letourneur in the eighteenth century—most of which was
due to the hand of Madame Guizot—to which he prefaced
an introduction on "Shakespeare and Dramatic Poetry."
This essay discusses the comparative merits of the romantic theater, as represented by the great Englishman, and
the classical stage, as conceived by Voltaire.   Guizot,
with the great men of his time, was a romanticist.   In
1828 he also assumed the editorship of the *Revue Française*, the forerunner of the *Revue des Deux Mondes*.

An election to the Chamber of Deputies in 1830, and
the July Revolution, which quickly followed, once again
transformed the historian into the politician.   The latter's
views had not been modified during the years of opposition to royal authority.   He still held for a constitutional
monarchy based on restricted suffrage.   For a time this
moderate measure was satisfactory to the nation.   Guizot
successively filled various offices of public trust, in which
he came into contact with Thiers, who was just beginning
his long career of varied success, which was to culminate
in the presidency of the third and lasting Republic.   In
the most notable of the ministries formed between 1830
and 1840 our author won the gratitude of the country by
his reorganization of the system of public education.
When he retired from power in 1836 he found the doors
of the French Academy open to him.   Before this emi-

nent body, composed of the great names of France, he was destined to repeat the oratorical triumphs of the parliamentary tribune. His chief contribution to literature during this decade was one well calculated to attract the attention of Americans. At the request of the trans-Atlantic editors Guizot chose from Sparks's "Washington" what he judged to be best suited to interest and instruct the French people. He translated and published this selection with an essay on Washington's life (1840), which at once took first rank among the masterpieces of biography. There is little doubt that Guizot thought he saw in the calm equipoise of the great leader of our own Revolution a counterpart of his own political moderation, and we may safely assume that the firmness of Washington in the midst of the turmoils of his public life inspired Guizot in maintaining a rigidity of principle which was not justified by the surroundings of a later generation.

A short residence in London, as ambassador to the court of Saint James, preluded a greater participation of Guizot in the political affairs of France. Though in the ministry which was formed in the autumn of 1840, he was nominally the Minister of Foreign Affairs (State) only, yet he was the guiding spirit of the whole cabinet, was responsible for its measures of both foreign and domestic policy, and when Marshal Soult, the figure-head, finally retired from the presidency of the cabinet, Guizot was forced to assume the authority in name as well as fact. In his relations with other powers he was able and discreet. An open collision with England over the eternal Eastern Question, made acute in 1840 by the attitude of the viceroy of Egypt towards his suzerain at Constantinople, was averted by his reasonableness and personal acquaintance with the English ministers, and the next year his ability succeeded in putting an end to the isolation of France in European affairs, which had been the result of this temporary disagreement. Not long afterwards the conquest of Algeria was definitely assured, and French influence became firmly intrenched beyond the Mediterranean. Other measures, such as joint action with England in regard to the slave trade, and marriages between the princes of the House of Orleans and the royal family of Spain, were conducted to satisfactory conclusions. In the words of one of his recent biographers, Guizot possessed a "patriotism better conceived (than that of the multitude)—broader, into which entered a general sentiment of justice together with love for humanity."

If Guizot's foreign policy was justified by its fruits the exact reverse is true of his domestic administration. It was an increasing failure from start to finish. It was directly responsible for the destruction of the throne and the ruin of constitutional monarchy in France. We can only explain this apparent anomaly in a historian of the first magnitude by the assumption that he was endowed with unusual self-esteem, with a disposition unyielding in the extreme, and that these natural, innate qualities were fortified by arbitrary preconceptions supported by a limited number of deductions from the teachings of history. But whatever our explanation may be, the fact remains that the political Guizot of 1840 was the political Guizot of 1815. And yet a generation of men had come and gone. Times had changed, even if we suppose that in 1815 he was in harmony with the times. He alone had not changed. Theoretically he believed in a constitutional monarchy based on a limited electorate, determined by the amount of direct taxation assessed on the individual citizen. Practically he stood by the first statutes for determining this amount, which had been voted in 1831, and no pressure nor argument could move him from his position.

With this question of suffrage was connected the accidental one of the propriety of deputies holding offices under the government, for which they might receive pecuniary emolument. Deputies who were also office-holders were naturally the objects of suspicion. Their financial interests were bound to affect their votes. Guizot apparently did not deny this accusation, nor did he consider the electoral body of his day an ideal one. He seems to have wished to adjourn discussion on either subject, in the belief that agitation and change would be harmful to the government. The two questions were in no way associated. It was the opposition of the administration to the consideration of either of them that joined them together in the public mind. In 1842 an attempt was made to modify existing regulations in both instances. The number of electors at that time approximated 224,000, out of a possible 7,000,000, had universal suffrage existed. Of the deputies sitting in the Chamber about one-third were salaried government officials. Guizot approved of the limitations which made the upper *bourgeoisie* the rulers of the country, a business man's government. He saw no peril in the large proportion of legislators attached by self-interest to the administration.

He defends in his "Memoirs" his attitude regarding the electorate by claiming that as society had become more united, homogeneous, one man represented more people than he had done in a less consolidated community. Hence the uselessness of universal suffrage and the desirability of a limited body of truly representative men, who possessed to a greater degree than those less successful in worldly affairs the capacity for political action. But the democratic spirit of the Revolution and Empire, which had worked less openly under the Restoration, had been rapidly gaining ground under the July monarchy. The Napoleonic tradition had recovered from the reaction of the days following the destructive campaigns of Napoleon, had joined itself to the democratic movement, and lent it the luster of military success. Guizot himself had furthered this sentiment during the months of his residence at London, when, at the instigation of Thiers, he had obtained from the English authorities the permission to bring back to France the remains of the great Emperor. In the minds of a large faction such glory as the Empire had won for the nation had been tarnished by the sordid pursuits of business. It was also evident that the *bourgeois* electors were rapidly confounding the interests of the state with those of their own families. Corruption entered into elections despite the fact that none of the electors were exposed to financial want.

As the decade advanced the debates in the Chamber grew more vehement. The aroused partisans of Napoleon, conscious that the country was behind them, hurled at Guizot the accusation of the famous trip to Ghent during the Hundred Days. He retorted with equal vehemence. The apostles of universal suffrage, no less insistent than their Bonapartist allies, harried the government with accusations of undue conservatism, with blindness to the general interests of the country, with corruption within its own chosen body of voters. All of these charges were true, but none was conceded to be so by Guizot. With a fatuity which seems incredible in a student of governmental origin and changes, he rejected all propositions to broaden the electoral body, and assumed that the voice of the upper *bourgeoisie* was the voice of the people. It was either bend or break. Guizot did not know how to bend, and February, 1848, found the "Man of Ghent" a fugitive with the king. But to his dying day Guizot could not discern wherein he had erred in thought or deed.

The Revolution of 1848 put an end to all plans of public life on the part of Guizot. His unpopularity knew almost no limit. Universal suffrage, which had come to stay, whether in republic or empire, considered him its greatest enemy, and would have none of him. The passions his rule must have aroused may still be felt in the contemptuous hostility which both the literary class—the *élite* of the social reformers—and the populace still feel for the self-absorbed, wealth-begetting *bourgeoisie*. For they build their hopes for a regenerate France on the nullification of this materialistic middle class.

Guizot's exile was of short duration. He returned to France in 1849, and settled down on the estate of Val Richer, in Normandy, which he had owned for some years. A widower, his house was managed by one of his married daughters. Politics were lost to him. He busied himself in the world of affairs with his duties as an academician, and his interests as a Protestant. The various orations he pronounced on the reception of new members by the Academy proved to that enlightened audience that separation from the debates of a legislative assembly had in no wise impaired the wonders of his eloquence. His voice was also heard in the consistories held at regular intervals by the Reformed Church, and the services of his pen were enlisted in the struggles occasioned by the schisms of the Protestant sects. Nor was he estranged from writings of a larger content. Early in the fifties he consigned his "Memoirs" to manuscript. He had no apologies to make. He had learned nothing by his failures as a statesman. Later he undertook the well-known popular "History of France Told to my Grand-children," which was planned on an extensive scale, and finished by one of his daughters after his death. Hack work also demanded his attention. For though often accused of corrupting others, he himself remained incorruptible, and retired from years of undisputed political power poor in purse and unimpeached in integrity.

He was destined to survive all of his family save one of his daughters. It was his misfortune also to outlive all the friends of his youth. One by one they passed away, widening about him the void of loneliness. He was paying the penalty of longevity. He also witnessed the humiliation of his native country in 1870 and 1871. "I leave the world much disturbed," he had written to one of his friends; "how will it be born again? I do not know how, but I believe it will be." "We must serve France," he used to say to his daughter, Madame de Witt, "a country hard to serve, without foresight and fickle. We must surely serve it; it is a great country." After a few weeks of increasing weakness, affirming to his last breath his love for the land he was leaving, and his belief in the world to come, peopled with so many near and dear to him, he expired on September 12, 1874, within a few days of his eighty-seventh anniversary.

A striking feature of the inner life of Guizot is the influence of woman. First his mother, slender in form, simple in manners, but clear-sighted, determined, forceful. To her training the boy, orphaned of his father, owed the directness and persistency of his later career. Her religious beliefs, Calvinistic, but not intolerant, if we may judge of them by her son's attitude, remained in him, a constant spring of hope and justice. Their years of intimate intercourse were prolonged beyond the wont of nature. She went into exile with him in 1848, and died in England. She had outlived her two daughters-in-law. The first, who was a woman of unusual strength of character and of considerable literary reputation, a disciple of the skeptical philosophy of the eighteenth century, had been married to Guizot in 1812, her junior by fourteen years and more. He owed much of his ambition to her. He confesses this obligation more than once, and on his ill-omened trip to Ghent, writes to her in these words: "Do you know what decided me to go? The desire to become everything that I should be, so that nothing may be wanting to your happiness. It is on your account that I do not wish to miss any occasion to distinguish myself from other men; without our union I should have lived on in my natural indolence." Their happiness was not destined to last. Worn out by an existence which drained her nervous force, she spent her last strength on an educational treatise, and ceased to live in 1827. We have noted the part she took in preparing the collections of memoirs on French and English history.

Guizot's second wife, a niece of the first, had inherited the former's fondness for literature and aptitude for details. Much of the drudgery connected with the publication of the *Revue Française* was performed by her.   She also assisted her husband in gathering the material for his great lecture courses of the years 1828–1830.   But her strength, too, was unequal to the task.   In 1833 she was gone, and Guizot was left to the care of his mother and daughters during the remainder of his life.   From the evidence at hand there seems to be no doubt that his literary work suffered seriously from the loss of these two devoted collaborators.   In after years his daughters replaced them to some extent, but rather as scribes than as co-workers.

In reviewing Guizot's public career, one must not forget to mention his services to the cause of education.   It forms his most enduring monument as an administrator. For the results of his diplomacy were ephemeral, while his whole internal policy, with the important exception of public instruction, was a fatal mistake.   He was Minister of Education from 1832 to 1836.   Within that short period of four years he found time to revive the Academy of Moral and Political Science, a branch of the Institute of France, which was established in 1795, but had been suppressed by Napoleon, in 1803, to found the French Historical Society, which should publish historical works, and to begin the collections of mediæval chronicles and state papers which succeeding governments have faithfully continued and completed.   The school system of France also became an object of his special care. Convinced that popular education should be impregnated with religious feeling, he opposed all attempts to alienate school and church; a separation "destructive of the moral value of the school."   Laws to increase the number of public schools were passed, and their direct control lodged in boards of education, in which both clergy and laymen had a voice. A system of school inspection was instituted, and inspectors were appointed to visit the schools and advise with their instructors. The effect of these measures was immediate and beneficial. His view of the higher education is best told in his own words, taken from a letter written to his intimate friend, the Duc de Broglie, in 1832:

"There is in it [the higher education] something which no longer answers to present conditions, to the natural bent of society and mankind. I don't know exactly what it is. I am groping. In no way would I like to abolish or even weaken that study of language, the only study really vigorous and learned at this time. I insist on the few years which we pass in familiar intercourse with antiquity; for he who does not know it is but a *parvenu* in the matter of intelligence. Greece and Rome are schools of good breeding for the mind of man, and in the midst of the ruin of all the aristocracies we must try to keep that one still on its feet. I also consider college life full of occupation and freedom, as intellectually excellent on the whole. From it alone come the strong minds, natural and keen at one and the same time, minds well trained, well developed, without any factitious bent, without any particular stamp. I am more and more struck with the advantages of classical education, and yet I admit I see, in the person of my son, that there is something to be changed there, and something important. The instruction is too thin and too slow. The distance between the intellectual atmosphere of the real world and that of the college is too great. The methods are calculated to fit large classes, and the result is that good students are sacrificed to mediocre ones. The classes are very large because a mass of children cannot find what they need, and wish to learn, taught anywhere. To tell the truth, the college and almost our entire system of public instruction are still patterned on the model of former social conditions. The dreamings of the eighteenth century, the follies of the Revolution in this particular, have rightly disgusted us with the new attempts which turned out so badly, and in returning to the old way we have fallen into the old rut. We must get out of it, but very carefully and cautiously.''

With an opinion like this so uncertain, fluctuating between theoretical and practical ideas, it was useless to expect any satisfactory outcome of the educational problem. Besides, the body of the French *bourgeoisie* was not prepared—and does not seem prepared to-day—to accept the principle of freedom of instruction, lay or clerical, which Guizot always championed. The laws he proposed were not voted by the upper house.

Conservative as he was in the matters of suffrage and representation, Guizot was ahead of his times in the theories of education. Perhaps because he was from the south of France, perhaps because of his historical studies, he believed in the advisability of decentralizing thought and increasing the number of centers for its dissemination. Paris, with its Institute, its schools of art and science, had drained the country and the smaller towns of their intellectual men. To be sure, there were some few groups of teachers employing university methods scattered through the provinces. But these did not suffice to stem the current setting steadily towards the great capital. Guizot wished to try heroic measures. He would estab-

lish in the four parts of France—at Strassburg, Rennes,
Toulouse, and Montpellier—universities in fact as well as
in name, great foundations equipped with the best of
buildings and apparatus, manned by men of the highest
eminence, offering to students instruction of the highest
grade in every branch of learning. These new universities should be true centers of study and wisdom. Another
ideal of the great historian which was not realized, and
he effected but little else than placing the teaching of
philosophy and history on a new and higher plane.

For history was his avocation and his life. Ambition
could lead him into the political arena, but could not give
him the victory. Unfortunately, like many other men of
letters, particularly of his day and of his school, the time
he spent in politics was lost to his reputation with posterity. The disastrous effects of public life may be seen in
the fact that nearly all his historical works, and those
which are most original and most lasting, were written
before 1830. Victor Hugo has said that "old age has no
hold on minds which follow ideal pursuits," and the saying is based on observation of facts. Guizot's best work
should have been done after he was sixty years old, especially as advancing years did not at all impair his physical
vigor or mental acuteness. But the intervening duties of
administrator and diplomat had raised a barrier to his historical investigation which he did not surmount.

From the beginning of his professorship at the Sorbonne, in 1812, when but twenty-five years of age, he had
formulated the principles which were to revolutionize
historical research. In his mind the duty of the historian
was "to discern the dominant ideas, the great events
which have determined the destiny, the character of a

long series of generations'' rather than make of himself
a mechanical chronicler of legislative and military happen-
ings. In other words, he should look behind facts for
their causes. The results would then follow of themselves. The historian should also be a philosopher. He
should take for his guide his reason, and follow its ''postu-
lates through the uncertain labyrinth of facts.'' His
principles were thus determined *à priori*, and facts were
made to fit them, too often perhaps in a purely arbitrary
way. Yet Guizot did not neglect the study of historical
documents. We have seen that he both made collections
of texts himself and incited the government to publish all
the material which its archives could yield. And on the
whole his method remains the method of the present day.
Individuals to him were of slight moment. They were
borne along on the surface of the social stream. Rarely
would he admit that they could impede its progress or
direct its flow. So his influence was optimistic. He was
a fervent Protestant. He believed in an overruling Providence. Moral and social progress went hand in hand with
him.

As we have seen, in the case of his ''Life of Washington,'' he used his historical studies to guide his political
career. The important element in the development of
nations, he claims, is contributed not by the upper or
lower classes, but by the opulent middle class, which is
given over to industry and ever seeking to advance its
sway. Some later historians, evidently of Guizot's school,
have affirmed that no war of conquest is ever undertaken
without a material object in view, namely, the increase of
the wealth of the assailants. Guizot may not have formulated such a statement, but he could hardly have disowned

it. His political theories were definitely crystallized by his investigation of the English Revolution, the results of which were to establish on a firm foundation the institutions of modern England, at one and the same time Protestant and liberal. These outgrowths of many centuries he hoped to adapt to the needs of France.

It was philosophical history, then, which he cultivated; human events interpreted by man's reason. The danger of such a system is obvious. The reason is individual and consequently the interpretations may be as numerous as the minds which interpret. But such a theory is a great advance over the chronological and biographical method, and with all its defects it is not easy to see how it can be replaced by any other view. To this theory Guizot made three notable contributions, all of which were the products of his lecture courses at the university: the "Essays on French History," in 1823, and the "Histories of Civilization," in 1828–1830. In the "Essays" he shows how from the beginning France and England differed in their political institutions; how these institutions in France were the result of the destruction of the middle classes by the fiscal administration of Rome. The middle classes gone there was no bulwark left to withstand the Germanic invasion of the fifth century. What civilization was saved from the wreck was due to the clergy, who preserved to some extent the laws and customs of Rome. Through the clergy these laws and customs were handed down to the communes of the Middle Ages. So with feudalism. Its origins are to be found in the personal relations of men at a period when these relations were peculiarly influenced by the ownership of land or the lack of such ownership. Its reasons for existence lay in the needs of the individual. Its growth and decay were alike due to his demands. The lesson of this period is that France of the Middle Ages was individual, while England was national.

The great works of Guizot are his two histories of civilization, in Europe and in France. The first general, the second special and illustrative of the first. In these new lectures the views of the "Essays" are taken up and carried out with a greater wealth of material, wider illustrations, and more convincing logic. France, for Guizot, is the center of European civilization, hence the close connection between the two courses. Distanced at times by its sister nations, France nevertheless has in the long run maintained her supremacy over them. She shows most clearly the workings out of the development of all the states, through the progress of the individual on the one hand and of society on the other. The history of Europe has been told by the struggles of these two antagonistic principles. And the conflict between the government on the one side, and the people on the other, has not yet reached a solution. The nearest approach to a lasting truce is found in England, where the church and state developed side by side, as also the aristocracy and democracy. On the Continent the growth of each of these elements was antagonized by the other, and the essence of Protestantism—freedom of investigation of truth—has constantly clashed with the tendency towards the centralization of power.

In France the upper classes of society, the nobility and the *bourgeoisie*, have remained constantly hostile to each other. The French people once in possession of an idea follow it out to its logical extreme, to a point where retreat becomes inevitable. On the contrary, the individual and society in general have advanced together in France. Ideas and facts have been intimately united. Speculative thought and its practical application have never remained far apart. The one has closely followed in the footsteps of the other, as witness the eighteenth century and the reforms induced by its philosophers. The cause for this association is found in the reasonable character of the different classes which compose French society. The clergy, learned and active in parochial work; the lawyers and magistrates, steeped in sound doctrine and insistent in experimentation; above all, the moderation, the avoidance of extremes, which is the distinctive trait of French character from one generation to another. So civilization in France, in Guizot's opinion, reproduces most faithfully the general type of civilization. Its visible tendency towards national unity, and therefore towards political unity, reveals the final goal of the more halting civilizations around it.

This study of civil society was to be followed by studies of religious society in its relation to the state and the papacy. A further extension of the plan would embrace the history of the human mind as shown in the modern tongues, the national literatures, and the Latin language, the vehicle of theological and philosophical thought. But the July Revolution interrupted this masterful program, and it was never resumed. Yet what was committed to manuscript and given to the public has proved a model and guide for subsequent students of the historical sciences.

EXTRACTS FROM THE WRITINGS OF GUIZOT

The Opening Lecture of "The History of Civilization in Europe"

[Guizot resumes his lectureship after some years of governmental injunction.]

Gentlemen:—I am deeply touched by the greeting I receive from you. I will allow myself to say that I accept it as a pledge of the sympathy which has not ceased to exist between us in spite of so long a separation. I say that the sympathy has not ceased to·exist, as if I found again in this hall the same people, the same generation which was accustomed to come here seven years ago, and share in my labors. (Guizot seems moved and stops a moment.) I beg your pardon, gentlemen, your kindly welcome has affected me a little. . . . . Because I return here it seems to me that all should return, that nothing is changed. Everything is changed none the less, and much changed! Seven years ago we used to enter here uneasy, preoccupied with a sad, burdensome thought. We knew we were surrounded with difficulties, with perils; we felt ourselves drawn along towards an evil which we vainly tried to turn aside by dint of seriousness, calmness, reserve. To-day we all come, you as well as I, confidently and hopefully, our hearts at peace and our thoughts free. We have but one way of worthily showing our gratitude for this, and that way is to bring to our reunions and studies the same calmness, the same reserve we used to bring when we thought every day we should see them hindered or forbidden. . . . . We have but a very short time before the end of the year. I have had very little time to think over the course I should offer you. I have tried to find the subject which could be best treated in the very few months which remain, and in the very few days allowed me for preparation. It seemed to me that a general picture of modern European history, considered in its relation to the development of civilization, a general glance at the history of European civilization, its origins, progress, goal, and character—it seemed to me, I repeat, that such a picture could be fitted to the time at our disposal. This is the subject I have settled upon to talk to you about.

I say the civilization of Europe. It is evident that there is a European civilization, that a certain unity is manifest in the civilization of the different states of Europe, that in spite of great differences in time, place, circumstances, this civilization takes its rise in facts that are almost alike, is attached to the same principles, and tends to bring about like results almost everywhere. There is, then, a European civilization, and I wish to call your attention to its general features.

On the other hand, it is evident that this civilization cannot be found, that its history cannot be traced, in the history of a single one of the states of Europe. If it possesses unity, its variety is none the less prodigious. It has not developed in its entirety in any special country. Its features are diverse; we must look for the elements of its history, now in France, now in England, now in Germany, now in Spain.

We are well placed to give ourselves up to this research and study European civilization. We should not flatter any one, not even our country. However, I believe we may say without flattery that France has been the center, the hearth of European civilization. It would be too much to claim that she has always marched at the head of nations in every direction. At various epochs she has been outstripped, by Italy in the arts, by England from the standpoint of political institutions. Perhaps in other particulars we would find other countries of Europe superior to her at certain moments. But it is impossible to deny that every time France has seen herself outstripped in the career of civilization she has taken on a new vigor, has rushed ahead, and has soon found herself on a level with all the rest or ahead of them. And not only has the peculiar destiny of France been such as I have said, but the ideas, the civilizing institutions, which had their birth in other territories, when they wished to transplant themselves, to become fruitful and general, to act to the common profit of European civilization, have been seen in some degree obliged to undergo a new preparation in France; and it is from France, as from a second fatherland, that they have gone forth to the conquest of Europe. There is hardly any great idea, any great principle of civilization, which, in order to spread everywhere, has not first passed through France.

The fact is that there is something sociable, something sympathetic, in the genius of the French, something which is propagated with more ease and energy than the genius of any other people. Whether because of our language or the turn of our mind, of our manners, our ideas are more popular, present themselves more clearly to the masses, penetrate among them more easily. In a word, clearness, sociability, sympathy, are the peculiar characteristics of France, of its civilization, and these qualities have made her eminently fitted for marching at the head of European civilization.

From the Opening Lecture of "The History of Civilization in France"

Gentlemen:—Some of you recall the object and nature of the course which finished some months ago. It was very general, very rapid. I tried to make the historic picture of European civilization pass before your eyes in a very short time. I ran, as it were, from peak to peak, limiting myself almost constantly to general facts and assertions, at the risk of not always being clearly understood, nor believed perhaps.

Necessity, as you know, had imposed that method on me, and in spite of the necessity I should have hardly resigned myself to its inconveniences had I not foreseen that I could remedy it in subsequent courses; had I not proposed at that time to fill out some day the frame I sketched and make you attain those general results, which I had the honor of unfolding to you, by the same way which had led me to them, by an attentive and complete study of the facts. This is the design I come to-day to try to accomplish.

Two methods of attaining this end are offered to me. I might begin again the course of last summer, and take up again the general history of European civilization in its entirety, relating in detail what I could present only in a mass, going over with slow footsteps the road we almost breathlessly traveled. Or I could study the history of civilization in one of the principal countries, with one of the greatest peoples of Europe where it developed, and thus limit the field of my researches in order to tell it better. . . . .

I decided to prefer this second method, to abandon the general history of European civilization among all the peoples who contributed to its formation, in order to busy myself with you on an especial civilization only, which, in taking differences into account, can become for us the image of the great destiny of Europe.

The choice of method once made, the choice of the country offered no difficulty to me. I took the history of France, of French civilization. I certainly shall not deny that in making this choice I felt a feeling of pleasure. All the emotions, all the susceptibilities of patriotism are legitimate. The important thing is that they be avowed by truth, by reason. Some people seem to fear to-day lest patriotism may greatly suffer from the extension of sentiments and ideas which spring from the present condition of European civilization. It is predicted that it will become enervated, and be lost in cosmopolitanism. I cannot share such fears. The love of one's fatherland will fare to-day as all opinions, all actions, all human sentiments, will fare. . . . . I think I can affirm that if any other history in Europe had seemed greater to me, more instructive, more suited than that of France to represent the course of general civilization, I should have chosen it. But I am right in choosing France. Independently of the special interest which her history has for us, European opinion has long proclaimed France to be the most civilized country of Europe. Every time that national jealousies are not excited, when you look for the real and disinterested opinion of peoples in their action and ideas, where it is indirectly manifested without taking the form of controversy, you recognize that France is the country whose civilization has appeared most complete, most communicative, and has struck the imagination of Europe most vividly. . . . .

You recall, I hope, the definition of civilization which I tried to give on opening last summer's course. I tried to find the ideas which the good, common sense of men attached to this word. It seemed to me that in the general opinion civilization consisted essentially in two facts, the development of the social state and the development of the intellectual state; the development of the external general condition of man, and the development of his internal and personal nature. In a word, the process of perfecting society and humanity.

And not only these two facts constitute civilization, but their simultaneousness, their intimate and rapid union, their reciprocal action, are indispensable to its perfection. I have shown that if they do not always happen together, if now the development of society, now the development of the individual man, proceeds more quickly and goes farther, they are none the less necessary to each other, and soon or late incite and lead on each other. When they go for a long time, one without the other, when their union is greatly delayed, the sense of a painful gap, of something incomplete, of regret, seizes on the spectators. If a great social amelioration, a great progress in material comfort, is revealed in a people, without being accompanied by a fine intellectual development, by an analogous progress in the minds of men, the social amelioration seems precarious, inexplicable, almost unlawful. . . . .

When, on the contrary, a great development of the intellect shows itself anywhere, and no social progress seems attached to it, we are surprised and disturbed. You seem to see a fine tree which does not bear fruit, a sun which does not give heat, nor fertility. We are seized by a kind of disdain for such sterile ideas, which do not take possession of the outside world. . . . . So firmly seated in man is the feeling that his duty here below is to have ideas embody themselves in facts, to reform, to regulate the world he inhabits, according to the truth he conceives. So closely united to each other are the two great elements of civilization, intellectual and social development. So true it is that its perfection consists not only in their union, but in their simultaneousness, in the extent, the facility, the rapidity with which they mutually summon and produce each other.

Let us now try to consider the different countries of Europe from this standpoint. Let us seek out the particular characteristics of each one of them, and the extent to which these characteristics coincide with that essential, fundamental, sublime fact which now constitutes for us the perfection of civilization. In this way we shall succeed in discovering which of the different European civilizations is the most complete, the nearest akin to the type of civilization in general; which consequently has the first claims on our study, and best represents the history of Europe in its entirety.

BIBLIOGRAPHY

Guizot's many writings have nearly all been translated into English and published by various editors.

M. Guizot in Private Life. By his daughter, Madame H. G. de Witt.

Guizot. A. Bardoux.

Articles in *Overland Monthly*, Vol. XIII, pp. 410 ff.

Littell's Living Age, Vol. CXXIII, pp. 749 ff., and Vol. CLXIV, pp. 387 ff.

FRANÇOIS MARIE CHARLES FOURIER

CHAPTER III

FOURIER AND SOCIALISM

[FRANÇOIS MARIE CHARLES FOURIER, born at Besançon, April 7, 1772; served in the cavalry, 1794-1796; died at Paris, October 10, 1837. Principal works: "Theory of the Four Movements and the General Destinies," 1808; "Treatise on Domestic Rural Association or Industrial Attraction" (later called "Theory of Universal Unity"), 1822; "The New Industrial and Social World," 1829.]

During the last half of the eighteenth century discontent with the social conditions existing in England and on the Continent was rapidly increasing. In a famous essay on the effects of progress on the human race, Jean Jacques Rousseau had bitterly attacked the works of civilization as detrimental to both goodness and happiness. Art and industry, instead of strengthening the virtues of man, were rapidly multiplying his vices. Private property was based on plunder. The growth of communities only widened the gulf between the strong, the rich, and the weak, the poor. No relief was to be hoped for from institutions which had grown out of the so-called development of the world. To bring back justice and peace these institutions must be destroyed, and their works must perish with them. Mankind was originally happy. All things were then held in common. Envy was absent, and violence. Restore this Golden Age by returning to nature. Leave the cities, dwell in the country, cultivate the soil, establish pure democracies. So Rousseau argued.

The French Revolution was one answer to his plea. It made all men equal before the law. It could not or did not change their natures, nor did it touch the principles of individual ownership. When its agitation had ceased, and men could take an account of what it had accomplished, it was seen that the essential causes of social inequality had in no way been overthrown by its political reforms. So far as the general bearing of its results were concerned, the world's future was to resemble the world's past.

Many who had hoped for some kind of a utopia on earth were discouraged by the failure of such a vast effort. Their exaltation sank back into indifference or bitterness. Others were inspired by the failure to seek other means. The great mathematician Condorcet took refuge in optimism, and wrote, while in hiding from the agents of the Terror, a treatise on human perfectibility, in which he defends the civilization that Rousseau had scourged, and deduces from the lessons of the past that inequality of privilege between nations and classes will gradually disappear, and the individual will come at last into complete moral, intellectual, and physical freedom. We now call this view of the world's destinies the theory of evolution. On the other hand, Babœuf could not await the tardy steps of justice. Allying himself with like-minded associates, he plotted to seize the government and found by force a communistic state which should realize to some degree the theories of Rousseau.

Another consequence of the fiasco of the Revolution was the formulation of doctrines for the production and distribution of wealth, which have since been defined by the term "socialism." They are to be distinguished from the programs of the reformers antecedent to the Revolution by their acceptance of the results of the world's labors. They start with the industrial conditions of modern life, so stimulated by the inventions of the end of the eighteenth century and the beginning of the nineteenth, by which manufacturing and the mechanical trades passed through a veritable renaissance. They would adapt themselves to these new conditions by improving them, not by destroying them. In France the leading expounders of these doctrines are Fourier and Saint Simon. Like the men of their day, and of the generations since their day, these expounders were primarily interested in the physical sciences. They sought in science a universal truth which should solve all special problems of labor and life. Saint Simon, later in date, but more popular, based his system on charity and merit. All social institutions should aim at the improvement of the poorest class. All the members of society should work with brain or hand, and each laborer should be paid according to his merit or capacity. Saint Simonism is also deeply religious. Its principle is brotherly love.

Fourierism is much more complex and less popular. Its founder, Charles Fourier, was born at Besançon, in eastern France, in 1772. His father was a dealer in cloth, of some means, and his son, though orphaned of him in 1781, received the education of his time, and won prizes at school for Latin composition. He also showed unusual inclination for the study of geography, was passionately fond of flowers, and possessed much aptitude for music. He himself wished to make engineering his vocation. But his plebeian birth forbade, and after some years of travel he invested his patrimony in foreign wares and started in business at Lyons. This was in 1793. The attack on that town by the government troops a few weeks later consumed his cotton bales in works of defense, and his rice, sugar, and coffee in support of the defenders. He lost his property and almost lost his life, escaping from Lyons only to find himself imprisoned at Besançon. The conscription authorized by the Convention that same year gathered him in. He served as cavalryman from June, 1794, to January, 1796, when he was retired for reasons of health. Now he could give himself up to plans of social reform which had long been germinating in his brain.

It is said that the evils of existing conditions had been impressed upon him when still a young boy. He had told the truth to some of his father's customers regarding his wares, and had been punished for it. He was then but five years of age. As a consequence, in the language of his disciple and eulogist, Victor Considérant, "he had taken Hannibal's oath against business. . . . . This oath, which he kept so well, is the origin of his discovery [system]; for it was in seeking the means of introducing truth and loyalty into the mechanism of trade that he reached in later years the Rural Association, the great Seriary Law, and the immortal theorem of the Attractions Proportional to the Destinies." This early conception of the world of affairs was strengthened in 1799 by an errand he was forced to perform for the firm which employed him as a commercial traveler. He had to order a cargo of rice thrown overboard in the harbor of Marseilles, because the firm in question had allowed it to rot rather than break a "corner" in grain, which they themselves had artificially created. This wanton destruction of food almost under the eyes of a starving population marks the culmination of Fourier's resolution to exert all his energies to put a stop to crimes against society committed under the name of trade. For several years yet he supported himself by the brokerage and commission business, occupied his spare moments with the preparation of his economic views and wrote articles on the events of the day. One such article in the *Bulletin de Lyon*, of December 17, 1803, shows how Europe was fast coming into the control of France, Russia, Austria, and Prussia. The last, and weakest, it argues, would become the victim of the other three. Then Austria would be dismembered. And finally, either France or Russia would engulf the other and become the master of the world. If France did not give heed to her ways the victor would be Russia. This article attracted the attention of Bonaparte, and its tenor bears a curious likeness to the policy he afterwards inaugurated.

In 1808 Fourier's ideas of social reform appeared in print under the title of "The Theory of the Four Movements and the General Destinies." The caption is formidable. The contents are no less so. The "movements" are social, animal, organic, and material, of which the first three, we are told, are new to mankind. The fourth, the "movements" of the material world, had been discovered by Newton, and their laws had been revealed by Leibnitz. Fourier had discovered the laws of the other three, a discovery which seems to have been directly provoked by the destruction of the rice at Marseilles. The failure of the French Revolution to benefit mankind had led him to consider the possibilities of a new social science which should do away with "poverty, lack of work, the success of trickery, maritime piracies, commercial monopoly, the slave trade, and many other misfortunes which need not be named, but which cause us to wonder whether civilized industry is not a calamity invented by God to chastise the human race.'' To find the natural order of things he adopted the principle of universal doubt, which Descartes had once ''partially'' used, together with the principle of the rejection of all known theories. To test his method he began with the consideration of ''rural association,'' a means of land cultivation agreeable to all concerned in it, and ''the indirect suppression of insular commercial monopoly.'' The solution of the first problem entails the solution of the second. By steadily working on this question Fourier saw that the law of the material universe, formulated by Newton, the ''law of attraction,'' as he terms it, was the true law of the social, animal, and organic world as well. Give this law free play and every man will desire to work. He will be drawn to it by his natural propensities. ''Emulation, self-love, and other motives compatible with self-interest'' will spur him on.

Exploitation in common will prove that the net profits of labor will be increased. Take a village, for instance. Assume that it holds one thousand people coöperating with one another. Each has some special aptitude. The men of brain will perfect the instruments of toil. One barn well cared for will replace three hundred poorly kept. One laundry will do the work of three hundred. The number of fires necessary can be reduced to three or four. ''They will send to the city but one milkwoman with a barrel of milk hung on cart wheels, and so will save a half-day's work of one hundred milkwomen carrying one hundred jugs of milk.'' Hence a greater profit for the community by this coöperation, and consequently a greater gain for each individual in it. With greater gain a greater control of the good things of life. And the conclusion here reached by Fourier gives the substance of his doctrine: "To summarize, this theory of Rural Association, which is going to change the lot of the human race, flatters the passions which are common to all men, and allures them by the seductions of profit and pleasures; this is the guaranty of its success with savages and barbarians as well as with civilized peoples, for the passions are the same everywhere."

These statements are perfectly clear. Fourier's "discovery" was the fact that the emotions or "passions" are the mainspring of human action. "The passions," he says, "which we have thought hostile to concord . . . . tend only to concord, to the social unity from which we thought them so far removed; but they can be harmonized only so far as they develop regularly in the Progressive Series or Series of Groups of people. Outside of this mechanism the passions are but unchained tigers." And he illustrates by showing how mankind is led along by the love of riches and pleasures. Instead of repressing the passions he will increase their intensity and their control of the individual by keeping them in a constant state of tension. He will excite envy by proving that the men of his "associations" live better and have more physical enjoyment than those outside of their circle. "When men notice that residence in a Phalanx (the name I shall give to the association which cultivates a district [Canton]) affords such fine fare that you have a service three times as delicate and abundant for one-third the expense of a private table . . . . besides avoiding the trouble of buying provisions and preparing them; when, besides, they see that in the relations between the members of the Series you never experience deception, and that the people who are so false and boorish in civilization become surprisingly truthful and refined in the Series, they will come to hate private households, cities, civilization; . . . . they will want to join a Phalanx of Series and dwell in its building."

This theory of association led Fourier to the discovery of two new sciences: One was the theory of passionate Attraction, capable of mathematical statement, the laws of which are in every way like those of material attraction as explained by Newton and Leibnitz. They prove that there is "unity in the system of movement for the material world and for the spiritual." This theory in turn led to the discovery of the other fixed science: "the Analogy of the four movements—material, organic, animal, and social—or the Analogy of the modifications of matter with the mathematical theory of the passions of man and the animals." These sciences pointed the way to others which embraced the whole domain of human activity and learning. By their harmony and unity the riches in reach of man will be multiplied. All classes of society will be sheltered from want. Wealth is the goal of humanity. The Theory of the Destinies will assure it this opulence. Our present civilization is a scourge which properly belongs to the primitive periods of existence. The pride or the negligence of the philosophers had already unnecessarily prolonged it two thousand and three hundred years. All the grades of savage, patriarchal, barbarous, and civilized society are but steps towards "a better social order, the Order of the Progressive Series which is the Industrial Destiny of man."

To further illustrate this progression from the unfinished to the complete, Fourier draws a picture of "the vegetable career of the globe," which he embraces in a cycle of eighty thousand years. The first five thousand, or one-sixteenth of the whole, he ranges under the head of Ascending Chaos, or the Reign of Ignorance and Philosophy, Collision of the Passions through the Lack of Social Art. This era is in turn divided into seven periods, of which Civilization is the fifth, "Guaranteeism" the sixth, and "Outlined Series" the seventh. Here we get a glimpse of the "dawn of happiness." This dawn becomes full day in the next era of thirty-five thousand years, or seven-sixteenths of the whole, classed under the head of Ascending Harmony or Social Light, Vigor of the Globe and the Creatures, Development and Interlinking of all the Passions. This era is subdivided into nine periods, one of the Simple Series Combined, seven of the Composed Ascending Series, which are distinguished by seven "Harmonic Creations," at intervals of four thousand years each, and the ninth of the First Septigeneric Creation and Ascending Plenitude. Following this creation comes the Pivotal or Amphiharmonic Period, of about eight thousand years, which is the Apogee of Happiness. In this era of thirty-five thousand years, directly after its first period, the "Boreal Crown" comes into being, and "the seas are disinfected and perfumed by the boreal fluid," while the Crown sheds aromatic dew upon the earth.

In the next cycle of thirty-five thousand years, the cycle of Descending Harmony, our planet will enter on an epoch of decline, which is divided into nine periods. It will witness in the first period a Second Septigeneric Creation and Descending Plenitude, in the next seven, of the Composed Descending Series, seven more Harmonic

Creations, during which the seas will return to their original taste through failure of the boreal fluid, and the aromatic dew will cease to fall because of the exhaustion of
the Boreal Crown. In the ninth period the Boreal Crown
will become extinct. As from the first to the second cycle
the world rose from chaos to harmony, so at the end of
the third it falls from harmony into chaos, and its last
cycle of five thousand years, divided into seven periods,
and called Descending Chaos (General Overturn by the
Eighteenth Creation, Clash of Passions because of Failure
of Luxury), repeats in inverse order the stages of the first
cycle, and ends in the physical death and dissolution of
the globe. The first two cycles are grouped together
under the head of Ascending Vibration. The Apogee of
Happiness separates them from the last two, of Descending Vibration.

Thus Fourier mixes geology and ethics. Harmony in
the one science is reflected in the other. The coöperation
of mankind in the production of wealth under the guidance of its passions changes, in the long run, the nature of
the earth's surface. Two ages of Combined Order will
give birth to the Boreal Crown, a luminous ring which
will turn the North Pole into an arable region whose fertility will endure for seventy thousand years. So with the
laws of the dependence of human progress on mathematics. "Without this dependence there would be no
harmony in nature and God would be unjust," for he
would be arbitrary in his dealings.

The exposition of these views, as might be inferred
from the outline already given, offers a mixture of fact
and fancy which is perplexing rather than interesting. At
times Fourier's criticisms of the waste of our present

social methods impress us with their justness. His remedy of coöperation appeals to us most strongly. But directly afterwards he starts upon a line of argument and illustrations which seem to be the empty vagaries of a disordered brain. Clearly his strength lies in his critical remarks. His constructive powers are questionable. His jumble of science and morals, and his claims of the influence of the fraternity of man on the productiveness of matter, calls his very sanity into question.

In the explanation of the meaning of his tabular view of the world's life, and the explanation of his terms, with which he continues his treatise, there is the same mixture of sense and nonsense. Take, as an example, his ideas of the Boreal Crown. They are based on the assumption that the earth will give birth to new creations, but these creations will not begin until humanity has reached the Simple Combined Series of the Ascending Harmony. By that time the increasing concord of the passions will have allured into domestic use such wild animals as the zebra and ostrich. The earth will have been brought under cultivation as far as the sixty-fifth parallel of latitude. The temperature of the planet will have been raised. "The Aurora Borealis, more and more frequent in its recurrence, will finally fix itself at the pole, and enlarge into the shape of a crown. The fluid which to-day is only luminous will acquire a new property, that of distributing warmth with light." Therefore the heat of the polar regions will exceed that of the temperate zone, and will therefore favorably affect the temperature of that zone. Excess of cold will be prevented as well as excess of heat. Two harvests will become the rule. Late springs and early winters will not be known. Another result of the action of the Boreal Crown will be to change the taste of sea water, "by decomposing or precipitating the bituminous particles through the expansion of a borealic citric acid. This fluid combined with salt will give sea water the taste of a kind of lemonade which we call *aigre de cèdre*." This water can then be easily distilled and used on shipboard. It will also give birth to new sea animals which can be taught to draw ships and fish, while it will kill the useless and destructive denizens of the ocean, "those infamous creatures, images of the fury of our passions, which are represented by the deadly wars of so many monsters."

So much for the nonsense, which goes on and on. But in the very midst of it we meet this striking passage, prophecy of the future. The natural result of the heat of the Boreal Crown will be to make the northern seas and their tributary rivers, now closed by ice, navigable. God has intended this, as we see by the grouping of the continents about the North Pole. However, "we might complain that God has carried the Magellaic point [Cape Horn] too far, which causes a temporary obstacle [to commerce]: but his intention is that this route be abandoned, and channels navigable for large vessels be made at the Isthmuses of Suez and Panama. These works, and so many others which terrify the minds of the civilized, will be but children's games for the industrial armies of the Spherical Hierarchy."

The social system of Guaranteeism which follows on the present period of civilization is thus defined: "It still preserves family life, marriage, and the principal attributes of the philosophic system [the present]: but it already reduces revolutions and indigence to a marked degree."

Civilization has been responsible for many evils: "There are other calamities which would spring from it and which the philosophers can in no way foresee; such is Commercial Feudalism, which would not have been less odious than the reign of the Clubs [of the Terror]. It would have been the result of the influence which the commercial spirit daily acquires over our social system." Fourier will furnish by his theory the means to avert this new tyranny.

The passions which we should cultivate, rather than repress as the moralists tell us, because they are in consonance with nature, include "the five appetites of the senses which exercise more or less sovereignty on the individual"—taste, touch, sight, smell, hearing—"the four simple appetites of the soul, to wit: the Group of Friendship, the Group of Love, the Group of Paternity or Family, the Group of Ambition or Corporation," all of which are known to these same moralists, "although they possess but very imperfect ideas regarding the four principal ones," and finally three others discovered by Fourier and now revealed by him under the collective name of "distributive" passions. These twelve passions naturally divide into three groups. The first five, of the senses, form the Group of Luxury. The next four, "called affective," form "the Groupism or desire for Groups." The last three form "the Seriism or desire for Series." They all combine and unite in "Unityism, a passion which comprises the three primary branches and is the result of their combined development." This Unityism "is the tendency of the individual to harmonize his happiness with the happiness of all that surrounds him and all the human race, now so hateful to him. It is a limitless

philanthropy, a universal good will which can be developed only when the entire human race shall be rich, free,
and just, conformable to the three groupings of passions
under Luxury, Groupism, and Seriism, which demand,
as a first development, graduated riches for the five
senses, as a second, absolute liberty for the four "affective" groups, as a third, distributive justice for the "distributive passions." These last are not easily named.
After a few trials Fourier settles down on Dissident or
Cabalist, Variant or Papillonne, Engrenant or Composit.
He also calls Unityism "Harmonism."

In other words, Fourier argues that all our passions
should be given free rein. Any other course is contrary
to nature, and with him, as with Rousseau, nature is the
model. By allowing them full play they will give rise to
higher forms of passion, create new ones, and eventually
lead to the perfect state of harmony and happiness. Here
Fourier becomes the ally of the theory of human perfectibility put forward by Condorcet. It will be noticed that
he demands "absolute liberty" for the four "affective"
passions, which are Friendship, Love, Paternity or Family, Ambition or Corporation. He scouts the notion of
duty "which has no relation to nature; duty comes from
men, Attraction comes from God. Now, if one wishes
to know God's views he must study Attraction, nature
only, without any acceptation of duty, which varies in
each age and in each region, while the nature of passion
has been and will remain invariable among all peoples."
The practical result of this theory is obvious. Friendship
should be free, love should be free, paternity free, ambition free. That is, all ties of marriage and family should
be broken, for true attraction does not belong to compul-

sion or restraint. Children do not understand paternal authority, often abused as it is, and when grown they notice the discrepancy between its theory and practice. Hence a lessening of affection on the part of the child to the parent. The same reasoning applies to the marriage relationship, where the ideal and the facts are so discordant as often to produce repulsion. But it is by attraction that nature governs, and Fourier invites us "to the analysis of that Passionate Attraction, which appears vicious to us because we are ignorant of its goal."

The pages on family relations, husband and wife, children and parents, are filled with the same mingling of sound criticism of the present conditions and fanciful assumptions of the blessings of a pure state of nature, which we have already noted in the chapters on physical geography and ethics. The present isolated household with its permanent marriage relations will give way to the Progressive Household of the seventh period of the "Outlined Series." Some one hundred persons of unequal fortune will be grouped together as a "Tribe" in one building, eighty of one sex, the employers, and twenty domestics of both sexes. The eighty will be approximately divided into nine groups of nine people each. Each group will eat at a different hour or in a different room in order to avoid uniformity. Each Tribe will exercise three compatible trades. Each member will contribute his share of the capital, large or small. The buildings of the various Tribes will communicate with one another so that you may pass into the successive buildings without fear of heat or cold, rain or snow.

Suppose there are six Tribes, three of men and three of women. Emulation will arise. The poorer tribe will seek to gain as much wealth as the richer tribe. Expenses of the state administrations will decrease and the waste of housekeeping will diminish. Therefore, the same private income will purchase more comforts or luxuries. An *esprit de corps*, jealousy for the honor of each Tribe, will cause coarseness and uncleanliness to disappear. The vexations of domestic service—which are principally due to three causes, low wages, incompatibility of disposition, and multiplicity of functions—will cease, because fewer servants will be required than in isolated households, the servants can choose the employers they like best and also the kind of employment they prefer. Old people, now a burden, will find vocations suited to their years, and helpful to the Tribe, and women who dislike housekeeping will be relieved by those who like it. The men also will choose the occupations they prefer. Division of labor according to taste will replace the jack-at-all-trades necessity of the isolated household. Close upon the sketch of this possible existence follows a graduated plan for the gratification of the animal passions and the propagation of the race, by which women may choose husbands, paramours, and lovers at will. As the choice lies with woman, she will rise in the social scale. This is one of the objects of Fourier's system. In his own words, "the extension of the privileges of women is the general principle of all social progress."

If liberty in family relations is entirely desirable, so is liberty in business, the passion of Ambition or Corporation. The present system "subordinates the social body to a class of parasitical and unproductive agents, who are the merchants." In the Sixth Period, of Guaranteeism, this class is to be subordinated "to the interests of the pro-

ducers, manufacturers, cultivators, and proprietors."
The merchant to-day is independent. The system of free
competition prevails. Under this system the social body
is a prey to bankruptcy, to "corners" in the necessaries
of life (Fourier's experience at Marseilles in 1799), which
"doubles the price of a raw material of which there is no
real scarcity," and thereby disorganizes manufacturing,
merely in order to enrich a coalition of gamblers. A
third despoiler is found in brokerage, which plunges financial markets into panics. And a fourth is the undue mul-
tiplication of middlemen, of agents who stand between the
producer and consumer, and who for the most part are
ruined by their own numerical excess, after a fierce struggle which is productive of deceit and disorder. As a
bulwark against this state of anarchy the period of Civilization is evolving commercial feudalism, or the restriction
of trade to the control of a few large companies. Thus
civilization rushes from one extreme to the other, never
resting at a golden mean. The antidote to all these contradictions and this social waste is found in the Societary
Competition of the period of Guaranteeism, which carries
on the great corporations "without constraint or exclusive
privileges, economizes capital, restores the middlemen to
labor, and subjects business to taxation." An epilogue on
the Social Chaos of the World, eloquent and hortatory,
ends this singular treatise.

No attention was paid to Fourier's "Theory of the
Four Movements." It seems to have attracted but very
few readers. The wars of the Empire did not favor the
propagation of humanitarian theories; or it may be that
such an attack on civilization was confused with Rousseau's, and the outline of the advance of mankind with

Condorcet's picture. Fourier continued to live on in
obscurity, gaining now and then an adherent, notably Just
Muiron, in 1814. In 1816 he retired to the small town
of Belley to the house of a sister, and there gave himself
up to elaborating his discovery and his theory. In 1822
his "Treatise on Domestic Rural Association" saw the
light, or as he preferred to call it, the "Theory of Universal Unity."

It is quite out of the question to analyze this book.
The ideas of the "Theory of the Four Movements" are
taken up again and commentated, now with a free use of
musical terms as well as mathematical. Economic and
philosophical questions are touched on and summarized in
bewildering confusion. Criticisms of society, attacks on
other social reformers, answers to criticisms of his own
views, are thrown together in a most haphazard manner.
The designs of God in creating the world, the immortality
of the soul, the training of children and youth, past, present, and future, take up quite as much space as the chapters on passionate attraction and coöperative association.
According to Pellarin, his biographer, Fourier would have
based his "Treatise" on the dictum of the German philosopher, Schelling, that "the universe is made according
to the pattern of the human soul." But whatever the
subject and the digression, the author rarely proceeds far
in his discussion without recurring to his main point of
Industrial Attraction, which makes work a pleasure, and
to its embodiment in a laboring household of four hundred
to sixteen hundred souls.

The public ear proved quite as deaf to this longer
harangue as it had to the shorter one of 1808. Nor did
a summary of it in 1823 have any greater success. No

one came forward with the capital sufficient to put the main plan to a test. Fourier spent some years in a vain search for this desired capitalist, and then losing hope for the time being, hired out to a Lyons firm in 1825, and a year later to an American house doing business temporarily at Paris. During 1826 and 1827 he gave his attention to the preparation of another volume on his system, an abridgement of the "Theory of Universal Unity." No publisher for it could be found at Paris. In 1828 he went back to Besançon; a printer was ready for his service, and "The New Industrial and Social World" appeared in 1829.

This book is distinguished from its fellows by a clearer construction and a more logical exposition. After a criticism of the existing social state, its author passes on to an analysis of Passionate Attraction and the twelve passions which lead to Unityism. The three "distributive" passions are defined—they had been loosely indicated in the "Theory of Universal Unity." The Cabalist passion is partisanship, intrigue. It mingles calculation with passion. Its office is to excite emulation between the Groups, both in production and consumption. The Papillonne passion is the need of variety in man, change of scene, novelty which stimulates the senses and also the soul. This need of variety "is felt to a moderate degree every hour, and keenly every two hours." If it is not satisfied man relapses into lukewarmness and ennui. The labor and the pleasures of civilization weary by their duration. Fourier shows how a judicious variation of work and recreation in the Harmonic state may constantly keep mind and body on the alert. He prepares two schedules of a daily occupation, one for the beginning of the Harmonic existence, the other for the period of its development. They differ in two ways. The first varies occupations or amusements every two hours as a rule, while the second varies them every hour. The first begins the day at half-past three, provides for three meals, and ends the day at ten. The second begins the day at the same hour, provides for five meals, and ends it at half-past ten. He explains the increase of meals in the complete Harmonic state as due to the active life, the habit of short and varied sessions which "will give a prodigious appetite." The limited space assigned to sleep is attributed to the "refined hygiene, joined to the variety of sessions," which will cause little fatigue and physical waste. The Composit passion finally is a state of exhilaration, a blind enthusiasm "born of the conjunction of several pleasures of the senses and soul, enjoyed simultaneously." It is called "bastard" when formed of pleasures of one kind, sensual or spiritual. Together with the Cabalist passion it gives Harmonic society its motives for action. But the important passion of all is the Papillonne, the need of variety, so decried by our present-day moralists.

From the theory and explanation of the passions of this perfected stage of humanity we pass to its mode of existence. The Phalanx is the nucleus, as we have seen. From the experimental Tribe of one hundred persons of the "Theory of the Four Movements" it had reached in the "Theory of Universal Unity" the Association of fifteen hundred to sixteen hundred, cultivating a square league. All classes and conditions, male and female (the males slightly in excess, according to nature's laws), rich and poor, should inhabit the same building and work together in friendly rivalry. The distribution of profits, according to the "Theory of Universal Unity," should be five-twelfths to manual labor, four-twelfths to capital, three-twelfths to theoretical and practical knowledge (talent). In the "New Industrial and Social World" the ideal phalanx numbers sixteen hundred and twenty persons, of whom two hundred and twenty are under four and a half years of age, forty-five extremely old, and one hundred and twenty ill, infirm, or absent. The others are classified according to their years and character. This body lives in an immense building called the phalanstery, modeled somewhat on the architecture of the French palaces, with arcades, gardens, stables, barnyard, theater, church, ball-room, and all the appurtenances of a city in miniature. The inhabitants of the phalanstery, in the complete Harmonic state, will be divided into four hundred and five series, each composed of individuals of like tastes, who will give themselves up to their favorite occupation. For the incomplete state but one hundred and thirty-five series will be formed, of which fifty will busy themselves with the vegetable world, thirty with the animal, and twenty with manufacturing. The remaining thirty-five are divided among domestic service and professions, in the widest acceptation of the term. All labor, of course, is prompted by the natural tendency of the twelve passions already described and their concord in Unityism, the desire for universal harmony.

The problem of the rearing of children and their education becomes of primal importance in a state founded on passionate attraction, for children lack such an attribute. Yet they do possess the desire for luxury, bestowed on them by nature. This desire is to be excited and turned towards the useful by the various allurements of playthings, games, and emulation. Such is Fourier's fondness for details and analysis that he mentions some twenty-four means of diverting a child of two years of age. Afterwards, their natural talents are cultivated by being allowed full play. Even those children inclined to filthiness are to be trained to care for sewers, drains, and the like! They should study books only on stormy days, because they prefer to be out of doors during fine weather. Above all, no constraint. As they grow older the same attraction will work on them which prevails over the passions of adults. Industrial life is the goal, and all training should tend to industry. But "all the passions go together, and the agreeable is always allied with the useful." The question of marriage is not again considered, probably because of the criticism of the views previously expressed, but the right of woman to teach and practice medicine is affirmed, and her supremacy in the world of art asserted.

More attention was paid to this last work of Fourier than had been given to his former publications. It was reviewed by the press, and its doctrines attacked. A few disciples came forward, among them a future leader of the sect, Victor Considérant. Some deserters from Saint Simonism, which was then meeting with considerable favor, came over to the Phalanstery camp. In 1832 a weekly was started, *Le Phalanstère ou La Réforme industrielle*. An experimental phalanstery even was projected, but was soon abandoned because of lack of capital. Courses of lectures on the theory were given, however, at Paris and elsewhere. In 1835 Fourier published a defense of himself and an attack on his critics, under the title of "False Industry." In 1836 *Le Phalanstère* (dead in 1834) was succeeded by another journal. The public became well informed of the movement. But no money was available to make the experiment, and Fourier, whose health had been steadily declining, died on October 9, 1837, without seeing the desire of his heart realized.

Shortly after Fourier's death his system seemed on the point of gaining a firm foothold. It was brought to America and made the subject of many experiments, the most notable of which was that faint reproduction of a phalanstery known as Brook Farm, in which Charles A. Dana, Margaret Fuller, and other celebrities of the world of letters took part, and which gave Hawthorne the material for his "Blithedale Romance." In France, after some years of halting, a stove manufacturer, in 1860, built a phalanstery at Guise (called *Familistère*), and rented it to his workmen. Many of the ideas of Fourier are here found in practical application. Some eighteen hundred people inhabit the building, which includes shops and a theater, young children are cared for in a day nursery, and the comfort of the sick and old is secured. A scheme of profit-sharing on the coöperative plan furnishes an incentive to industry. But the occupation of the community is manufacturing, while Fourier evidently considered a return to nature and agriculture an essential factor in his new world.

The general interest excited by Fourier's views, an interest which has led to so many attempts to realize the practical side of them, and which has only recently suggested the theme of Zola's regenerative novel, "Labor" ("Travail"), seems capable of a rational explanation. In spite of his extravaganzas, his irrelevancies, his absurdities of thought or statement, Fourier quite consistently advocates two principles which commend themselves to the judgment of modern thinkers. These principles are those of evolution and private property. Perfection is not to be suddenly attained by Fourier. The world is not to change its habits over night. Through a series of centuries, of epochs only, eras of constant improvement in the dispositions and manners of men, are we to reach the perfect social state. The human mind will react with beneficial results on nature. The better spirit of mankind will make the wilderness blossom as the rose (the theory of the Boreal Crown). There is some truth at the bottom of all this. And it satisfies the universal longing for the future of the race. It is in imaginative accord at least with the present teachings of science.

Furthermore, this ideal future is not to be reached by sacrificing the individual to the extent that communism and other doctrines of socialism would sacrifice him. In Fourier's social unit, the phalanstery, each associate retains his own property, and thereby the incentive to increase it. Each can hand it down to his children or friends. There seems no reasonable solution of the problem of society which ignores the predominant factor of individual effort. Fourier's plan preserves this essential agent. It goes even farther, and gives this agent a wider scope by the economies gained in coöperative work, and the division of labor according to personal inclinations. Coöperative housekeeping, for instance, is becoming more and more desirable, provided the family privacy is not endangered. It may be possible that the general trend of the arguments urged by Fourier may one day lead to a practical solution of this vexatious problem.

SELECTIONS FROM THE WORKS OF FOURIER

Extracts from the Introduction to Fourier's "New Industrial and Social World."

A means of suddenly quadrupling the products of industry; of bringing all the masters to the conventional enfranchisement of negroes and slaves; of refining barbarians and savages without delay; . . . . of spontaneously establishing all unities in language, measures, money, typography, etc.! This is some charlatanry, the wits will say. . . . .

A modern has rightly said: "The last wrong we pardon is that of announcing new truths."

This is the wrong I have done, to unveil many new and eminently useful sciences; the most precious novelties were rejected at first; potatoes and coffee were proscribed by parliamentary edicts; vaccination, the steam engine, were likewise slandered when they appeared. . . . .

But let us stop this discussion; it is more urgent to acquaint the reader with the subject in hand, the scale of the social states superior to civilization, whose mechanism has been discovered at last. Humanity in its social career has thirty-six periods to cover; I give here a schedule of the first, which will be sufficient for the documents contained in this volume:

SCALE OF THE FIRST AGE OF THE SOCIAL WORLD

Periods anterior to industry.	K. Bastard, without men. C. 1.
	1. Primitive, called Eden. C. 2.
	2. Savagery, or inertia. C. 3.
Industry fragmentary, deceitful, repugnant.	3. Patriarchal, petty industry.
	4. Barbarism, mean industry.
	5. Civilization, great industry.
Industry societary, true, attractive.	6. Guaranteeism, half-association.
	7. Sociantism, simple association. C. 4.
	8. Harmonism, combined association. C. 5.

NOTE.—The letter C indicates the epochs of past and future creations of which we speak farther on.

I do not mention period 9 and following periods, because we can at present rise to period 8 only, already infinitely blessed in comparison with the four societies now existing. It will suddenly and spontaneously extend to the whole human race, by the mere influence of profits, pleasures, and especially industrial attraction, a mechanism not at all known to our politicians and moralists. . . . .

In order to create this attraction we had to discover the method called Passionate Series, explained in this work. It is gradually established during the periods 6, 7, 8 of the above schedule. Period 6 creates but a half-attraction, and would not allure the savages. The 7th would begin to attract them. The 8th will win over the idle rich also. We can pass over the 6th and 7th periods, thanks to the invention of the Passionate Series, which forms the mechanism of the 8th period. . . . .

Civilized peoples are persuaded that they are hastening to perfectibility when they are overwhelmed with new and recent calamities; . . . . among others the scourge of public debts, ever increasing, and which at the first war among the western nations would bring on universal bankruptcy, followed by revolutions.

There are many other wounds unperceived. Such is the encroachment of commerce, which threatens to invade everything, and which is finally alarming the governments. The societary theory can alone teach the means of striking down this political Titan. . . . .

For three thousand years philosophy has not been able to invent anything new in industrial and social politics. Its innumerable systems are based only on a distribution by families, the smallest and most ruinous unity.

Here are new ideas at last, a theory adapted to the views of governments, instead of tormenting them by philanthropic visions, true masks for agitators. Every minister will appreciate a method which, while quadrupling the revenue available, will at once allow taxes to be doubled, while really decreasing the burdens of the tax-payers by one-half. (They will pay but double on a quadruple product.) . . . .

A more brilliant effect will be to operate on the entire world, savage, barbarous, and civilized; to change it all by an experiment limited to a square league and eighteen hundred people. What a contrast with philosophy, which overturns empires without any guarantee of good results. . . . .

Poor civilization makes gigantic efforts for nothing; sending armies and navies to deliver *perhaps* one-tenth of Greece; revolutions and massacres, as attempts to emancipate the negroes; fruitless endeavors to aid poverty. All this pygmy labor is going to cease. The human race is going to be enfranchised and delivered *altogether*. It will rally everywhere to attractive industry as soon as it knows, by an experiment on one district, the prodigies of riches, pleasures, and virtues reaped from it.

There the chimeras and furies of party spirit will end. Each one, seeing the true destiny of man, *the mechanism of the passions*, will be so confounded at the absurdities of civilization that he will elect to forget them as quickly as possible. . . . .

At Paris they are trying to extirpate begging. . . . . Those in charge of this attempt do not know that they must operate on the country before operating on the city, effect industrial reform in agriculture, manufacturing, commerce, and housekeeping.

BIBLIOGRAPHY

French and German Socialism in Modern Times. Richard T. Ely.

Fourierism New International Encyclopedia.

The Guise *Familistère* is described in *The Fortnightly Review*, Vol. LIII (1893), pp. 418-426, and *Harper's Monthly*, Vol. LXXI (1885), pp. 912-918.

CHAPTER IV

THIERS AND THE GROWTH OF REPUBLICAN PRINCIPLES

[LOUIS ADOLPHE THIERS, born at Marseilles, April 16, 1797; journalist at Paris from 1822; deputy from Aix, 1830; Minister of the Interior, 1832; member of the French Academy, 1834; in exile, 1851–1852; deputy from Paris, 1863; President of France, 1871–1873; died at St. Germain, September 3, 1877. Principal works: "History of the French Revolution," 1823–1827; "History of the Consulate and Empire," 1845–1862.]

There were many in France, like Fourier and Guizot, who had profited by the great Revolution, but to whom it had not been an unmixed blessing. Fourier had lost his property in it, Guizot his father. Their attitude towards the movement, in common with the opinion of a large number of their countrymen, particularly those who belonged to the higher *bourgeoisie*, was one of approval with reservations. The greater measure of liberty it had brought they enjoyed. But they wished this liberty to be held in check, controlled by a conservative moderation. On the other hand, the mass of the population indorsed the ideas of the Revolution and approved of its acts. The peasant had become owner of the soil he had tilled for centuries, confiscated from the clergy and nobility. The small tradesman, roofed in by the ledge of caste, had suddenly found the rock above him blasted away, and the fields of opportunity lying at his feet. The peasantry and the petty *bourgeoisie* easily outnumbered the other classes.

LOUIS ADOLPHE THIERS

They had no apologies to proffer for the way in which their social status had been transformed. After the despotism of the Empire they quickly found their leaders, and chief among these stood Adolphe Thiers.

This champion of democracy, and president to be, was born at Marseilles, in 1797. Of a family that was not particularly prosperous, he had obtained his education in the local schools by means of a scholarship. Going in 1815 to Aix to study law, he found there, as fellow-student, the future historian Mignet, with whom he formed a lasting friendship. During this residence at Aix Thiers's political leanings became manifest. It is told that on the occasion of a prize competition proposed by the Academy of Aix, in 1820, Thiers, who had just graduated from the law school, offered a eulogy of the eighteenth-century philosopher and essayist, Vauvenargues. It was the best of all the pieces submitted. But the name of its author was revealed, and the reactionary Academy could not make up its mind to thus publicly reward a defender of the Revolution. So the competition was annulled for that year. The year following Thiers submitted his eulogy again under his own name, and also a second piece which purported to come from Paris, and which did not bear a signature. The Academy, thus tricked, awarded the prize to the latter essay, and gave honorable mention to the former.

In 1821 Thiers and Mignet went to Paris. Thiers was soon admitted to the staff of *Le Constitutionnel*, and was also assigned the political review of a weekly paper. *Le Constitutionnel* was radical in its leanings. It supported the cause of the Revolution. Thiers took the side of democracy against the aristocracy of the Restoration.

He also tried art criticism, and wrote up the picture exhibit (*Salon*) of 1822 for the romantic journal, *Le Globe*. In 1823 a book on the Pyrenees and South France, ostensibly a narrative of travel, but really a political pamphlet against the proposed expedition into Spain—to restore Ferdinand VII—illustrated in a concrete way his powers of argument and satire.   Some years afterwards, in 1830, he was active in founding a new journal, *Le National*, in which he continued to sustain the work of the Revolution.   In practice, however, he considered, with Guizot, that liberty would be best conserved by a constitutional monarchy after the pattern of England, not a republic like the United States.   As he himself expressed it: "We must cross the Channel, and not the Atlantic."   This position, once assumed, seems to have been maintained by him to the end.   The name mattered little.   He was ready to uphold any government which should guarantee to the governed the liberty won by the Revolution.   The great obstacle to the furtherance of this liberty, he claimed, was the divine right of kings, which the Bourbons still maintained.   Now the monarch, emperor, or president of the modern state should derive his powers from the consent of the governed.   Specifically he would be an Orleanist, were the opportunity given.   The opportunity came in 1830, and Thiers entered public life.

During these ten years of literary and political activity the journalist had shown himself an historian also.   His "History of the French Revolution," begun in 1823, had expanded to ten volumes by the time it was finished, in 1827.   When he first proposed it to a publisher, the latter required that he add as collaborator the name of Félix Bodin, a well-known writer of historical summaries for

popular use, books of facts and dates rather than of judgment and description. The first two volumes of the
"History" bore, therefore, the names of both Thiers and
Bodin. From the third the name of Thiers appears alone.
Nor is there any reason to suppose that he had received
much assistance from Bodin, unless indeed in the suggestion of the work itself. Thiers's method of historical
writing is quite the reverse of Guizot's. If the latter's
may be rightly called philosophical, the former's may perhaps be termed journalistic. Thiers certainly did not shut
himself up in his study and absorb himself in the contem-
plation of the principles of the world's progress, illustrat-
ing these principles by documents in hand. On the
contrary, he went out into the street, entered cafés,
joined groups in the public squares, frequented *salons*,
questioning the men and women who had played a part
in the great drama, or who had accounts of it from eye-
witnesses. This is the reportorial way of gathering news.
It has its merits. The facts collected are quick with life,
the impressions received glow with passion, the opinions
expressed still quiver with the emotion of personal experience. But all the notes thus made, however vivid their
content, are quite untrustworthy in their application to
events. They cannot lay claim to impartiality at least.
They are personal, partisan. And so it was with the
history which Thiers made up from them. It was vivid,
clear in expression, vibrating with feeling, but superficial
as to the exposition of causes, and filled with party spirit
in the narration of events. Inevitably, certain of the
great figures became heroes in the author's eyes; others
quite as great suffered by his hostility. His prejudices
were those of the Third Estate, and the lower Third Estate

at that. He had suffered nothing in property or in life by the political and social changes of the revolutionary period. He had gained rather by the general results of the changes. Therefore, he comes forward as their defender. It is the radical republican daring to praise what had been condemned by the writers of the Restoration. He was not actuated by sentiment. There is little that is romantic in his inspiration. Thiers belonged to the class of materialists who recognize facts because they are facts, and accept them because they are. So the general thought of his "History" is stamped with fatalism. What must be must be, the creed of that embodiment of the Revolution, Napoleon Bonaparte. The style and content go well together. Both are equally clear, direct, forceful.

Consequently the success of this book was unusual. The passing generation, of whatever shade of belief, found in it the recital of its exploits or its wrongs. Partisans of every sort denounced it or defended it, but all read it. Furthermore, its publication came at what is generally called the "psychological moment." A new generation had come forward, contemporaries of Thiers, who knew of the excesses of the Terror by hearsay only, as he did, but who saw that whatever injustices had been done in the name of liberty, the fact remained that liberty had been acquired and the class privileges of the *ancien régime* had gone forever. These people had benefited by the change. They were tired of the denunciation of the methods by which the change had been wrought. They were beginning to feel their power and they hailed the daring protagonist of their views as the champion of the new democracy. The "History of the French Revolution" laid the foundations for Thiers's political career. Henceforward he felt behind him a party, increasing in numbers and growing in wealth and influence. Relying on its support he had helped found *Le National*, its votes had elected him to the Assembly in the same year, and he represented it in the ministry of the new government which was formed after the Revolution of 1830.

Thiers was not a republican yet. He still held to the idea of a constitutional monarchy based on the model of the English government. He thought it best adapted to preserve the liberties which had been won by the French against both despotism and anarchy. In this respect he agreed with Guizot and for a time we find these two working together. But Guizot, as we have seen, possessed but a restricted notion of political liberty. Not only should it be conserved by a monarchy, but it should also be guaranteed by a choice body of voters selected from the upper *bourgeoisie*, to which Guizot himself belonged. Now Thiers was of the petty *bourgeoisie*. He could see no harm in bringing his own social caste into participation in public affairs. It was soon evident that the advocate of the wider democracy could not dwell in peace with him who saw all political wisdom concentrated in the upper *bourgeoisie*. In 1840 they came to an open separation.

The intervening ten years, 1830 to 1840, had confirmed Thiers in his attitude of political progress, and had introduced him to the public as an orator of the first rank. His maiden speech, however, as one of the secretaries of the Treasury Department, had been a failure. Monotonous in tone and hesitating in speech, his physical appearance, short, ugly, had added to his discomfiture. But his

reappearance on the floor the following year, 1831, in a
debate on foreign affairs, had at once convinced his fellow-
members of their wrong judgment. Clear, logical, inci-
sive, witty, passionate, his emotion and his energy transformed his very body. Such merits could not be neglected
by the government, and in 1832 he became Minister of
the Interior, thus entering on a career of administrative
responsibility which lasted four years, and during which
he was closely associated with Guizot. Both retired at
the same time in 1836. Thiers resumed power for a few
months in 1840, this time, however, to be replaced by
Guizot, whose attitude of conservatism stood higher in
the favor of the king.

During this decade the reaction against the condemnation of the Revolution had been steadily gaining headway.
The glory of Napoleon, obscured for a time by the
remembrance of the wretchedness his wars had brought
to the homes of France, had also come out from its
eclipse. The splendor of his conquests illuminated all his
deeds. The legend of the Little Corporal began, fostered
by the sentimentality of the veterans of the Grand Army
and by the fireside poetry of a Béranger. A Bonapartist
revival was well under way. Certain public events had
been created by it, and had assisted it in turn. In 1833
the statue of the Emperor had been restored to the pedestal on which it had formerly stood, the Vendome column,
cast by Napoleon out of the cannon captured in his European campaigns. In 1836 the Arch of Triumph, begun
by him to celebrate his victories and turned from this plan
by the government of the Restoration, was restored to its
original purpose and finished by Louis Philippe. Finally,
in 1840, during the short interval that Thiers was head of

affairs, Guizot, then ambassador to England, acting at Thiers's instigation, obtained from the English ministry the permission to remove Napoleon's remains from St. Helena to French soil. Bonaparte had said in his will: "I wish my ashes to repose on the banks of the Seine, in the midst of that French people I have so loved," and the popular desire had long looked forward to a consummation of this wish. In November, 1840, his body arrived at Cherbourg. From that port to Paris the funeral cortége moved along escorted by the acclamations of the whole population. So slow was the progress in the midst of the unbounded enthusiasm, that it was the middle of December before the final resting-place was reached under the dome of the church of the Invalides.

Thiers may not have aided this apotheosis of Napoleon with his own political interests in view, but he as surely aided it. His "History of the French Revolution" had pointed that way. His speech at the time of his reception to the French Academy (1834) further showed the inclination of his mind. In the midst of the praise of his predecessor, the dramatist Andrieux, the newly elected Academician found room for the eulogy of the times in which Andrieux had lived. This eulogy better than any words of paraphrase or comment can throw light on the attitude of a large group of the French people towards the Revolution and the Empire: "What a time, what things, what men, from that memorable year of 1789 to that other year no less memorable of 1830! The old French society of the eighteenth century, so polished but so badly ordered, ends in a frightful storm. A crown falls with a crash, carrying with it the august head which wore it. Immediately and without respite the most precious and illustrious heads are stricken low: genius, heroism, youth, succumb to the fury of factions, which are irritated by all that charms men. And from out this bloody chaos an extraordinary genius suddenly arises, who seizes that society, stops it, gives it at the same time order, glory, realizes civil equality, the most genuine of its needs, postpones the liberty which would have impeded its progress, and hastens to carry through the world the puissant truths of the French Revolution. One day his tri-colored banner shines forth on the heights of Mount Tabor; another day, on the Tagus; finally on the Borysthenes. He falls at last, leaving the world filled with his works, the human mind full of his image. And the most active of mortals goes away to die, to die of inaction, on an island of the great ocean! . . . . We have seen a forum as bloody as that of Rome; we have seen the heads of orators borne to the tribune's seat; we have seen kings more unfortunate than Charles I, more sadly blinded than James II; we see every day the prudence of William of Orange; and we have seen Cæsar—Cæsar himself! Among you who are listening to me there are witnesses who have had the glory of approaching him, of meeting his gleaming glance, of hearing his voice, of receiving his orders from his own lips, and of hastening to execute them through the smoke of battle-fields.''

The bearing of such eloquent sentences is unmistakable. Thiers, willingly or not, was already a pronounced admirer of Napoleon, and saw in him the personification of the principles of the Revolution. But apart from this admiration of the man he still stood for a constitutional monarchy, and not for an empire. Throughout the eight years of political opposition that followed 1840, the years

in which Guizot's "doctrinaire" ideas of a *bourgeoisie*
administration, stubbornly adhered to, were ruining the
cause of a constitutional monarchy, Thiers abode by that
principle. He argued for an extension of the suffrage,
and the incompatibility of office-holding with the function
of a deputy to the Assembly, but he never spoke for either
republic or empire. In the last days of Louis Philippe
he carefully abstained from overt acts of disapproval, and
when at the supreme moment Guizot was forced to give
up the direction of affairs, he even consented to head a
more liberal ministry. But it was too late. The day of
compromise had passed. Universal suffrage triumphed in
the Revolution of 1848.

Thiers accepted the Republic as he would have accepted
any form of government which should preserve the results
attained by the French Revolution. Shortly before the
fall of the monarchy he had affirmed his position before a
hostile house in these words: "I am not a radical, gentlemen; the radicals know that very well, and to read their
journals is enough to be convinced of it. But listen well
to my opinion, I am of the party of the Revolution, both
in France and in Europe. I hope the government of the
Revolution may remain in the hands of moderates. I
shall do all I can to have it remain there. But even
though this government should pass into the hands of men
who are less moderate than I and my friends, into the
hands of ardent men, even were they radicals, I shall not
abandon my cause on that account; I shall always belong
to the party of the Revolution." He accepted an election
from Paris to the new house of representatives, and in its
deliberations ranked himself among the conservatives.
To combat the theories of the socialists, which were

attaining prominence at this time, he published a witty
defense of the rights of individual ownership ("On Property," 1848). In the house itself he led the majority
against a proposition of the socialist writer, Proudhon.
Later, in the presidential election, he supported the can-
didacy of Louis Napoleon, perhaps because of his devotion to the cause of the first Napoleon, perhaps because
he considered the nephew of the great Emperor more
conservative than the other candidates, and did not fear
any reaction in the government. Napoleon was elected
by an overwhelming majority, and with him an Assembly
which numbered but very few partisans of a republic.
The sequel of this election is well known. Greeted by
the sober mass of the population as the restorer of law
and order, crowned with the halo of the Napoleonic glory,
supported by the clergy and the advocates of clerical
authority, Louis Napoleon dared affront the men who had
aided his advancement, gained control of the regular
army, and established despotic power in France by the
coup d'état of December 2, 1851. Thiers had foreseen
the catastrophe, had striven to avert it by recalling his
countrymen to the defense of the law. On the dissolution of the Assembly, he was arrested by order of the
conspirators and sent into exile. A few weeks later the
famous *plébiscite* voted the Second Empire into being.

The *coup d'état* gave Thiers back to the duties of private life. The decree of his exile was revoked in the summer of 1852, and he returned to France, to the meetings
of the Academy, to the *salons* of Paris, mainly hostile to
the new master, to new studies in the natural sciences and
astronomy, to attendance on the lectures of Pasteur at
the École Normale, above all, to the composition of his

greater historical work, "History of the Consulate and the Empire." He had begun this sequel to his "French Revolution" in 1845, while still engaged in parliamentary work. Five volumes had been published in that year, two each in 1847 and 1849, and three in 1851. The period of exile had interrupted him. Some time elapsed before he could settle down to his task again. Not till 1856 was publication renewed, and 1862 first saw the completion of the undertaking. The same success was won here that was gained by his "French Revolution." The methods employed in writing the two books varied, of course. The men who had taken part in the politics and wars under Napoleon, while still numerous, retained impressions of events that were less vivid than those of the survivors of the revolutionary period, in 1823. Many details had escaped them. Their passions had cooled in the thirty years and more of interval. From them Thiers gleaned what he could. But other sources were open to him. The government archives, the memoirs and correspondence of contemporaries and participants, the judgments pronounced by predecessors—how much use he made of this written material cannot be determined. He is accused of restricting himself to the files of the government organ, *Le Moniteur*. An unjust accusation probably, but which might well be true, in view of the fact that he wholly neglected the accounts of English and German authorities. Consequently, from an historical standpoint, the "Consulate and Empire" possesses little value.

The public at large, however, did not look so closely. It was attracted to the work by the same qualities which had furthered the vogue of the "French Revolution." The same clear style, the same rapid sequence of events narrated, the same disregard of philosophical meditation on cause and effect. Heroes come and go. Those who succeed are praised, those who fail are condemned. Such are the fortunes of war, and Thiers was not an idealist. Even the great hero, the genius whose career was so eloquently outlined in the speech delivered at Thiers's reception into the French Academy, shares like fate with the heroes of less eminence. All conquering he was all wise. But his campaigns in Spain and Russia demonstrated his fallibility. Thiers's critics attribute this alteration of eulogy in the case of the great Napoleon to the political deeds of the "petty Napoleon," as Hugo delighted to call him. Between the first volumes of the history and the last the *coup d'état* had intervened. It may be these reproaches of undue influence are right. Yet it was Thiers's way to reward success with praise, failure with blame. It was this characteristic of his work which gives it the name of "fatalistic." Napoleon was no exception to his rule.

No sooner was this second great literary undertaking ended than an indication of liberalism in the policy of Napoleon III called Thiers once more into the political arena. In the election of 1863 he was returned to the house ("corps législatif") as member from Paris. His appearance was a political event. The old guard of constitutional liberty in France reëntered the parliament of France with him. This idea was clearly affirmed in his first long speech. He asks for liberty—individual, electoral, parliamentary; liberty of the press and ministerial responsibility. He asks for these "necessary liberties" quietly, dispassionately. Yet he points out the danger of refusing them. And he continued on this course, a critic

or the administration, but not a hostile one, more desirous
of seeing the return of representative government than of
accomplishing the ruin of the Empire. He was not an
extremist. He was not even a republican by conviction.
He still modeled his opinion on the English constitution.
He often stood alone, between the imperialists on the one
hand, and the radicals on the other.

But even a temperate critic found occasions enough to
employ all the resources of his talent. The Second
Empire was tossed from one mistake to another. The
Emperor was a mixture of an autocrat and a humanitarian. At times he was more than suspected of socialistic
views. He constantly wavered in both his domestic and
foreign policy. Extreme measures in one direction were
soon balanced by extreme measures in the opposite direction. For a while at least the people of France were not
affected by his home policy. All classes were satisfied—
the workmen, peasants, business men, and clergy. But
the French have always been peculiarly sensitive to their
standing among nations. They would play a large part
in the politics of the world. Napoleon III recognized
this trait, and tried to suit it. The Crimean War was
one consequence of his attempts to please, a war which
estranged both enemy and ally. Another endeavor was
the war against Austria for the independence of Italy,
which was brought to an abrupt close without Italy's consent. The war in Mexico grew out of a mixture of business with dreams of a Latin empire. French pride was
touched by its unfortunate conclusion. So with the other
events of the day, the Schleswig-Holstein imbroglio, the
war between Prussia and Austria in 1866, the failure to
secure Luxembourg, the expedition into Italy in 1867.

Every undertaking of the Emperor, the result of his own emotions, or the country's ambition, with which he had no real sympathy at heart, alienated some portion of the nation because of its lack of decision and thoroughness. Finally the elections of 1869 showed that the peasants alone remained loyal to the government. The cities were all in active opposition. A liberal administration was tried. A constitution was submitted to popular vote. It was overwhelmingly ratified. The pure Bonapartists took courage. Absolutism seemed possible again. A successful war might confirm its hold on the nation for another generation. Urged on by partisans, by dynastic considerations, by popular jealousy of Prussia, the fatalistic Emperor yielded to the importunities of his advisers and consented to a breach of peace. The Empire paid the price, but the humiliation of France was complete.

Throughout these years of unrest Thiers had remained a critic, and an ally as well. He had deplored the mistakes in the foreign policy, had urged vigorous measures at the time of the Danish war in 1864, and again on the occasion of the Austrian defeat in 1866. Opponents even assert that he was partly responsible for the final catastrophe of 1870, because of his insistence on military interference with Prussia in these other affairs. And indeed, his foreign policy as a minister under Louis Philippe had not lacked in aggressiveness. However all this may be, when in July, 1870, it came to the point of declaring war against the German state, he opposed the declaration with all his might. For hours this old man, of more than threescore years and ten, pleaded with the excited Bonapartist majority and endured its insults. He knew that France was in no condition for war, and that Prussia was ready. Yet, when his advice was disregarded, when the Emperor had gone to the front and the first reverses were pushing the French armies back onto their own soil, he did not stand aloof. He made common cause with the Empire in the defense of the fatherland, and accepted a nomination to the Council of Defense. And he continued at this post even when all his protests were unheeded.

Sedan came. The Emperor was deposed. The Third Republic was proclaimed on September 4th, by the citizens of Paris. The deputies of the capital accepted the situation, the Corps Législatif was dissolved, and an unauthorized government took charge of public affairs. Thiers would not consent to become a part of it, though he did undertake at its request a mission to foreign courts. For more than a month this wonderful septugenarian made the tour of Europe, to London, to Turin, to Vienna, to St. Petersburg, pleading with unsympathetic governments for intervention in behalf of France. He obtained the expression of a desire for an armistice, and Bismarck consented to open negotiations. But once again Thiers was baffled, this time by his very friends. Gambetta, in the provinces, did not wish to link the name of republic to an inglorious peace, the inevitable result of an armistice under existing conditions. The populace of Paris, agitated by theories of social reforms, and irritated at the incapacity of its generals, coerced the authorities, and would not listen to Thiers's proposals. The siege and the desultory war dragged on. Paris was starved into submission in January, 1871, and all resistance disappeared with its surrender. At last it was seen that some regular administration should replace the temporary expedient of the government of national defense. General elections

were held throughout France, and in February a new
Assembly met at Bordeaux.

This Assembly wished for peace. It was elected with
peace in view. Because the republic had stood for war,
under Gambetta's leadership, only a minority of the
deputies were republicans. The large majority was composed of monarchists of different stripes. A few were
imperialists. Yet all factions united to put at their head
the man whose opposition to the war and whose efforts
for peace had made him the most prominent figure in the
country. Thiers was chosen Chief of the Executive
Power of the French Republic, with the mandate to make
a treaty with the Germans, a duty which he performed
with considerable difficulty. The Prussian demands had
been already indicated. France was to pay for the cost
of the war and in addition was to lose her eastern provinces, Alsace, always a German-speaking land, and part of
Lorraine, including the fortress of Metz. It was the
territorial concession which made Thiers's task peculiarly
painful. The deputies from Alsace-Lorraine opposed
their denationalization by voice and petition. But no way
of escape could be found. Belfort, on the southern edge,
was the utmost concession allowed by Bismarck. Under
the stress of necessity the Assembly ratified the preliminaries of peace, and in May the treaty was concluded.

Meanwhile another evil had threatened to destroy the
enfeebled vitality of the nation. Discontented with the
management of the war and the conditions of peace,
smarting under the rebuffs administered to the national
honor by the victorious alien, suspecting the royalist
majority in the Assembly of attempting to do away with
the republican form of government, lured with the pic-

tures of utopias where labor would possess all the rewards
and pure democracy would protect true liberty, equality,
and fraternity, above all without occupation in the weeks
of transition between siege and peace, the laborers of
Paris, under the leadership of daring dreamers, rose in
rebellion and endeavored to establish an independent government. The Commune was an echo of the French
Revolution, fostered by the social theories of Saint
Simon, Fourier, and their successors. It was hostile to
all restraint of law or property. A less resolute man
than Thiers would have yielded to discouragement and
given the country over to anarchy. He had neither army
nor means at hand. But he saw that the revolt must be
suppressed. At his suggestion the seat of government
was transferred from Bordeaux to Versailles. An army
was concentrated there, made up for the most part of the
troops who were returning from German prisons. The
conquest of Paris was attempted. In spite of a desperate
resistance, which lasted over six weeks, and desolated the
very streets of the capital, Thiers's wisdom and energy
triumphed. The revolt was attended by all the horrors
of a civil war. Class hatred intensified its bitterness,
and Rousseau's argument for the ills born of civilization
was given a concrete example. Many of the public buildings were burned. The intention of the communist chiefs
was to involve the whole city in destruction. Prompt
action saved the French from this catastrophe, but the
fall of the Commune left its aftermath of dissension and
ill-will.

From this chaos of ruined and tottering governments
the French Republic finally emerged. It is probable that
the personality of Thiers contributed in great measure to

this result. During the last years of the Second Empire he had been gradually led to the opinion that a republic, and not a constitutional monarchy, would be the outcome of the natural political movement of the nation. When Sedan was over he did not associate himself with the government of national defense, though he served it and his country to the best of his ability, and after the new Assembly was elected, he strictly adhered to the agreement to free France from invasion before raising the question of her future administration. This work had been done. The Republic had got the credit for it. The Commune had been ruthlessly crushed. Thiers could therefore expect the support of all conservatives. Supplementary elections in July, 1871, had added to the number of republican deputies. All these things conspired to make the moderate royalists acquiesce in the conditions existing. Agitation was feared. The republicans thought they saw signs of a royalist plot. The royalists trembled at the prospect of a Jacobin revolution. The firmness and tact of Thiers, who was now wholly convinced of the desirability of continuing the republican form of government (a conviction, it is alleged, which was strengthened by the dictates of his private ambition), succeeded in drawing together the more reasonable of all groups. On August 30 he was formally elected president of the French Republic, and given the power to constitute a cabinet. But he was made subject to the vote of the Assembly. In reality his attributes were little other than those of a prime minister. But the name had come, and, as the sequel showed, the thing followed.

In the treaty of peace it was stipulated that the withdrawal of the German armies should be in proportion to the payment of the indemnity. This indemnity was fixed at five milliards of francs—about one billion dollars. It was thought that a country overrun and demoralized as France had been could not soon rally, and there is no doubt that the Germans looked forward to a somewhat protracted residence. But the outcome of the government appeals to provide for the indemnity was most unusual. Thiers had made his first appearance in public life as a secretary in the Treasury Department. At the age of seventy-four he was called upon to justify this early office. The Germans were paid off ahead of time, and their last regiment withdrew in September, 1873. "Liberator of the territory" is the title which public opinion conferred on the man who had achieved this great result. It settled Thiers's position with posterity, and yet it was fatal to his further career as a statesman.

The Assembly, the only legislative body of the nation, was supposed to dissolve when the Germans withdrew, and allow new elections, free from the emotions of war, to decide the future of France. But the Assembly was anti-republican. The majority in it was united in opposition to a republic. Late in 1872 Thiers brought this opposition to a head by proposing that the Assembly proceed to discuss plans for a permanent constitution. The majority feared that such a measure would establish the Republic beyond a doubt. They now sought to undermine Thiers and replace him with a president in harmony with their views. The radicals unwittingly aided this plan. Thiers's intimate friend De Rémusat was defeated in a Paris election by Barodet, whom Gambetta championed. At a new session of the Assembly in May, 1873, a resolution was proposed for discussion which Thiers declined to accept. The discussion was voted, and the first president of the Third Republic resigned at once. He was succeeded by Marshal MacMahon.

But the conservative coalition was still only a negative one. Partisans of the old dynasty, known as Legitimists, the Orleanists, and the Bonapartists, could unite against the Republic, but could not agree on any other form of government to take its place. Shortly after the accession of MacMahon a deputation from the royalist factions had waited on the Comte de Chambord, the representative of the Bourbons. It seemed as though a throne would rise again in France. But his conditions were impossible, particularly a sentimental one, which demanded the substitution of the old fleur-de-lis banner for the tricolor of the Napoleonic and Franco-Prussian wars. MacMahon consequently was given a term of seven years. He urged a constitution. In 1875 it was adopted. It provided for a Senate and a Chamber of Deputies. Thiers had voted for it, though he had taken little part in the debates on this or other subjects. His attention was mainly given to reconstructing his house which the Commune had destroyed, and the preparation of a treatise on scientific philosophy. But he stood again for election in 1876. Belfort named him senator and Paris deputy. He chose the latter mandate, which seated him in the legislative body that was nearer the people. The country had returned a republican majority, and MacMahon was forced to form a cabinet which should represent its opinions. This cabinet was short-lived. The Marshal's reactionary advisers forced his hand. He dismissed the ministry, and went so far as to dissolve the House. A royalist *coup d'état* was feared. Excitement grew apace.

All shades of republicans, seeing that the crisis had come, united to save the Republic. Thiers was among them. He consented to stand for Paris. His electoral manifesto had been partly written. But before it could be finished a stroke of apoplexy brought his busy life to an end, on September 3, 1877. He had passed his eightieth birthday.

The death of Thiers only preluded the triumph of that republic in which he had come at last to believe. It still endures. Its foundations seem fixed. It will transmit with its permanence the name of its first president to posterity. But Thiers's services to the state in the time of its great need transcend the bounds of governmental polity, and appeal to all Frenchmen of whatever political creed. He had the satisfaction of enjoying this reward in advance. An accident had revealed it to him. Just before the dissolution of the Chamber of Deputies, in June, 1877, one of the members of the cabinet, in alluding to the liberation of the territory from the German troops, had given the credit for it to the old Assembly. The effect of this statement was electrical. Leaping to his feet, with all the impetuosity of his nature, Gambetta stretched out his hand towards the white-haired states-man, "There is the liberator of the territory!" he cried, while with almost one accord the deputies rose in their places to do homage to their acknowledged benefactor.

Thiers had no descendants. His will bequeathed to the nation the collection of pictures and statuary which had adorned his house in Paris. The Thiers Prize in history had previously been established by him with the prize money awarded him by the French Academy, in 1861, for his "History of the Consulate and Empire." But his chief memorial is the Thiers Foundation, maintained by the estate left by his widow, through which five scholars of promise, nominated by the scientific associations of France, are generously supported for a period of three years.

SELECTIONS FROM THE WRITINGS OF THIERS

Preface to the "History of the French Revolution"

I propose to write the history of a memorable revolution which has moved men deeply, and which still divides them to-day. I do not hide from myself the difficulties of the enterprise, for passions which were supposed to be stifled under the influence of military despotism have just been awakened again. All of a sudden men overwhelmed with years and labor have felt sentiments revive in themselves which had seemed to be appeased, and have communicated them to us, us their sons and heirs. But if we have to sustain the same cause we have not to defend their conduct, and we can distinguish the liberty of those who served it well from the liberty of those who served it ill, while we possess the advantage of having heard and observed these old men who, still full of their recollections, still agitated by their impressions, reveal to us the spirit and character of the parties, and teach us how to understand them. Perhaps the moment when the actors are about to pass away is the time best suited to write history; we can listen to their testimony without, however, sharing all their passions.

Be this as it may, I have endeavored to still all sentiment of hatred in my soul. I have in turn fancied to myself that, born under a roof of thatch, animated by a just ambition, I have wished to acquire what the pride of the upper classes had unjustly refused me; or that, reared in palaces, heir to ancient privileges, it was painful for me to renounce a possession which I used to consider a legitimate right. Henceforward I could not feel any irritation. I have pitied those who waged the warfare, and I have found a recompense in adoring the noble souls.

*From the Speeches on the Preliminaries of the Treaty of
Peace between France and Germany*

[The treaty was attacked in the Assembly by Victor Hugo and
others because it looked to the separation of Alsace-Lorraine.
Thiers replied supporting it.]

If there was, in my eyes, one single chance of keeping up the
struggle, with prospects of success, never would I have imposed
on myself one of the greatest griefs of my life in signing the preliminaries of the treaty I have brought to you. It is the absolute
conviction of the impossibility of continuing that struggle which
has constrained me to bow my head under the might of the
foreigner. I beg you not to ask me to give the motives for my
conviction. My silence is a sacrifice which I make to the safety
and the future of my country. Yes, it is my deep conviction that
in making peace to-day, in submitting to a great sorrow, we are
saving the country's future, we are making its future greatness
sure. It is this hope only, this hope alone, which was able to
bring me to a decision.

I give the Assembly no advice. I cannot advise it except by
my example. I repeat I have imposed on myself one of the most
cruel sorrows of my life. (He is so moved as to be obliged to
stop a moment amidst the applause of the Assembly.)

(He speaks a second time.) I will say but a few words; but
it is necessary that the question be clearly put and the responsibilities exactly assigned. The war had two periods, one which
followed the famous declaration you have just condemned and
punished, the other which succeeded the 4th of September. I
judge no one, I condemn no one; I am convinced that every one
did his best. I was a stranger to both periods. If the war was
not successful, neither I nor the colleagues the Assembly gave me
a few days ago can be accused of its failure.

When I was obliged to negotiate I found Sedan, Metz, and
Paris lost, and the armies dispersed which were to go to aid the
capital, but could not reach it. I have conducted the negotiations
with all the patriotism of which I was capable. I struggled for
days with all my might. I was not able to do better than I
did. . . . .

I do not doubt France's strength, but I doubt its present organization. Its military organization is broken; here is the secret of its weakness.

Why was that organization broken? I will say but one word on the subject, without going into details. When they had the madness to declare war last July, I said from the start that France was not ready. When they had infantry regiments of thirteen hundred to fourteen hundred actual men, how could they in a week raise them to a war-footing of three thousand men? It was impossible. I said to the ministers: "Set me before the Minister of War and I will prove to him that you are not ready, that you can't be ready." . . . .

Well, let some one come now and tell me we can resist an army of five hundred thousand regular troops. I will tell him we cannot. You would ruin France, you would impoverish it, you would squander its last resources and take from it the means of reaching that future you hope for, and of which I catch a glimpse with the sole satisfaction I can feel to-day.

Yes, gentlemen, you wish other destinies for the fatherland. So do I. I eagerly wish for them, and what supports me at my advanced age is the hope of being able to aid in their coming, not for very long, but for some time still. To accomplish this purpose you must know the truth, you must have the courage to tell yourselves the truth and to believe it. . . . .

To my last hour I shall not change my line of action and I will do all I can to make my countrymen hear the entire truth. Six months ago they would not listen to it. More recently still they would not listen to it. But I am not discouraged. If you, in your turn, will not listen to it, you will make me very unhappy for my country. But if I dared say so, while being very unhappy about my country, I would perhaps be happy for myself because you didn't believe me. I would have thrown off the burden you had confided to me, and I would thank you for it, though weeping over my unfortunate country.

Gentlemen, hear the truth. But if you do not know where truth is to be found, if you do not wish to listen to it and believe it, you may boast of our nation's future, it will be a vain boast. You will ruin it at the very moment you are boasting of it.

BIBLIOGRAPHY

A. Thiers.   P. de Rémusat.

Life of Thiers.   F. Le Goff.

Articles in *The Century Magazine*, Vol. I, pp. 439 ff., and *The Chautauquan*, Vol. XXV, pp. 239 ff.

CHAPTER V

GAMBETTA AND THE THIRD REPUBLIC

[LÉON MICHEL GAMBETTA, born at Cahors, April 2, 1838;
educated at the Lycée of Cahors and Law School at Paris;
admitted to the bar, 1860; the Baudin trial, November 14,
1868; elected to the Corps Législatif from Paris and Marseilles, 1869; Minister of the Interior in the Government of
National Defense, 1870; elected to the Assembly, 1871; leader
of the majority in the Chamber of 1875; President of the
Chamber, 1879; Prime Minister, 1881; died at Ville d'Avray,
December 31, 1882.]

The present government of France has lasted full
thirty-three years, a generation of humanity. When it
was established few believed in its permanency, and it
must be confessed that this unbelief was reasonable.
Since the French Revolution of 1789 the nation had seen
half a score of administrations of greater or less endur-
ance, but none so robust as to reach their majority. The
Second Empire, the longest of them all, died in its nineteenth year, the monarchy of Louis Philippe in its eighteenth, the Restoration and the First Empire at an earlier
age even. As for the republics, they had shown still less
vitality, and the more recent one of 1848 had proved
weaker even than the older republic of 1793. So many
political overturnings in such rapid succession could well
be taken as indications of the future. They showed
unusual instability, greater even than the restlessness of
which the pulpit orator Bossuet had accused England in

LÉON MICHEL GAMBETTA

the seventeenth century.   Besides it was well known that
republicans, pure and simple, were comparatively rare in
France.   In 1852, when Napoleon III put the Empire
to the test of a popular approval, but half a million votes,
representing all sorts of opposition, were polled against
it.   In 1870 the half million had increased to a million
and a half, but this number was still a hopeless minority.
How many republicans it included cannot be known.
There is good reason to believe that it counted more
advocates of a constitutional monarchy than sincere partisans of a republican form of government.   Elections
after 1870 showed this fact plainly, though there was an
apparent drift, as we have noticed in the case of Thiers,
from Orleanism to republicanism as the only possible
solution of the political problem.

The elections of 1863 had returned a handful of republicans, together with Thiers, to the Corps Législatif.   The
election of 1869 had multiplied their number.   Among
the newcomers was Gambetta, borne into political life on
the crest of a legal plea of a political nature.   If Thiers
was to found the republic on the discord of its opponents,
this younger, genuine democrat, Gambetta, was to
strengthen its foundations by winning over the opposition.   He was a Southerner like Thiers.   His father was
a Genoese grocer, who had settled at Cahors and married
there.   He named his first child, a son, born April 2,
1838, Léon Michel.   He gave this son the education
within his reach, and after the Cahors lycée (high school)
made the sacrifice of sending him to Paris to study law.
Young Gambetta reached the capital in 1857.   In spite
of his liking for argument and debate, his delight in
companionship and fondness for popularity, in spite also

of the loss of one eye from an accident when he was but
eight years old, he seems to have made a fairly diligent
student, and early in 1860 was admitted to the bar.

It was these first years in Paris, years of work and
good fellowship, that formed Gambetta's character and
showed him the road he was to follow. Like all students
of his day he lived in the students' district, the Latin
Quarter. The glory it had inherited from the men of
1830, sculptors, poets, painters, dramatists, novelists,
physicians, still lingered in its tortuous streets and
weather-stained garrets. The flowing locks of the
romanticists and the red waistcoats of the night of
Hugo's "Hernani" still distinguished its more devoted
denizens. The evening life of the region was in the
cafés. There art, philosophy, religion, literature, politics,
furnished abundant material for nightly debate. In the
cafés the eloquence and wit of Gambetta found ample
room for display before an admiring circle. Alphonse
Daudet, the novelist, has chronicled for us the impressions made upon him at that time by the future ruler of
France: "The Gambetta of those days was sowing his
wild oats, and was deafening with his thundering eloquence the cafés of the Latin Quarter. But make no
error, the cafés of the Quarter at that epoch were not
merely the saloon where you drink and smoke. In the
midst of Paris, muzzled by the Second Empire, without
public life, without newspapers, those reunions of a studi-
ous and noble youth, true schools of opposition, or rather
of legal resistance, remained the only places where a free
voice could still be heard. Each of them had its own
orator, a table which at certain moments became almost a
speaker's desk, and each orator in the Quarter had his

admirers and partisans. . . . . Doubtless some of our
young speakers never progressed, grew old without advancing, spoke constantly, and never did anything. . . . .
But Gambetta was not of that number. If he fenced under
the gas at the café, it was only after he had filled his day
with real labor. As the factory gets rid of its steam at
night, he came there to let his surplus vigor and ideas
overflow in words. This did not at all prevent him from
being a serious student, from having his triumphs at
Molé's lecture-hall, from being promoted in his courses
and winning his diploma. . . . . Not stout as yet, but
squarely built, stoop-shouldered, with familiar gestures,
already liking to lean on a friend's arm while walking
and talking, he spoke a great deal, at every opportunity,
with that hard, strong voice of the South which cuts off
phrases like a pendulum and stamps words like medallions.
But he also listened, questioned, read, assimilated everything, and was laying in that enormous supply of facts
and ideas so necessary to any one who claims to direct a
time and a country as complicated as ours. Gambetta is
one of the rare politicians who like art and suspect that
literature may occupy some place in a people's life. . . . .
These strolls through the Art Exhibitions and the Louvre
Museum . . . . had given Gambetta a reputation for
laziness with certain verdant statesmen, stiff and starched
since childhood. These same men, now grown up,
always full of themselves and always hermetically sealed,
take him to be a frivolous man and a politician lacking in
seriousness, because he likes the company of a witty actor.
At the very most this would prove that then, as to-day,
Gambetta knew men, and knew the great secret of making
them useful, which is by winning their affection. A char-

acteristic trait will finish the portrait of the old Gambetta. That speaking-trumpet of a voice, that terrible talker, that great Gasconizer was not a Gascon. Is it race influence? On more than one side this mad son of Cahors came near to Italian prudence. . . . . Speaking often, always speaking, he never let himself be carried away by the whirlwind of his speech. Very enthusiastic, he knew in advance the precise point where his enthusiasm should stop.''

Daudet's sketch indicates the traits which made Gambetta a power in France. He was friendly to all men. He was careless in dress and companions, thereby disarming the jealousy of his more severe and better bred rivals. His voice overwhelmed all others, and the flow of his words swept opposition from its feet. With all this, while seemingly on fire with enthusiasm, heating the emotion of his hearers to a glow, he himself was a cool, observant master of his own actions and the actions of those he had inspired. Assiduous in the collection of information, he gradually amassed a knowledge of things and men which fully atoned for his lack of breeding and the narrowness of his home life.

Admission to the bar had been gained in 1860, but his life at Paris had weakened his constitution. A few months' rest became imperative. He returned to Cahors to recruit. Restored to health, the question of locating himself for the practice of his profession arose. The father felt he had done all he could. The son longed to try Paris. The financial difficulty was solved by the devotion of an aunt, who moved to Paris in 1861, and on her small income started housekeeping, in which she figured as both servant and mistress. In this way her nephew was given a home and support, until the slow remunerations from his infrequent briefs should bring him a livelihood.   Entering law offices as a student or clerk he got now and then a case of a political nature, and gradually became known.   His native eloquence stood him in good stead.   Lawyers admired it.   It brought him more clients.   At last it brought him success.

The *coup d'état* of December 2, 1851, had met with slight resistance.   Little blood had been shed.   Yet among the victims was Baudin, a member of the Assembly, shot down on the only apology for a barricade that had been built.   Baudin, however, had been forgotten, until a book on the *coup d'état*, published in 1868, revived his memory.   Then the republicans seized upon his fate as a means of annoying the government.   Speeches were made at his grave.   Certain newspapers began to collect funds for a statue.   The authorities took the matter up and prosecuted some of the journalists concerned.   Among the lawyers appearing in their defense was Gambetta, and his speech was the speech of the trial, and the beginning of his political career.   In it he denounced the *coup d'état*.   He contrasted the adherents of Napoleon III with his opponents.   He dilated on the dishonor and loss of prestige which the foreign policy of the Empire had brought on France.   He satirized the pretenses of the government in the light of its accomplishments.   And all this in a great voice that drowned all answers, and a torrent of invective which the imperial lawyers could not stem.   Gambetta had seized on the "psychological moment."   He had expressed what the nation was feeling.   His words penetrated the utmost corners of France, and carried with them the celebrity of his name. This was in November, 1868. The following May two districts elected him to the Corps Législatif. He declined the Paris mandate and sat for Marseilles.

During the months that followed, so long as the so-called "Liberal Empire" endured, under Ollivier's premiership, Gambetta continued in parliament the attitude of opposition he had assumed before he entered public life. As is seen by the circumstances of his birth, he represented a lower social class than had either Thiers or Guizot, and consequently having less to lose than either of these statesmen, and more to gain, his tendency was more radical than theirs. He was a democrat from the start, an advocate of a republican form of government, not a constitutional monarchy. His political platform included the separation of church and state and the election of all public officers by the people. Universal suffrage was his idol, and in words at least he never forsook it. Napoleon III did not hold his mandate from universal suffrage, he said, therefore the Empire should give way to an administration which the nation should sanction. All *plébiscites* were thus a mockery. With Thiers and the straight-out republicans he opposed the declaration of war against Prussia. Once declared he voted for the measures in its support. When Sedan fell and the Corps Législatif, by its procrastination, allowed itself to be overrun by the mob, Gambetta, with other deputies from Paris, retired to the City Hall, and there from one of the windows, by Gambetta's voice, the Republic was proclaimed. This was on September 4, 1870.

In the hastily formed organization which now undertook the defense of the country, Gambetta held the post of Minister of the Interior. When the Germans surrounded Paris, and it was necessary for the central committee there to keep in touch with their adherents in the provinces, Gambetta was chosen as ambassador. With his secretary he escaped in a balloon from the capital, beyond the lines of the enemy, who almost perforated his carriage, and from Tours first, afterwards from Bordeaux, directed what remained of national resistance. Filled with the traditions of 1792, when the citizen soldiery of France met and vanquished the trained veterans of monarchical Europe, he would not be discouraged by defeat or discord. With his burning appeals to the honor of the nation he roused the dormant spirit of all factions. All united to furnish men and means to resist invasion. But supplies were lacking, officers were lacking, even maps and charts were not at hand. Hastily raised levies under such conditions could be little else than a half-armed rabble when brought in contact with Von Moltke's perfectly equipped armies, led by most capable generals.

To add to his trials Metz surrendered. Its beleaguering forces were thrown at once on his patriotic bands. Some doubtful battles were fought, a victory or two were won. But such scattered successes could not affect the general results. The odds were too overwhelming. Still Gambetta labored and planned, encouraged and ordered. Even the fall of Paris found him undaunted, but the entreaties of his colleagues, who now could reach him, broke down his obstinacy. Elected to the Assembly which met at Bordeaux in February, 1871, he sat for an Alsatian district, and when the preliminaries of peace were agreed to by the House, he left the session together with the other representatives of the ceded provinces. He left France also, and during the whole outbreak of the

Commune lived in retirement at St. Sebastian, just across the Spanish frontier. If it was rest he sought he had well earned it. The amount of work he had performed since the previous October was well nigh incredible. For four months he had practically been the dictator of France.

The Commune had been crushed, the treaty of peace signed. Elections to fill vacancies in the Assembly had been fixed for July. Gambetta returned to contest a seat. His program, as before, was a government elected by universal suffrage, with the education of the lower classes, particularly the peasant, the center of political conservatism, to an appreciation of their duty towards society. Such a government would naturally be a republic. He was elected by several constituencies, and chose to sit for Paris. His course as a deputy was in harmony with his platform. He lost no occasion to preach republicanism to the royalist majority, and he opposed the declaration made by the Assembly, when Thiers was elected president, that it had the right to vote a constitution. It should have been dissolved when peace was once assured.

During the winter and spring of 1872 he kept on with his political proselyting, traveling about the country and addressing the electors on each and all occasions. In these speeches he developed his ideas of the mission of the Republic. It should uphold the good results of the French Revolution. It should look for support to the lower social classes. It should subordinate the church to the state and restrict the range of the evils arising from clericalism. When these things were done a new and happier life would prevail in France. Between times he employed his surplus energies in editing *La République Française*, a daily he had founded in November, 1871. Such persistency in pleading for a larger democracy naturally displeased the majority in the Assembly. Debates grew fierce. His endeavors also reacted on Thiers, and caused the breach between him and the House to widen. Finally, as we have seen, in April, 1873, the election of a radical in Paris, whose cause Gambetta undertook, over a member of the Thiers cabinet, brought on a crisis. The majority in the Assembly insisted on a vote committing the government to greater conservatism. Thiers replied with the proposition to found a republic. He was outvoted and resigned. His resignation brought Gambetta to the front.

MacMahon was president, the Duc de Broglie prime minister. The policy of the new administration was openly anti-democratic. It soon showed its animus by suppressing a radical newspaper. Gambetta's speeches themselves became subject to discipline. It was at this time that the throne was offered on the part of the majority to the Comte de Chambord, and declined by him unless it carried with it the white flag of the *ancien régime*. The failure of this negotiation resulted in a vote fixing Mac-Mahon's tenure of office at seven years. Meanwhile the republicans were steadily gaining in strength. The extremists among them were quiet. The divisions among the monarchists became accentuated after the demands of the Comte de Chambord were seen to be inadmissible. The royalists were disheartened and the Bonapartists encouraged. The latter began to display unusual activity. It was an opportunity for the republicans. Under Gambetta and Thiers, now united in a common purpose, they began to detach adherents from the cause of a constitutional monarchy, the Orleanists in particular, by showing the hopelessness of their case and the imminence of a Bonapartist restoration. Gambetta, radical and petty *bourgeois* as he was at heart, also changed his tone, and took occasion to compliment the upper *bourgeoisie*, to which he had been steadfastly hostile. Thus led on by one motive and another, by fear of despotism and by dread of lawlessness, the moderate men of the Assembly joined together in a series of compromises which resulted in the adoption of a constitution for France. The final vote was taken on February 25, 1875. Its most important provisions established a Senate and a Chamber of Deputies, gave to them conjointly the election of president, and fixed the latter's tenure of office at seven years. Gambetta was one of the most important factors in bringing about this result. To do this he had to sacrifice much of his personal opinion, and retract many of his former statements. The choice of a president by an electoral college rather than by universal suffrage, his political cure-all, must have been a particularly hard concession for him to make. But he made it, and France for a while was saved the dangers of a monarchical reaction.

But only for a time. The ensuing elections resulted favorably to the republicans, though the Senate, chosen for the most part by the councils of the various "departments" into which France is divided, showed a reactionary majority. In the Chamber the republicans prevailed, but soon split into factions. Besides, MacMahon, who owed his election to the monarchists, and was not dependent on popular favor, thought that his duty lay in the direction of conservatism, and gave the country cabinets which were not in accord with the legislative majority. Still Gambetta was for peace. He counseled moderation everywhere. Only the clericals and their pernicious influence incited him to invectives. Finally this idea of clericalism became too strong to be suppressed. The republican majority adopted it, pressed it to a vote, with the result that MacMahon, who stood for quite the opposite, lectured his last prime minister, who had not yet been defeated in the Chamber, for his subservience to Gambetta, and practically forced his resignation. This proceeding was not constitutional. Furthermore, it was a challenge to that part of the government which alone represented universal suffrage.

Gambetta, now the leader of the majority, lost no time. That very day he gathered the republicans together, proposed and carried a resolution not to support any ministry which should not govern according to republican principles. At the regular meeting of the Chamber on the day following the majority ratified the resolutions of the republican meeting. MacMahon answered with the appointment of a royalist cabinet, and adjourned the Chamber for a month. The republicans, under Gambetta's guidance, took the country into their confidence with a manifesto. All factions were now thoroughly united. The Chamber met again for a few days in June, long enough for Gambetta's dramatic reference to the "liberator" Thiers, and was then dissolved. General elections followed. Again the republicans were united, the monarchists divided. Gambetta caught the popular ear with the cry of "irreconcilable opposition" to the Empire, and with the statement that after the poll was once known the Marshal could do nothing but submit or resign ("*se soumettre ou se démettre*"). His newspaper was prosecuted by the authorities for contumacy, and Gambetta was fined. Yet in the end he won a victory. The elections did not return the desired number of republicans, the three hundred and sixty-three who had opposed the Marshal in June, but the party still had a majority, and used it in the new Chamber to unseat its opponents. It also refused to recognize a new ministry appointed by the marshal-president. Furthermore, following Gambetta's lead, it declined to vote the budget. MacMahon yielded at last. The republicans controlled the next cabinet of December, 1877.

Though the conservative Marshal refused him a ministerial office, Gambetta was now the acknowledged head of the governing majority. Unfortunately for his reputation, the merits of statesmanship, which had shone out so brightly in times of adversity, were somewhat beclouded or even eclipsed during this period of prosperity. Far from conciliating the opposition and winning over its less extreme adherents, he antagonized it in word and deed. During the senatorial elections of the autumn of 1878 he repeatedly assailed "the enemy" of clericalism and its connection with the schools, and asked for the suppression of nonauthorized religious communities—practically the measures that the French administration is pushing to-day. He also demanded the discharge of all magistrates and office-holders who were not republicans. The newly elected senators now gave him the control of the upper house, and MacMahon, weary of the fruitless contest, concluded to resign. Jules Grévy was elected in his stead. Gambetta, who might have been president perhaps, was chosen to be Grévy's successor in presiding over the Chamber.   This office he discharged with fairness and vigor.

His assumption of the presidency of the Chamber was the beginning of the decline of Gambetta's influence in public affairs.   His policy, which aimed at compromises, moderation, made use of accidental circumstances, such as divisions among the reactionary elements, and for this living from hand to mouth had been, perhaps contemptuously, dubbed "opportunism," was not based on any enduring principle of government, and of course satisfied none of the out-and-out partisans, who are always in a majority.   Consequently, from the day that MacMahon resigned and the republicans took entire control of the administration, he, as the leader of the republicans, the man who had done most to bring about the existing conditions, was attacked on every side, by the extreme royalists, by the imperialists, and also by the radicals to whom he by nature and environment really belonged.   He was accused of all kinds of misdeeds, of aiming to make himself dictator, of secret intrigues with state officials, of a desire to provoke foreign wars, of enriching himself at the public expense.   As a rule these attacks were passed over in silence.   Occasionally he would come down from his desk and reply to them on the floor of the House.

There was one reform on which his heart was set and which was destined to prove his undoing.   Seeing how parliamentary government was made impossible by the number of parties of various shades, from legitimists to radicals, into which the deputies were divided, he determined to try to change the mode of election from the district to the "department."   For instance, he would have the deputies from Paris and suburbs elected together on a general ticket (*"scrutin de liste,"* the plan was called), representing the whole department instead of singly by subdivisions of the departments, or congressional districts (*"scrutin d'arrondissement"*). In this way he claimed that men of larger caliber would be nominated, of broader views, less dominated by local interests. He also hoped that such a measure would diminish the number of factions, and force the people into two great political parties. The Chamber, which might be supposed to oppose such a law, as tending to diminish the importance of the individual deputy, finally passed the bill, in May, 1881. But the Senate rejected it.

General elections ensued in August. Gambetta stood for two Paris districts, and was elected in one. His platform was one of opportunism and reform combined. In his addresses he particularly inveighed against violence, which by its prominence during the French Revolution, and again in the Commune, still kept many conservatives away from the republican ranks. When the new Chamber met, the cabinet was engaged in the expedition to Tunis. Its policy was opposed and it fell. Gambetta, who had been considering the question of the premiership, consented to form a new ministry. His efforts met with little response from the leading republicans, and he was forced to fall back upon his personal following. The impression thus made was unfavorable. Various measures of administration contributed to the irritation of the Chamber, particularly the creation of a ministry of agriculture and one of fine arts, and the appointment of conservatives to prominent positions. Finally the program of the new cabinet, which included reforms in the civil service, as well as in the other departments of government, and a project for election by a *"scrutin de liste,"* brought the opposition to a head.   After but sixty-six days of service the Gambetta ministry surrendered its charge.

Its head returned at once to his newspaper work, while continuing to discharge his duties as a deputy, and speaking occasionally in the Chamber.   His last speech, in July, 1882, was on the Egyptian question.   In the autumn of that year he retired to Ville d'Avray, near Versailles, to the house of Les Jardies, which Balzac had once occupied, and which he had recently bought.   There, on November 27, he was wounded by a pistol shot, whether accidentally or by design has never been satisfactorily proven.   It was reported and commonly believed that his mistress had shot him in a quarrel.   His friends claimed it was only an accidental wound.   Whatever may have been the occasion, the consequences were not directly serious.   But this injury preluded a severe malady.   No sooner was the hand healed than a disturbance became manifest in the abdomen.   The symptoms described by the attendant physicians resemble those that are caused by appendicitis.   However, no operation was attempted. The disease went its way, and Gambetta's body, spent in many years of storm and labor, and so lately shocked by the injury to his hand and wrist, offered but a poor resistance to its encroachments.   For weeks his strength steadily decreased.   He alone seemed unable to appreciate his decline, but talked and read and occupied his thoughts with the affairs of the political world.   The crisis drew near.   On the night of December 31, 1882, he passed away.

With the death of the great republican the voice of calumny was stilled.   The antagonisms he had aroused subsided.   His mistakes, his weaknesses, were willingly forgotten.   He ceased to be the leader of a party in the public mind.   He became the representative of the whole nation.   For it was he alone who had appealed to national honor in the day of direst calamity.   He alone, rallying the sons of France, had led them undaunted to a glorious defeat.   This is the memory which France cherishes of Gambetta.   Some of the measures he advocated, notably those against clericalism, have since become laws.   But his name is not connected with them.   What the French people think of Gambetta, the idea which he stands for in their minds, is expressed in unmistakable terms wrought out of stone and bronze.   After a state funeral had been accorded to his remains, and official eulogies had been duly pronounced, a popular subscription took it upon itself to perpetuate his memory.   In the outer court of the Louvre, fronting a broad highway which connects the two great divisions of the city of Paris, stands a granite pedestal upholding a shaft of granite.   Allegorical figures of bronze surround and crown the stone.   But in relief against the shaft, clothed in his customary civilian dress, Gambetta rises erect among a group of the French people hovering under the folds of the French flag.   And above his head is inscribed the words of his Tours proclamation in that sad autumn of 1870: "Frenchmen, raise your souls and your resolutions to a level with the perils bursting on the fatherland.   It still depends on you to show to the universe what a great people who will not perish is "

SELECTIONS FROM THE WORKS OF GAMBETTA

Extracts from the Speech at the Baudin Trial

[Gambetta is defending the journalist Delescluze for having solicited funds for a statue to Baudin. He begins by alluding to the speech of the prosecuting attorney, and continues:]

I agree with him on what is really the question here. Like him, and following him, I come to discuss that terrible question, the highest we can submit to men whose profession is to respect justice and to those whose calling it is to defend justice. Here is the question: Can there exist for a nation, in the bosom of a civilized society, a moment when state policy, when state violence, can with impunity, under pretext of public safety, violate the law, overturn the constitution, and treat as criminals those who defend the right at the peril of their lives? . . . .

I do not know whether I am deluding myself, but it seems to me that the last place where such assertions should be made and such crimes should be glorified is the court of a judge, for here law alone should speak and be heard. Law alone should be the interest and the passion of the magistrate, since without it there is nothing lasting and respected, since without it all social certainty disappears, and we inevitably end in anarchy, with all the disorders and meannesses it involves. I ask myself whether it is in this especial sanctuary of justice that it will be allowed to contradict me?

Do you recall what December 2 is? Do you remember what happened? The annals have just been taken up and told again by M. Ténot, in their heart-rending episodes. You have read this story, limited to the facts, and all the more avenging because of its impartiality. You know what blood, and griefs, and tears there are in that date. But what must be said here, what must be touched with the finger, is the machination, the consequences, the evil caused to France, the trouble made in consciences by this criminal attempt, it is this which constitutes the real responsibility. It is this alone which can make you appreciate how far you owe us aid and protection, when we come to honor the memory of those who fell defending the law and the constitution, which was being massacred.

Yes, on December Second, were grouped around a pretender men whom France had not known up to that time, who had neither talent, nor honor, nor rank, nor position, people such as, at every epoch, are accomplices of violence, people of whom you can repeat what Sallust said of the rabble that surrounded Cataline, what Cæsar himself said in tracing the portraits of his accomplices, eternal offscourings of regular society.

Aere alieno obruti et vitiis onusti

"A pack of men ruined by debt and crime," as Corneille has translated. It is by this kind of men that institutions and laws have been slaughtered for ages, and the conscience of mankind is powerless to react, in spite of the sublime procession of a Socrates, a Thraseas, a Cicero, a Cato, of thinkers and martyrs who protest in the name of immolated religion, of wounded morals, of right crushed under the heel of a soldier. . . . .

On which side was genius, morals, virtue? All had gone down under the foul conspiracy! . . . .

Those who seized the country put its freedom in fetters, made use of the new means given man by science to enter into communication with one another. Centralization and terror did the work. Paris was deceived by means of the provinces, the provinces by means of Paris! Steam and the telegraph became the instruments of power. They spread through all the departments that Paris had yielded! Yielded! It was assassinated. Yielded! It was struck down with bullet and grape-shot. I who am speaking to you, I had friends—do you understand?—who were killed as they came out of the Law School. They were unarmed. It is true that they were very rash and very guilty to have come to study law in a country where law is respected in such a way. . . . .

At the end of seventeen years of reign you perceive it would be a good thing to forbid the discussion of these facts by means of a posthumous ratification given out from a police court. No, it shall not be so. No, you will not give, you cannot give, this satisfaction, for there exists no court of appeals for this case. It was judged yesterday, it will be judged to-morrow, the day after to-morrow, forever, without truce or armistice, until justice has received its supreme satisfaction. This trial of December Second, whatever you may do, will remain living and ineffaceable at Paris, at London, at Berlin, at New York, in the whole world, and everywhere the universal conscience of man will pronounce the same verdict.

There is already something besides which judges our adversaries. Listen! For seventeen years you have been the absolute masters of France and governed it at your discretion—the statement is your own. We do not ask what use you have made of her treasure, blood, honor, and glory. We will not speak of her integrity compromised, nor of what has become of the fruits of her industry, without mentioning the fact that no one is ignorant of the financial catastrophes which at this very moment are exploding like mines beneath our footsteps. But what best judges you, because it is the witness of your own remorse, is that you have never dared say: "We will celebrate December Second as a national anniversary, we will place it among the festivals of France!" And yet all the governments which have succeeded one another in this country have honored the day that saw their birth. They have celebrated July Fourteenth, August Tenth. The days of July, 1830, have also been celebrated, as well as February Twenty-fourth. There are but two anniversaries, the Eighteenth Brumaire and December Second, which have never been put among the national festivals, because you know that the universal conscience of man would reject them if you wished to place them there.

Well, this anniversary which you have refused, we claim it, we take it for our own. We will always celebrate it, always. It will be, each year, the anniversary of our dead, until the day when the country, becoming master once again, will inflict on you the great national expiation in the name of liberty, equality, fraternity.

From a Speech of January 26, 1882, Defending the Scrutin de Liste

[Gambetta affirms the necessity of electing the deputies by departments instead of by districts. The vote which followed forced his resignation as premier.]

I hear very well the answer: No. Well, you will see, gentlemen, that the near future will prove the wisdom of my words, and for this reason, because I have the deep inner conviction, when I resist you, when I struggle against you, that it is my sad and imperious duty to declare to you that it is a governmental necessity. . . . .

I can only meet your apprehensions with my loyalty, the sincerity of my words, the plans we have made ready, my past, in short, and I appeal to your consciences.

Yes, I think that the republican legion with which I began my career, with which I have passed through the struggles and tests of years, will no more fail us on the day of success than it failed us on the day of battle. In any case it will be without bitterness, especially without the shadow of a wounded personal feeling, that I shall bow before your verdict. For whatever may have been said, there is something which I set above all ambitions, even lawful ambitions, and that is the confidence of the republicans, without which I could not accomplish—I indeed have some right to say it—my task in this country, the restoration of the fatherland.

BIBLIOGRAPHY

The Evolution of France under the Third Republic. Pierre de Coubertin.

Life of Léon Gambetta. (The Statesmen Series.) Frank T. Marzials.

Articles in *Littell's Living Age*, Vol. CLVI, pp. 667 ff. *Century*, Vol. III, pp. 708 ff. *Critic*, Vol. XXXVII, pp. 72 ff.

VICTOR MARIE HUGO

CHAPTER VI

VICTOR HUGO

[VICTOR MARIE HUGO, born at Besançon, February 26, 1802; educated at Madrid and Paris; prize poems, 1819; journalist, 1819; "Odes," 1822; "Hernani," 1830; "Notre-Dame de Paris," 1831; elected to the French Academy, 1841; peer of France, 1845; deputy to the Assembly, 1848; in exile, 1851; in residence at Guernsey, 1855; return to France, 1870; deputy, 1871; senator, 1876; died at Paris, May 22, 1885. Works: poems, dramas, novels, essays.]

The nineteenth century in France witnessed one of the greatest manifestations of her literary genius. It acknowledged, in fact, but two rivals in the annals of the nation. Once, when after the conquest of Sicily and England by the Normans, and the surging of the knights and peasants of the West to the invasion of Asia and the rescue of the Holy Sepulcher, the young society, born of these movements, broke out into Troubadour song. Again, when after the last bulwark of the Byzantine Empire had fallen, and Greek learning had finally been driven from its ancient seats, after Columbus had discovered a new world, and the rude soldiery of Charles VIII had discovered Italy, the revival of learning and ancient art and culture formed the Pleiades, inspired Montaigne, and shaped the talent of Corneille, Molière, Racine, and Bossuet. Deep social movements gave birth to the mediæval and the Greek renaissances. As profound a stirring of man's emotions, the humanitarian crusade of a Voltaire and a

Rousseau, the democratic crusade of the armies of the Republic and Empire, brought forth the romantic and realistic literature of the nineteenth century.

The writers of the nineteenth century were eminent in all branches of composition. They admitted the supremacy of the seventeenth in drama, in philosophical, oratorical, or epistolary prose. But they claimed the preëminence, even over the twelfth and the sixteenth, in lyric poetry, and over the seventeenth and the eighteenth in criticism and historical prose; and they stood without rivals in the field of fiction. Among their representatives some few authors united many of their excellencies. None combined them in a higher degree or showed greater originality and vigor than Victor Hugo, poet, dramatist, orator, novelist.

Hugo is deservedly called the great writer of the nineteenth century. His life was almost contemporaneous with its decades. He was born on February 26, 1802, at Besançon, in the west of France. The locality was of no consequence, for the family's stay there was but temporary, occasioned merely by the military duties of the older Hugo, an officer in the French army. For the same reasons the family soon moved south, wandered over the islands of Corsica and Elba, then to Paris (1805–1807), again to Italy, and again to Paris (1808). Finally, in 1811, it moved to Spain, where Victor attended school at Madrid, and received his first impressions of Spanish scenery and architecture. In 1812 it was once more the turn of Paris, and this time permanently. The father was away on campaigns. The young Victor was given over to the care of his mother and an ex-priest. He passed his leisure hours in the garden of the old convent, where they made their home, or in reading the literature of the century just gone. As he himself sings in his "Lights and Shadows": "I had in my blond infancy— alas! too fleeting—three masters, a garden, an old priest, and my mother."

Under the Restoration this irregular education was systematized by attendance at a private school which had affiliations with a Parisian lycée (high school). Victor showed proficiency in both language and science. He won honorable mention in physics at a general municipal examination of the pupils in his grade, composed French tragedies, and wrote poems, both original and translated. In the latter instance he showed particular fondness for Virgil, and Virgil's influence was to prove a lasting one. Some poetry, provoked by prize competitions under the auspices of the French Academy, received favorable mention (in 1817 and in 1819), and called the attention of the literary public to his precocious talent. In 1819 he competed for prizes which had been offered by the Academy of Floral Games at Toulouse, and won two. This success was partially repeated in 1820. In December, 1819, together with his two older brothers, he had begun a fortnightly review, *Le Conservateur Littéraire*, to which he contributed poetry, criticisms—among them an article on Scott's "Ivanhoe"—and fiction. A small pension from the king rewarded his efforts.

The tide of literature was now strongly setting towards romanticism. Already in school Hugo had imbibed the mysticism of the melancholy Ossianic poetry, which reflected the shadowy mists of the Scottish Highlands, filled with calm brooding over a vain and transitory life. He had also made himself acquainted with Chateaubriand, the idol of his generation, a noble, who during the Revolution, weary of a fruitless existence in his own land, had fled from its scenes of violence and had carried his bitter hopelessness across the Atlantic, had visited Niagara, skirted the old French settlements of western Pennsylvania, looked on the sources of the Ohio, and crossed its watershed to the ocean again. What he had seen of frontier life and the vastness of American forests kindled his imagination. He rose from the real to the conceivable, which he argued from the real, and seizing his pen, wrote the epic of the New World in his romances of "Atala" and "René." His was a *blasé* hero, seeking refuge for fanciful ills among the wild tribes of a virgin continent.

But Chateaubriand drew also from other springs of inspiration than nature's. The worship of nature he had found in Rousseau. His egotistic melancholy, which buried itself in nature, had come from within him. But his admiration for the Middle Ages, a large element in the broader manifestation of romanticism, and bearing with it a revival of the Christian faith, after the skepticism of the philosophers of the school of Locke and Hobbes had worn itself threadbare, he had inherited from his English and German predecessors. This he handed down to his compatriots in his "Genius of Christianity." He was Hugo's great teacher, after Virgil. In both of these masters, the romancer and the poet, thought and style blended to a charm.

By 1820, however, romanticism was no longer content with its conquest of prose. It was seeking an outlet for its feelings in another rhythm than the harmonious, picturesque period. Lyric poetry had for generations lain dormant in France. The new voice of passion and longing was now to arouse it, recall it to its younger days. Lamartine wrote his "Lake" and the "Meditations." To the French people of that time (1820) it seemed, as has often been quoted, that the world had changed during the night. Hugo could not remain untouched by this event, for his temperament was such that he vibrated with every motion of the nation. Though saturated with Ossian and Chateaubriand, his political ideas as a strict adherent of the Bourbons had hitherto kept him a regular, a classicist, in literature. He was also a devout churchman, and the new religion was suspected of heresy.

Certain domestic trials, however, shook his steadfastness to the legitimist and the classical cause. His mother, practically the only parent he had known, died in 1821. His projected marriage with a friend of long standing, Adèle Foucher, was opposed by her family, because of financial reasons. From these sorrows Hugo sought refuge in poetry, and in 1822 published his first volume of "Odes." It attracted little attention, for it lacked the personal note, and Lamartine, whose verse expressed the emotions of the individual soul, could not be dethroned by objective harmonies, however sonorous their cadence. Still the "Odes" advanced Hugo's fortunes, and his marriage shortly followed. But at the wedding banquet his brother Eugène went mad, a serious grief to Victor. In the following year he consented to give out something of his inner self to the public. The strange romance of "Han d'Islande," suggested by the blood-and-thunder school of English fiction, in which the hero cherishes a tender affection for a lovable woman, revealed some of the author's trials in his own courtship. And his inner nature was to be again stirred within him. A child was born to him. Its life was short, but Hugo's sorrow was lasting. It entered into his very being, and was reflected in the verses of his after years.

The romanticists by this time had formed a well-defined circle, and Hugo became one of the group. They met in the offices of a new journal, *La Muse Française*, and also at the rooms of one of the romantic pioneers, Charles Nodier, the author of fairy stories, romances, and "Trilby." They incited Hugo to the composition of new "Odes," which appeared (1824) with a preface that proclaims poetical liberty. These were followed, in 1826, by another fantastic romance on West Indian slavery and revolt, "Bug-Jargal," and the same year by a new volume of "Odes and Ballads," where Hugo's household poetry begins under the influence of his little daughter Léopoldine.

In 1827 he attempted dramatic poetry in a drama which was not intended for acting. As the tragedy of the seventeenth century, which was modeled after the drama of Greece and Rome, chose for a subject the interesting episode in the life of an individual, and studied that one event alone, so Hugo, now an out-and-out romanticist, sets over against this dramatic ideal the broader theme of the whole delineation of a man. This man was none other than Oliver Cromwell, whose various characteristics are brought out as he meets with enemies, friends, astrologers, or relatives. Accompanying "Cromwell" was a long preface, in which Hugo advocated at length the theatrical doctrines of the new sect. The great exemplar, he asserts, is Shakespeare. Like him the French playwrights should aim to present broad pictures of life, rather than restricted crises, should mingle the serious with the humorous, should no longer be bound by the time limit of twenty-four hours for the supposed action, nor by one single place for its exposition. But the scenery, plot, and characters should be true to nature, for "everything which is in nature is in art"—a dogma carried to the bitter extreme by later French novelists.

It is interesting to trace the development of a genius. By the beginning of 1828, when Hugo was as yet hardly twenty-six years old, he had passed his formative period and already was the great poet, dramatist, and novelist that we know. In the next ten years poem succeeded poem, play followed play, with marvelous rapidity. In a new edition of the "Odes and Ballads," in 1828, the poet breaks the traditional mold of classical rhythm. Under the influence of the great critic Sainte-Beuve, he adopts the measures of the Pleiades school of the sixteenth century, fails to always observe a fixed cæsura, or pause in the middle of the line, and deliberately carries the sense over from one line to the next, thus producing overflow verse, which had also been tabooed by the classicists. In politics he had undergone as significant a change. From the Bourbon of the beginning, and the fervent royalist, by successive steps he had grown into a Bonapartist, and in 1827 had welcomed the reviving glory of the Empire in his famous "Ode to the Vendôme Column."

Both of these conversions, the literary and the political, were in keeping with the march of events. For Hugo ever showed himself most sensitive to the currents of popular opinion. The Napoleonic legend was gaining headway, as the splendor of the imperial sway dimmed the memory of the suffering on which it was grounded.

Béranger's poetry had made the Little Corporal an idol of the fireside. He had sung, in Young's translation,

> "Ay, many a day the straw-thatched cot
> Shall echo with his glory!"

So Hugo, reminding his audience that his father had been a general under the Corsican, carried Napoleon's praises into a higher social circle. And together with these eulogies he couples the praise of a peaceful home, the meditations of a philosophic dreamer, the description of current events, or even the images of the mysterious East, with all its color and fire of passion.

He launched also a series of romantic dramas, beginning with "Hernani," in 1830. All the theories of "Cromwell" he here strives to convert into dramatic facts, and purposely applies to the versification of the play the heresies he had learned from Ronsard and his associates of the Pleiades. The classicists, who still stood for the dramatic ideals and verse of Corneille and Racine, were warned in advance that the gauge of battle was to be thrown down to them in "Hernani." They gladly took it up, but as they entered the theater on the fateful night of its first representation they found the strategic points occupied by their foes, a Spartan band of authors, painters, musicians, disciples of the new creed, gathered from the Latin Quarter, and led by the poet Théophile Gautier, whose costume, which included a scarlet vest and the flowing locks that are now typical of the artistic world, was in itself a shock and offense to the periwigged purists. The combat was unequal. The lungs of the recruits from the garrets and studios were invincible. Besides, they had a winning cause to champion, for French poetry contains few passages that can rival "Hernani" in lyric beauty. The classicists were routed, horse and foot, and though on succeeding evenings they returned to the charge, the advantage on the whole remained with their opponents.

Hugo followed up the success of "Hernani" with several other plays, but with the exception of "Ruy Blas" (1838), and also perhaps "Marion Delorme" (1831), they verged too much on the blood-and-thunder of his early romances, and have disappeared from sight. Finally the production of "The Burgraves," in 1843, met with such a chilling reception, because of its impossible events and stage effects, that it confirmed in itself the restoration of the classical drama which was already under way.

This interval of time (1828-1843) showed Hugo in other capacities than as poet or dramatist. He had continued his rôle as critic, already essayed while a journalist. He had begun his career as a reformer, by pamphlets directed against capital punishment, as the gruesome and harrowing "Last Days of a Condemned Man" (1829). He had become the recognized head of the new "Cénacle" of authors, artists, and contributors to the romantic organ, *Le Globe*, which numbered such celebrities as Alfred de Musset, De Vigny, Sainte-Beuve, the elder Dumas, and the painter Delacroix. He had published a narrative of travel in Germany under the title of "The Rhine" (1842). He had received the honor of an election to the French Academy (1841), after having solicited it three times to no purpose. But most important of all he had published, in 1831, his great novel of "Notre-Dame de Paris," composed under pressure in the short interval of six months, begun with the first drop of a quart bottle of ink, he says, and finished with the last drop.

In this romance, which mingles nineteenth-century ideas and fifteenth-century manners, we get a glimpse of the Hugo of "Les Misérables." It is the people of Paris under Louis XI which he endeavors to portray, their amusements, occupations, crimes, spirit. And throughout this narrative of the life of the crowded capital, with its courts, its squares, its thieves' quarter, the Cour des Miracles, its places of public torture and executions, runs the praise of its great center, the metropolitan cathedral, with its towers and buttresses, its volutes, sculptures, altars, and high arches, a steadfast, immovable rock amid the swirl of human passions that eddy about it, and flood at times its portals. Some of the book we have seen before. Characters and episodes have been drawn from the older stories of "Han d'Islande" and "Bug-Jargal," molded again and perfected. The long chapters of eulogy on Gothic architecture may have been suggested by Hugo's early admiration for Chateaubriand. But what had not been previously revealed, even in a glimpse, was the fairy-like figure of Esmeralda, a picture of youth, gayety, and innocence, in bright contrast to the ugliness of a Quasimodo and the gloom of cloister and hovel. In "Notre-Dame de Paris" we also catch the fondness of Hugo for symbolism. The cathedral is the material sign of the immaterial thought. With its slow accretions of chapels and naves, of decorations, grotesque or beautiful, it embodies the life of generations of the people, who have thus wrought their transitory being into its immutable forms. And in its larger meaning, the people of Paris taken as an epitome of humanity, the novel tells the story of man's struggles against his destiny, against the unseen, the supernatural.

Esmeralda, the young girl, is no doubt the ideal image of Hugo's devotion to his own children, particularly to his daughter Léopoldine. And up to the time of the publication of "Notre-Dame de Paris" nothing which was within his power had lessened the joy of his family life. We have noticed how he had wooed and won the love of his youth, triumphing at last over all opposition. He had been faithful to this love, and the union had been thrice blessed since the death of the first born. Here surely was a happy household, destined to greater happiness as the years rolled by, a constant source of inspiration for the talent of its father and protector. And as we know it did inspire him. From his poems on infancy and childhood a whole volume has been made, appropriately called "The Mother's Book." Why, then, was this picture torn, its brightness tarnished? Was it because of merited and continuous praise bestowed on one who after all was only a mortal, and who, unable to withstand its glorification began to look on himself as in all ways perfect and incapable of doing evil? Or was it a simple infatuation? It is difficult to decide. All we know is that one of the minor parts of "Lucretia Borgia," a tragedy by Hugo, played in 1833, was filled by an actress of mediocre fame, Juliette Drouet. But her beauty was alluring, if not her ability, for all critics unite in praising it. It touched Hugo. He renewed the romantic days of his early flame. He carried her away from her unworthy surroundings, domiciled her close to his own dwelling, and made her his lasting confidante and companion. Many of the finest passages of Hugo's verse were called out by this extraordinary association.

It was at the end of this period of unusual literary activity, when all things had conspired to secure the happiness of his genius and exalt his fame, that Hugo met with the greatest sorrow—if we may judge from its permanence—of his whole career. In 1843 his daughter Léopoldine had become the bride of Charles Vacquerie, a family friend of long standing. A few months later the young couple went for a sail on the Seine. The boat upset. The husband, unable to save the wife, preferred to die with her. They were found locked in each other's arms. To Hugo this event was a catastrophe. In a volume of verse, "The Contemplations," published in 1856–1857, he separates the poems written before 1843 from those written after that date. Many of the anniversaries of the accident are marked by his compositions, mile-stones on the road of sorrow. Here is a portion of one, written a year later, in 1844, as given in Dean Carrington's translation:

> When we our life together led
>   On the hillside, now long ago,
> Where waved the trees, and waters sped,
>   Where the house hugged the wood below—
>
> She was ten years—thrice ten was I.
>   I was the universe to her.
> How sweet the grass, how clear the sky,
>   Beneath the thick green woods of fir.
>
> My lot she glad and happy made,
>   My labors light, and blue my sky;
> When she "My father!" to me said,
>   My full heart would "My God!" reply.
>
> 'Mid thousand dreams, by fancy wrought,
>   I heard her prattle, fond and bright;

My forehead, shadowed o'er with thought,
  Her merry glance o'erflowed with light.

And when her little hand I took,
  Like a princess she proudly trod,
And always would for flowers look,
  And for the poor upon the road.

. . . . . .

She was like angels of the skies—
  How charmingly she greeted you!
Heaven's grace had placed within her eyes
  The look that could not be untrue.

I was so young when she was born
  To shine upon my destiny;
She was the child of my glad morn,
  The star of dawn that lit my sky.

. . . . . .

And then how glad she was—how gay,
  Sweet angel, with unspotted mind!
But all these things are past away—
  Gone like a shadow, or the wind!

The death of Léopoldine put a stop for a time to the
outward literary work of Hugo. He continued to write
poetry, and was already planning "Les Misérables," part
of which he committed to manuscript. But to the public
he was now an Academician and a politician. His taste
for the latter calling had been increased by his appointment to the peerage in 1845, under Louis Philippe. He
sat in the upper house and took part in debates, proving
himself to be an orator of considerable power. Political
changes were pending in France. Hugo, with his mobile
temperament, keenly alive to the veerings of the popular
compass, felt them. Already an ardent admirer of Napoleon, his humanitarianism, shown so strikingly in "Notre-

Dame de Paris,'' inclined him to democratic views of state management. He was a liberal now, perhaps in theory a republican even. But he did not openly advocate a republic. When the Revolution of 1848 came, and Louis Philippe fell, Hugo stood for a Paris constituency on a conservative republican platform. He failed once, but was elected a second time. In the following autumn he favored Louis Napoleon as presidential candidate. But in 1849, when he was reëlected to the Assembly, he suddenly appeared as a radical—his critics say because he saw greater possibilities of preferment in a party which could claim few members of eminence. From now on, instead of sharing in the Napoleonic revival, to which he had so greatly contributed, he opposed with word and pen the pretensions of Napoleon's nephew. No longer a conservative, he seized every opportunity to extol the French Revolution, and based his hopes for a future France on universal suffrage, with the attachment of what is now known as the referendum. Such extreme views only paved the way for the Second Empire. The *coup d'état* of December 2, 1851, came; Baudin was killed; Hugo escaped arrest, and for two days sought to incite resistance. But few responded to his appeals, and he soon fled in disguise to Brussels.

A new career was opened for Hugo by the *coup d'état*. It added to his endowments as an author the qualifications of a political agitator. From the time he reached Belgium until he came back to Paris, after Sedan, he did not cease to assail, in prose and verse, the Second Empire, its ruler, its leading men, its measures. He might have accepted the amnesty of 1859 had his hostility allowed him, but he preferred to remain a living protest against the crime of

December Second. At first his exile was vexatious.
Napoleon had been elected ruler of the French, and as
such was acknowledged the head of the state. Consequently, when Hugo put through the press, in 1852, a
most virulent attack on him in the prose work "Napoleon the Little," the Belgian government refused him
further shelter. He moved on to the Channel Islands
and took up his residence in Jersey, where his family
joined him. Here he produced that marvelous collection
of invective poetry, "The Chastisements" (1853), where
in a series of pen pictures we find that Napoleon's expiation for his crimes was not to be the Russian campaign,
nor Waterloo, nor yet St. Helena, but his nephew Louis.
He also composed the "History of a Crime," namely the
coup d'état, but this narrative was not published until 1877.
Soon further trials came to the exiles. France and England, having formed an alliance, were engaged in the
Crimean War. This was gall and bitterness to the band
of French patriots in Jersey, and often did they inveigh
against it in their newspaper, *L'Homme*. Finally, when
Queen Victoria visited Paris and met the Emperor, a letter
to the Queen, most insulting in its tenor, was printe in
this sheet. The inhabitants of the little island were
aroused. They called on the governor to act. He ex-
pelled the editors, and the Hugos sailed away to Guernsey. This removal took place in the autumn of 1855.

From 1855 to 1870 Hauteville House, on the island of
Guernsey, was one of the most notable buildings of Europe.
As the Second Empire waned and the protests of the French
radicals won a hearing Hugo gradually advanced in public
esteem until he became quite as important a figure as any
monarch of them all. And then his fame as an author

was constantly increasing. "The Contemplations," a collection of meditative, lyric, and philosophical verse, published in two volumes in 1856 and 1857, "The Legend of the Ages" (1859), where the history of mankind in its typical episodes is sung in almost epic strains, and the lighter themes of "The Songs of the Streets and the Woods" (1865) were accompanied by "Les Misérables" (1862), "The Toilers of the Sea" (1866), "The Man Who Laughs" (1869) for romances, and "William Shakespeare" (1864), a sounding eulogy of the dramatist and also of Victor Hugo; for the egotism of the latter had enough on which to feed. And pamphlets multiplied without number, appeals to this and to that, articles against slavery, remonstrances against the execution of John Brown, satires on the mal-administration of the Second Empire. No question debated in either hemisphere was foreign to Hugo's mind. Such a combination of political and literary renown has hardly been equaled. Pilgrimages to Hauteville House became the fashion. Everything was admired, the manuscripts of unpublished masterpieces, the sketches which whiled away leisure hours—for Hugo possessed considerable artistic talent—and adulation rose higher and higher, as one disciple crowded the other at the feet of "the master."

But a word or two regarding the novels which have entered into the world's literature. "Les Misérables," begun, as we have seen, before 1848, had been shaped and enlarged by that event and its political consequences, until it became quite truly the romance of the outcast and down-trodden. Somewhat of the symbolism of "Notre-Dame de Paris" is visible in its pages. There is the struggle of man, of the individual, this time not against fate, the intangible, supernatural, but against his fellowmen, against society. There is the great material abode for the victims of social laws, the galleys, ever yawning to receive Jean Valjean. They dominate the scene, not so toweringly as the cathedral had done in "Notre-Dame," but quite as vividly. And then the agent of the law, typified in Javert, the police automaton, which cannot comprehend the fact that a lawbreaker may cease to be a criminal, and when the fact becomes too potent to be ignored, despairs of its own rightfulness and commits suicide. The young girl, too, reappears, transformed from the airy Esmeralda into the gentle Cosette, and the young man, whose early history is the history of Hugo himself. But the teaching of "Les Misérables" is not the doctrine of despair. In that respect it differs from "Notre-Dame." Jean Valjean, though he tries in vain to redeem his faults in the eyes of man, is justified by the infinite, and receives even in this life the reward of an upright conscience, free from all reproach. And the same hope is found in "The Toilers of the Sea," a story suggested by Guernsey scenery. The fisherman, wild and true, conquers in vain the ocean and its monsters. His light-headed sweetheart sails away, while he buries himself in the element he had overcome. But the symbolism is apparent. Man fights with nature, the waves, and the animate but unconscious devil-fish. And man wins the fight. Hugo is becoming optimistic.

The ruin of the Empire brought Hugo back to Paris amid the acclamations of the populace, which crowded the streets of the great town. He was shut up in the city by the Germans, occupied himself in encouraging resistance, appealed to the enemy to cease their warfare, wrote poems on scenes and events suggested to him by the times. After the siege he was elected to the Assembly from the "department" of the Seine, and spoke in favor of continuing the war rather than abandon Alsace-Lorraine. He opposed clericalism, and resigned his seat, when attacked for a eulogy of Garibaldi. During the Commune he stayed at Brussels, where he had gone on a business errand. His sympathies were to a certain degree with the Communists, and therefore for a second time the Belgian government requested him to make his residence elsewhere. He afterwards failed of reëlection to the Assembly, and when in 1876 he was named senator it was too late for him to exert much influence in political life. But as a private citizen he never ceased to champion the cause of the oppressed, whether they were oppressed wrongfully or rightly.

Apart, then, from these early months of 1871, Hugo's attention after his return from exile is almost entirely given up to literature. The poetry he had written, and in which Napoleon III, the Prussians, and the priests came in for denunciation, was published in 1872, under the title of "The Terrible Year." Before this, during his stay at Guernsey, the wars of the Reds and the Blues, in Vendée during the French Revolution, had suggested an historical novel, which saw the light in 1874, as "Ninety-Three." Its manner is the manner of "The Toilers of the Sea." Inanimate nature furnishes once more the symbolism. A feudal castle is the central picture, the fight of a man with a ship's cannon, which had broken loose from its moorings, recalls the struggle of the fisherman with the devil-fish. Here again man triumphs, mind conquers matter. Children occupy a prominent place in the narrative, and it is a mother's love which solves the plot, by inciting the leader of the Blues to rescue her little ones at the sacrifice of his own freedom, and the future of his cause. But the mass of new publication consisted of poetry. "The Legend of the Ages" received considerable additions, while philosophical, satirical, and lyric verse filled several good-sized volumes.

The last fifteen years of Hugo's life, 1870 to 1885, were passed in the midst of such popularity as rarely falls to the lot of a mortal. Adulation almost reached the heights of apotheosis. With the exception of some political opponents, the extreme clericals, whom he had offended by his attacks, and the more aristocratic set of the nobility, all France looked upon him as the embodiment of the nation's genius. Pilgrimages to his house at Paris multiplied, literary men and those wishing to be such, natives of Besançon and exiles from Alsace, tourists and notables from foreign lands, schemers in finance or politics, the needy and the hare-brained, all crowded into his drawing-room in gratification of curiosity or in hope that a word from the great man might be used to their temporal or professional advantage. There were daily receptions, almost daily addresses from individuals or delegations, an existence that truly seemed founded on declamation. And yet Hugo reserved time for work—eight volumes of poetry between 1877 and 1883, a drama, "Torquemada," which was not played, and the "History of a Crime." For his habits had become fixed. He gave his forenoons to intellectual pursuits, and the regularity of his hours produced in the long run unusual results. He was fond of recreation also. Frequent excursions to the suburbs of Paris, to which his favorite conveyance was the top of an omnibus or a third-class seat in a railway coach, formed his chief delight. His white head and beard, his pink cheeks and sparkling dark eyes, became one of the few sights of the capital that were known to all its inhabitants. He even took part in balloon ascensions, whereby he showed his Gallic temperament.

But the ideal side of these later years is most strongly seen in his relations with his grandchildren. Since the death of Léopoldine, in 1843, he had been called upon to mourn his wife, who had passed away at Brussels in 1868, his son Charles, stricken down with apoplexy in 1871, while on his way to his father's rooms, his other son, François, who succumbed to a long illness in 1873, and his youngest child, Adèle, who had inherited the family insanity. There were left to him his friends, the ever-faithful Madame Drouet, and Charles's two children, Georges and Jeanne. His delight in childhood, always keen, grew even greater in the presence of these comforts of his declining years. They became his chief concern. Their joys, sorrows, health, maladies, games, studies were his constant occupation, and furnished his muse with a never-failing source of literary material. In 1877 a number of the poems addressed to them were collected in a volume called "The Art of Being a Grandfather." The art is a simple one—indulgence. Do whatever the grandchild asks you to do. This grandfather did so, and boasted of it in many a line of delightful rhythm. And as Hugo's household poetry is perhaps not so well known abroad as his other work we cite the "Grandfather's Song," a rhyme for children's rounds, also from Dean Carrington's translation:

Dance, little girls,
  All in a ring;
To see you so pretty,
  The forest will sing.

Dance, little queens,
  All in a ring;
Lovers to lasses
  Sweet kisses will bring.

Dance, little madcaps,
  All in a ring;
The crabbed old mistress
  Will grumble and fling.

Dance, little beauties,
  All in a ring:
The birds will applaud you
  With clapping of wing.

Dance, little fairies,
  All in a ring;
With corn-flower garlands
  And fair as the spring.

Dance, little women,
  All in a ring;
Each beau to his lady
  Says some pretty thing.

But all things have an end here below, and Hugo was
but a mortal in spite of his fourscore hale and hearty
years. His health was spared to the last. In May,
1885, after one of his field excursions he seemed ailing.
Pneumonia set in, and nine days later, May 22, he died.
His obsequies were notable. The nation took them in
charge. Under the great sweep of the Arc de Triomphe,
which was draped in black, the body lay in state at the

head of the Champs Élysées, and visible from the heart of
Paris.   And when it was removed it was only to be borne
down the wide avenue, over the Seine to its resting-place
in the church of the Panthéon, which the government now
set apart for the burial of the illustrious dead of the land.
Thousands followed behind the little black hearse—the
hearse of the poor people, which Hugo had himself
desired—and tens of thousands lined the way to witness
perhaps the greatest pageant of the century.

The funeral rites of Hugo were a wonderful tribute to
the power of the mind, paid by a people who have ever
shown a peculiar admiration for military power.   It was
an homage done to art, to literature, to the intellect, and
in doing it France recognized what constitutes her true
and lasting glory.   For Hugo's work did not die with
him.   We might say even that his literary activity did
not cease.   In spite of the great amount of publication
in prose and verse, carried on with slight interruptions for
nearly seventy years, his productiveness had not been
exhausted.   From the material which his executors found
in his papers, half a dozen more collections of poetry
have been made, two volumes of dramas, and as many of
travel and narrative.   And through the same self-sacrificing filial devotion the house which Hugo occupied in
the Place des Vosges (old Place Royale) from 1832 to the
Revolution of 1848, has recently been set apart for a
museum of the author and made the property of the
nation.

SELECTIONS FROM THE WORKS OF VICTOR HUGO

Beginning of Monologue from Act IV, Scene 2, of "Hernani." (Bohn's Translation.)

[Don Carlos (the future Charles V) is before the tomb of Charlemagne at Aix-la-Chapelle, and is considering the Holy Roman Empire.]

DON CARLOS (*Alone*)

Forgive me, Charlemagne! Oh, this lonely vault
Should echo only unto solemn words!
Thou must be angry at the babble vain
Of our ambition at thy monument.
Here Charlemagne rests! How can the somber tomb
Without a rifting spasm hold such dust?
And art thou truly here, colossal power,
Creator of a world? And canst thou now
Crouch down from all thy majesty and might?
Ah, 'tis a spectacle to stir the soul,
What Europe was and what by thee 'twas made!
Mighty construction with two men supreme,
Elected chiefs to whom born kings submit.
States, duchies, kingdoms, marquisates, and fiefs,
By right hereditary most are ruled.
But nations find a friend sometimes in Pope
Or Cæsar; and one chance another chance
Corrects; thus even balance is maintained
And order opens out. The cloth-of-gold
Electors, and the scarlet cardinals,
The double sacred senate, unto which.
Earth bends, are but paraded outward show.
God's fiat rules it all. One day He wills
A thought, a want, should burst upon the world,
Then grow and spread, and mix with everything,
Possess some man, win hearts, and delve a groove;
Though kings may trample on it, and may seek
To gag;—only that they some morn may see

At diet, conclave, this the scorned idea,
That they had spurned, all suddenly expand
And soar above their heads, bearing the globe
In hand, or on the brow tiara.   Pope
And Emperor, they on earth are all in all.
A mystery supreme dwells in them both,
And Heaven's might, which they still represent,
Feasts them with kings and nations, holding them
Beneath its thunder-cloud the while they sit
At table with the world served out for food.
Alone they regulate all things on earth,
Just as the mower manages his field.
All rule and power are theirs.

From " The Djinns " (" The Oriental Poems")

THE DJINNS

[The genii of the Arabs approach, pass, and depart.]   Translated by J. L. O'Sullivan.

> Town, tower,
> Shore, deep,
> Where lower
> Cliffs steep;
> Waves gray,
> Where play
> Winds gay,
> All sleep.
>
> Hark! a sound,
> Far and slight,
> Breathes around
> On the night;
> High and higher,
> Nigh and nigher,
> Like a fire,
> Roaring bright.

Now on 'tis sweeping
With rattling beat,
Like dwarf imp leaping
In gallop fleet:
He flies, he prances,
In frolic fancies,
On wave-crest dances
With pattering feet.

Hark, the rising swell,
With each new burst!
Like the tolling bell
Of a convent curst;
Like the billowy roar
On a storm-lashed shore—
Now hushed, but once more
Maddening to its worst.

O God! the deadly sound
Of the Djinns' fearful cry!
Quick! neath the spiral round
Of the deep staircase fly!
See, see our lamplight fade!
And of the balustrade
Mounts, mounts the circling shade
Up to the ceiling high!

'Tis the Djinns' wild streaming swarm
Whistling in their tempest flight;
Snap the tall yews 'neath the storm,
Like a pine flame crackling bright.
Swift though heavy, lo! their crowd
Through the heavens rushing loud
Like a livid thunder-cloud
With its bolt of fiery might!

.   .   .   .   .   .

They have passed!—and their wild legion
Cease to thunder at my door;
Fleeting through night's rayless region,
Hither they return no more.

Clanking chains and sounds of woe
Fill the forests as they go,
And the tall oaks cower low,
Bent their flaming light before.

On! on! the storm of wings
Bears far the fiery fear,
Till scarce the breeze now brings
Dim murmurings to the ear;
Like locusts humming hail;
Or thrash of tiny flail,
Plied by the fitful gale
On some old roof-tree sere.

Fainter now are borne
Feeble mutterings still;
As when Arab horn
Swells its magic peal,
Shoreward o'er the deep
Fairy voices sweep,
And the infant's sleep
Golden visions fill.

Each deadly Djinn,
Dark child of fright,
Of death and sin,
Speeds in wild flight
Hark, the dull moan,
Like the deep tone
Of Ocean's groan
Afar, by night!

More and more
Fades it slow,
As on shore
Ripples flow—
As the plaint
Far and faint
Of a saint
Murmured low.

Hark! hist!
Around,
I list!
The bounds
Of space
All trace
Efface
Of sound.

*From "The Shooting Stars." "Songs of the Streets and
the Woods"*

(Dean Carrington's translation.)

Lovers twain, beneath the night,
  Dream, a young and happy pair;
Through the sky-space infinite,
  Suns are seeded everywhere,

Athwart th' heav'n's loud-sounding dome,
  White from the night's extremest way,
Showers of sparkling dawn-dust roam,
  Stars that pass and fade away.

Heaps of falling stars are shed
  Through the vast dark zenith high;
Kindled ash, which censers spread,
  Incense of infinity.

And beneath, which dews bedew,
  Showing pinks and violets shy,
Yellow primrose, pansy blue,
  Lilies, glory of July.

By the cool mist, nearly drowned,
  Lies the meadow far away,
Girded by the forest round,
  Shivering, so that one would say

That the earth 'neath veil of showers,
Which the tear-wet forest sheds,
Wide its apron, decked with flowers,
To receive the stars outspread.

The Wave and the Shadow (*"Les Misérables,"* Book II,
Chapter 8)

[An allegory which contains the thought of "Les Misérables"
—the abandonment of the criminal by society.]

Man overboard!

What matters! The ship does not stop. The wind blows.
That somber ship has a route it must pursue. It passes on.

The man disappears, then reappears; he sinks and rises again
to the surface; he calls; he stretches out his arms; he is not heard;
the ship, trembling under the hurricane, is wholly taken up with
its own handling; the sailors and passengers no longer even see
the man who has sunk; his wretched head is but a speck in the
enormous mass of water.

He utters despairing cries in the depths. What a ghost that
fleeing sail is! He looks at it, he looks at it madly. It goes
away, it grows dim, it grows smaller. A moment ago he was
there, with the crew; he was coming and going on the deck with
the others; he was enjoying his share of breath and sunshine; he
was a living being. Now, what indeed has happened? He
slipped, he fell, it is over.

He is in the monstrous water. Under his feet there is nothing
left but flight and crumbling. The billows, rent and torn by the
wind, surround him hideously; the rollings of the abyss carry him
away; all the tatters of the waters stir about his head; a populace
of waves spit upon him; murky openings half devour him; each
time that he sinks down he catches glimpses of precipices full of
night; fearful unknown vegetations seize him, tie his feet, pull
him to themselves; he feels he is becoming abyss; he is a part
of the foam; the waves throw him to one another; he drinks
bitterness; the cowardly ocean is bent on drowning him; enormity
sports with his death struggle. All that water seems hate itself.

Nevertheless he fights on.

He tries to defend himself; he tries to keep up; he makes an effort; he swims. He, that poor force at once exhausted, he fights against the inexhaustible.

Where, then, is the ship? Yonder. Scarcely visible in the pale shades of the horizon.

The blasts blow! all the particles of foam overwhelm him. He lifts his eyes and sees only the livid clouds. He witnesses, dying, the sea's vast madness. He is tortured by this madness. He hears noises foreign to man, which seem to come from beyond the earth and from some frightful alien region.

There are birds in the clouds, as there are angels above the distress of humanity, but what can they do for him? They fly, sing, and soar, and he—he gives the death rattle.

He feels himself entombed at the same time by these two infinities, ocean and sky; one is a grave, the other is a shroud.

Night falls; he has been swimming for hours; his strength has reached its limit; that ship, that distant thing where men were, has died away; he is alone in the formidable twilight gulf; he sinks; he stiffens to resist; he twists about; he feels beneath him the waves, monsters of the invisible; he calls.

All men are gone. Where is God?

He calls. Help! help! He keeps on calling.

Nothing on the horizon; nothing in the sky.

He implores space, the wave, the sea wrack, the reef; they are deaf. He begs the tempest; the imperturbable tempest obeys only the infinite.

Around him are shadow, mist, solitude, the stormy, insensate tumult, the confused curling of wild waters. In him are horror and fatigue. Under him, falling. No supporting crevice. He thinks of the darksome adventures of the corpse in the limitless shade. The bottomless cold paralyzes him. His hands stiffen, shut, seize on nothingness. Winds, clouds, whirlwinds, blasts, stars, are useless! What is to be done? The despairing man gives up; he who is weary concludes to die; he yields, lets himself go, relaxes his grasp, and there he is rolling forever in the mournful depths of the engulfing chasm.

Oh, implacable march of human society! Losses of men and

souls on your way! Ocean into which falls all that the law lets fall! Sinister disappearance of help! Oh, moral death!

The sea is the inexorable social night into which the penal system casts its criminals. The sea is wretchedness immense.

The soul floating in this gulf may become a corpse. Who will revive it?

BIBLIOGRAPHY

Translations from the Poems of Victor Hugo. Henry Carrington.
Life of Victor Hugo. Frank T. Marzials.
Articles in *Harper's Monthly*, Vol. CII, pp. 100 ff., and 444 ff.; *Scribner's*, Vol. XXI, pp. 108 ff.; *The Chautauquan*, Vol. XXV.

HONORÉ DE BALZAC

CHAPTER VII

BALZAC AND REALISM IN LITERATURE

[HONORÉ DE BALZAC, born at Tours, May 16, 1799; educated at Vendôme College, in Paris schools, and at the Paris Law School, 1807–1819; life of writing and reading at Paris, 1819–1820; at home at Villeparisis, 1821–1824; publisher at Paris, 1824–1825; printer, 1826–1828; novelist, 1829–1848; died at Paris, August 18, 1850. Leading novels: "Louis Lambert," 1832; "Eugénie Grandet," 1833; "Père Goriot," 1834; "Séraphita," 1835; "The Lily in the Valley," 1835; "César Birotteau," 1837; "Ursule Mirouet," 1841; "Cousin Pons," 1847.]

French realism in the literature of the nineteenth century differs from English realism in at least one essential particular, the amount of moral fiber in its heroes and heroines. While the realistic writers of both nations agree in presenting life such as they see it around them, with its trials and changes, the English author balances the evil of that life with the good. The French author, as a rule, does not. The reason for this striking divergence is not far to seek. The English novelists were not guided by a preconceived theory. The French were. As the French are at bottom a logical people, and demand conclusions which proceed strictly from accepted premises, so in their literature they wish consistency in argument. Now, the argument of realism is fidelity to facts, facts separated from everything which is imaginative or immaterial, absolute, scientific facts. French realism

147

added to this postulate the further one of man considered as an animate being.

France had received from England, from Locke, the doctrine of knowledge derived through the senses. The disciples of this philosophical school, carried away by their logical temperament, pushed this doctrine to an extreme, and claimed that man has no other sources of knowledge than through his body. The influence of the great teachers of medicine, who in France began to reorganize the study of that profession towards the last years of the eighteenth century, tended in the same direction. So much so, indeed, that under this combined pressure from philosophy and physiology few Frenchmen of the first half of the nineteenth century, save the most devout, seem to have looked on man as anything but an animal. If he receives all his knowledge through his physical being as the dog or the horse does, he differs from the dog and horse only in degree. When the sources of his knowledge cease, when the body dies, the man is dead. He has no mind apart from his body, no soul.

Apply this creed to literature and see the result. Realism is observation of the facts of life. Philosophy and science both limit the observation of man to the facts of his material existence. They do not show that he has any other existence. Consequently a study of man, if pursued in a scientific way, as realism claims it should be, resolves itself into the study of an animal, of its needs and its appetites. The animal wants something and seeks it. So does man. Neither is endowed with the capacity to resist its desires, so far as science shows. Man is higher than the brute in the order of creation. He has more brains. He is actuated by other instincts than hunger and thirst.   His faculties admit of ambition, avarice.   He loves power, luxury.   As the senses furnish no valid reasons why he should not get what he wants, he strives to get it by all the means he possesses, by violence, deceit, labor.

This is the principle of French realism.   In contrast to the English practice of assuming that man has both a spiritual and a physical nature, and that the two often clash, the French theory is more simple.   It does away with the inner struggle of the individual, and considers only the struggles between individuals, where the strong or the crafty destroy the weak or the simple.   In other words, French realism ignores the question of the individual conscience.   It deliberately confines itself to the description of that part of humanity which is not disturbed by ethical considerations.

Connected with this principle of French realism is another, subordinate to it, but still important in comparison with its relative across the Channel.   The French Revolution, as we have seen, made for the widening of those who are socially capable, for democracy.   Chateaubriand, Madame de Staël, both romanticists, remained aristocrats in their writings.   Hugo began as such, but was soon carried towards democracy by his surroundings and sympathies.   Yet he still believed in man's moral nature.   The remaining romanticists either remained aristocratic or mingled aristocracy with democracy, as Alfred de Vigny in poetry, Alexandre Dumas and George Sand in romance.   But the true realist could not be an aristocrat.   Political power had fallen into the hands of the Third Estate, and the realist must recognize that fact. The aristocracy was dying, was losing property and social position to the successful plebeian, the *bourgeois* banker, merchant, manufacturer. The new-school novelists must tell of the rise of the poor boy, with passions or ambitions to gratify, through the social strata, across the ruins of the upper layers, to prominence or indulgence. And they had before them a model, the embodiment of democracy and materialism, Napoleon, who without apparent regard for morals, individual or social, went straight about his work of leveling mankind to one huge democracy under him. He was the idol of the first realistic novelist, Stendhal, who exalts him in "Red and Black" and "The Chartreuse of Parma." His success was also ever present before the eyes of the greater realistic author, who began his genuine career at the flood-tide of the Napoleonic legend, Honoré de Balzac.

Balzac was born at Tours in 1799, on the calendar day of St. Honorius, from whom he took his name, as was the custom. His family was well to do, and had not suffered by the Revolution. The first four years of his life he passed with a peasant nurse in the country, also customary with French children of respectable parentage. At the age of eight he was sent to the college at Vendôme, where he spent six years without vacation or holiday. Our first glimpse at his character is obtained here, from the school register: "Honoré Balzac, aged eight years and one month. Has had the smallpox and is without infirmity. Temperament sanguine; easily excited; subject to feverish attacks." The confinement of this existence for a child who had passed nearly all his hours out of doors seemed at last to benumb his faculties, and he was sent home to recruit. So he hated these years, as many of his countrymen do the years of their prison-like education, and in his novel of "Louis Lambert" has left us the legacy of his abhorrence. In 1814 his family moved to Paris, and Honoré continued his study in the schools of the capital. He then entered the Law School, and also got practical legal experience in the offices of friends of his family. From these first years at Paris he gained his personal knowledge of Napoleon, whom he had seen, and his familiarity with legal terms, both of which were to enter widely into the composition of his future works.

By 1819 the Balzac family had retired to the country, and Honoré, refusing to practice law, had wrung from his father a reluctant consent to give himself up to literary pursuits. He established himself in a garret near one of the libraries of Paris, and read, wrote, and observed the life and occupations of the town. But he strangely misjudged his own talent. Filled with a desire for literary fame at all hazards, he took the shortest road to that goal in France. He chose a tragedy, and a tragedy on Cromwell. He composed the tragedy, read it to his family, and submitted it to friends. It was wretched, and resulted in his recall to the family home. There, although subject to many interruptions, he began to work on fiction. In 1822 he published five romances of four volumes each. In 1823, 1824, and 1825 he added three more to the number, all under pseudonyms, mainly that of Horace de Saint-Aubin. But these stories were always refused a place in his complete works by him. They are novels in the extravagant taste of the time, and are now of interest only because Balzac wrote them.

In 1823 he wished to take up his residence in Paris again. Unfortunately his career had not yet justified any further liberality on the part of his parents, and he was forced to rely on himself. Acting on the advice of a business acquaintance who lent him the money for the enterprise, he turned publisher, and got out the complete works of Molière and La Fontaine in one volume each, the first attempt, it is said, to make compact editions of the French classics. But nobody bought them, and Balzac was left in debt. Here begins the struggle against financial burdens with which he consumed his vitality. From publishing he went to printing, in a vain hope to retrieve his fortunes, using for his purpose the patrimony his family advanced to him, and when printing proved unsuccessful, he bought a type-foundry, a good speculation had he possessed sufficient capital. Indeed, it may be said of Balzac's financial schemes in general, that they were good ones, but he did not have the money to push them. And the close of the year 1828 saw him out of them all, but deep in pecuniary obligations. He owed, he says, about twenty-four thousand dollars.

His failures in business restored him to literature. In 1827 he had begun the first novel he was to acknowledge later, a story of the Vendean war—anticipating Hugo's "Ninety-Three"—which he named "Les Chouans." It was published in 1829 under his own name, and as the book has merit, and the fashion of the day favored historical romances in the manner of Walter Scott, whom Balzac here takes for a model, it brought reputation to its author, and encouraged further literary undertakings. Of these there was no end. Balzac's memory was unusual. His reading had been enormous, his observation long continued, his experience varied, and he had the habit of supplementing his after impressions by a kind of scrap-book he carried on his person. Our guide to his career in these first thirty years of his existence is his devoted sister, Madame de Surville. Speaking of his method of accumulation she says: "Wherever he went he studied what he saw—towns, villages, country places, and their inhabitants; collecting words or speeches which revealed a character or painted a situation. He called, rather slightingly, the scrap-book in which he kept these notes of what he saw and heard, his 'meat-safe.' "

Out of this faculty of observation of places and men grew many of his stories and novels. "Les Chouans" itself had been suggested by a visit to friends who lived in Brittany, and it contains descriptions of Breton scenery. So his early years had given him surroundings and events. Tours is celebrated ("The Curate of Tours"), the fertile valleys which lie near it ("The Lily in the Valley"), the residences of acquaintances as he visits them from time to time, towns he stays in, as Saumur ("Eugénie Grandet") or Angoulême ("Lost Illusions"). During his early solitary life in Paris he himself tells how he made a point of using even his exercise to gather material for fiction. He noticed people, their dress, their manners, drew near to listen to their conversation, and tried by it to enter into their beings and lead their lives. His imagination was so powerful he actually succeeded in this last instance. He claims he could feel the clothes of others upon himself, could share their angers and pleasures. He found in this kind of metamorphosis a relaxation from the fatigue of toil. And this trait grew on him with years. His sister shows how he considered the characters of his work as living beings, how interested he was in their plans and fortunes. Such a power explains the attraction which his writings exert.   He lived out his people.   He thus makes them vivid for us.   They are real flesh and blood, because for the time being they were a part of humanity.

Endowed with this gift, Balzac could not satisfy himself with the rather distant domain of historical fiction. With a few slight exceptions "Les Chouans" remains his only incursion into that field.   He was full of the world around him.   He had shared the passions, good and bad, of his contemporaries.   His observations of things and manners, attributes of these contemporaries and their environment, had led him along the way of actuality.   It is said that Stendhal, intent on his sketches of Parisian society, influenced Balzac to follow his example.   This is possible.   But it is not necessary to explain his course. His genius was realistic.   His material was objective. His own life even was a matter of analysis to himself.   His imagination consisted mainly in his transformation of himself into others, whose profession or trade he studied and embraced for the moment.   And then at bottom he was unemotional; or if not unemotional, he was surely unsympathetic.   The prizes of this world are for the strong, he argued.   You cannot spare the weak without falsifying the reality of life.   So his sister says that when she interceded with him in behalf of some unfortunate of his unfinished romances, he would answer: "Don't bewilder me with your sensibilities; truth before everything.   Those persons are feeble, incapable; what happens to them must happen; so much the worse for them."   Napoleon, the great realist, could hardly have spoken otherwise of the victims of his ambition.

"Les Chouans," therefore, was not repeated.   The year 1830 saw a large number of sketches and short stories from his pen, some fanciful, some historical, some drawn from life. Émile de Girardin, the great journalist of his time, opened to him the columns of his newspaper, *La Mode*, and also the doors of Madame Sophie Gay's salon, Madame Girardin's mother. There Balzac could meet the best minds of the nation. Hugo, Lamartine, artists, musicians, or politicians like Thiers. He also aided Girardin in founding a new weekly, devoted to literature and art. In 1831 he left his ugly quarters for an apartment which he was to occupy for seven years, and which he fitted up with considerable taste, though denying himself at the same time many of the necessaries of life. It is in this new house that he wrote the works which brought him fame, and where he conceived the plan of what he was pleased to call—surely in imitation of Dante—"The Human Comedy." And yet it was the spur of debt which goaded him on.

His method of work, of actual labor in writing out his stories, has been told so often that it has become legendary. Having prepared himself with subject, plan, and material, he would isolate himself from the world during the process of composition. One of his publishers tells us that he would retire at eight in the evening, rise by two in the night, and write as fast as he could carry his quill—it was before the time of steel pens—until six. A long bath at six, coffee at eight, when the publisher would call with proofs and to get copy, and writing again from nine to noon, lunch and writing again from one to six. Dinner followed, and at seven the publisher would call again, and occasionally Balzac's intimates. He himself gives a picture of his own manner of work to his sister, in the year 1833. It is practically the existence

sketched by his publisher, though the details are somewhat different: "I have begun hard work again. I go to
bed at six with my dinner in my mouth. The animal
digests, and sleeps till midnight. Then Auguste makes
me a cup of coffee, on which the mind works without a
break till noon. I rush to the printing-office to take my
copy and get my proofs, in order to give the animal exercise, who dreams as he goes. One puts a good deal of
black on white, little sister, in twelve hours; and after a
month of this existence there's not a little work done.
Poor pen! it must be made of diamond not to be worn
out by so much toil. To increase its master's reputation . . . . to enable him to pay his debts to all, and
then to give him, some day, rest upon the mountain—that
is its task."

Before this account, he had told his mother, in 1832,
of his experience in writing "Louis Lambert": "I was
worn out with the labor which 'Louis Lambert' caused
me; I had sat up many nights and drank so much coffee
that I suffered stomach pains which amounted to cramps.
'Louis Lambert' is, perhaps, a masterpiece, but it has
cost me dearly—six weeks of unremitting toil at Saché
and ten days at Angoulême." In other words, when at
work he would pass from six to eight weeks away from
every one but his publisher, turning night into day by the
free use of coffee. His actual time at his desk was twelve
hours daily.

This unusual existence has become attached to the
name of Balzac and stamped itself on his history. Yet
it did not fill up all his life, nor possibly the greater part
of it. For when once released from his self-imposed
prison, he was off, visiting friends and places, observing

men and landscapes, speculating on financial schemes, and
planning more books, the meanwhile writing letters, many
and long, to correspondents of all kinds.   During these
intermissions he attempted other vocations.   Once he
thought of turning politician, and actually stood for two
constituencies in 1831, one in 1832, and again in 1834.
But the party he belonged to was the Legitimist, the
Bourbon party, and the larger number of its members
protested against the July Monarchy by refusing to vote
under it.   Consequently Balzac had little support at the
polls.   His political program did not stop with affirming
the excellence of a limited constitutional government, with
the larger part of its legislative power lodged in an upper
house of peers, who represented landed property.   He
had views of his own regarding the liberty of the press,
and advocated the remission of taxation on newspapers,
so that many should be printed and the one-cent sheet
might be possible.   He also wished France to prepare for
foreign wars by a general conscription of the whole nation
after the model of Prussia.   This was in 1831.

And then Balzac had desires to shine socially.   His
writings had brought him many admirers among women,
who sent him letters eulogistic of his work — as
was the case of Madame Hanska, whom he afterwards
married—and who opened to him the doors of their
houses.   In this way he became acquainted with some of
the leaders of fashion, and drew on his experience at their
receptions for his episodes of high life.   The remarkable
thing of it all is, that in spite of these opportunities, and
notwithstanding that both here and in literary and family
circles he constantly met women of the greatest refinement, he seems to have never known what a lady was,

and his portraits of what he considered *grandes dames* are simply absurd—witness Madame de Beauséant and the Duchesse de Langeais in "Père Goriot." One would say their originals were bold, vulgar upstarts who had derived their ideas of breeding from the haughty heroines of flashy romances. In this respect his observation certainly failed him, perhaps the only respect. But this particular failure spoils many of the pages in which he evidently took unusual delight. The reflex influence on his private life is seen in the extravagance he indulged in, for a short period only, it is true, of a carriage and groom, with which ornaments he appeared in the favorite streets and parks of the French capital.

But politics and society occupied an extremely small fraction of Balzac's life. Nor does he seem to have fostered love affairs either. His mind was intent on books, always books. He carried the plots of several in his head at once. Two or three would actually be on the stocks at the same time. Quite likely he found mental relief in changing from one to the other and back again, just as he found recreation in embodying himself now in this now in that character. To one of his correspondents, Madame Carraud, he thus describes the state of his brain, in 1833: "I assure you I live in an atmosphere of thoughts, ideas, plans, labors, conceptions; which cross one another, boil, crackle in my head enough to drive me crazy. But nothing makes me thin. I am the truest portrait of a monk ever seen since the first hour of monasteries."

Yet with all this material on hand, and in process of casting, he was not careless in his use of it. Indeed, Balzac was the terror of type-setters. It was his custom to send to the printer an outline of his stories merely, which was set up and returned to him in separate columns on large sheets of paper. This sketch he would elaborate, correcting, adding, and with the return of this copy the next day would continue to change and amplify. Sometimes as many as eleven or twelve proofs would thus pass before his eyes. He was rarely satisfied even then, for though he possessed little artistic ability, he was always seeking to improve his style. The cost of so many alterations was, of course, enormous. The printers generally refused to pay for them, and he was forced to bear the burden. In one letter he speaks of a new publisher having paid for four thousand francs of proof corrections in order to relieve him. So we may not wonder that he had difficulties with the publication of his books, or that he antagonized many with whom he had business relations. He also had causes for disagreement with the journalists, not always of his own making, and after a lawsuit, in 1835–1836, with Buloz, the editor of the *Revue de Paris*, as well as the *Revue des Deux Mondes*, he found the columns of the press practically closed to him. So he seemed to wish an organ of his own. In 1836 he started the semi-weekly *Chronique de Paris*, which lasted less than a year. In 1840 he tried the monthly *Revue Parisienne*, which died with the third issue.

The years between 1832 and 1836, to which period these comments belong, established Balzac's fame on a lasting foundation. His manner of work, his working costume of a white cashmere dressing-gown, made like a monk's habit, and fastened with a cord around the waist, his frugal life of abstinence, all contributed to invest his person with interest. And his novels confirmed these exter-

nal signs of genius. In 1832, together with many short
stories, "The Curate of Tours" and "Louis Lambert"
saw the light; in 1833 "The Country Doctor" and
"Eugénie Grandet"; in 1834–1835 "Séraphita," "La
Recherche de l'Absolu," and "Père Goriot"; in 1835–
1836 "The Lily in the Valley." Nor were the following
years less productive. In 1838 he left Paris for the
suburb of Ville-d'Avray, where he bought land on a hillside, and built some buildings, to which he gave the name
of Les Jardies. He had long desired a country place.
Here he remained four years, then returned to Paris,
where he finally (in 1846) bought a house of his own, the
Beaujon Hotel in Rue Balzac (former Rue Fortunée),
which he filled with many curiosities and bric-à-brac. To
the first six years belong the voluminous "Lost Illusions,"
"César Birotteau" (1837), "Béatrix" (1839), "Ursule
Mirouet" (1841), and "Albert Savarus" (1842).

The year 1843 marks an epoch in Balzac's life.
Among the women whose attention had been aroused by
Balzac's first successes was, as we have noticed, Madame
Hanska, a Pole. The correspondence she carried on with
the novelist led to various interviews, as she visited France
or the neighboring lands. In 1843 her husband, who was
many years her senior, died, and that summer Balzac
visited her at her home. The affection which had been
steadily increasing in his heart was now aroused to a
passion. Unfortunately it was not to be soon satisfied.
Duties toward her daughter, a minor, unusual state regulations regarding property in Russia, and differences of
religion delayed the projected marriage. In 1846 they
became formally engaged. In October, 1848, Balzac
went to Poland to stay until he should return with his

bride. One circumstance after another delayed the wedding. Finally, on March 14, 1850, it took place. In April the bridal trip to Paris was begun, and May found the husband and wife installed in the Beaujon house.

But all these delays had left their impress on Balzac. The consequences of his unnatural mode of life, excessive hours, lack of sleep, and overstimulation were already noticeable by 1842. A letter to his mother, in April of that year, reveals discouragement, and speaks of his productiveness as diminishing. By 1844 the breakdown had become serious. He writes of fever and internal pains. Mental distress augmented his physical discomfort. The postponement of his union with Madame Hanska weighed upon him. The uncertainty attending the outcome of his courtship—an accepted lover and yet separated from his love, his "star" as he delighted to call her—distracted his mind. His work became more and more halting, the times of inspiration less frequent. Still with all these ills, physical and mental, when he did work his talent showed no signs of diminution. "Modeste Mignon" belongs to 1844, "The Peasants" to 1844–1845, "Cousin Pons" and "Cousine Bette" to 1846–1847. His art gallery of the Beaujon house did service in "Cousin Pons." But with his journey to Russia, in 1848, disease finally conquered. The climate aggravated his maladies, and when he returned to France, in May, 1850, it was only to die. Standing on the threshold of happiness, holding what he had so long desired, a woman's love, freed from his life incubus of debt, his frame was too weak to sustain any longer the soul which had overwrought it. On August 18, 1850, he passed away.

The extent of Balzac's work renders any detailed

analysis of it quite impossible. He had begun his career under Walter Scott's influence, and expected to write historical novels like him. But his own experience and the atmosphere in which he lived were both opposed to this idea, and after "Les Chouans" and several shorter sketches of an historical nature he settled down to put into fiction what he himself had seen or fancied. As early as 1830 he had recognized this bent of his genius, and affirmed that he was painting a picture of men and manners in the first part of the nineteenth century. In a letter to Madame Hanska, written in January, 1833, he states that he has "undertaken, rashly doubtless, to represent all literature in the whole of his work," and that "wishing to build a monument durable more for its size and accumulation of material than because of the beauty of its structure," he is "obliged to attempt every kind of subject so as not to be accused of lack of power." He had long been seeking for a general classification for this material. He had tried "Philosophical Romances and Stories" for some, "Scenes of Private Life," "Scenes of Provincial Life" for others; he had settled on a more comprehensive title for the latter varieties in 1834, with "Studies of Manners in the Nineteenth Century," and had changed the heading of the former to "Philosophical Studies" in 1835. Later he conceived the idea of grouping all his work of whatever nature under the name of "The Human Comedy," with the subdivisions of "Scenes of Private Life," "Provincial Life," "Parisian Life," "Military Life," "Political Life," "Country Life," "Philosophical Studies," and "Analytical Studies." And these titles appear in his final edition, begun in 1842.

This edition has a preface which contains Balzac's

literary theories, and a defense against his critics as well. In it he says that the underlying idea of his work was based on a comparison between man and animals. As the zoölogists had claimed that all animals came originally from one form, which had developed differently in different environments, and produced at last different species, so man is one in his origin, and differs from his fellow-man merely because of his environment. Buffon, the great naturalist of the eighteenth century, had written the chronicles of the animal kingdom. Balzac would now record the annals of humanity existing in organized society. Before 1842, in a preface to "Lost Illusions," printed in 1837, we can see the embryo of this idea: "When a writer has undertaken a complete description of society, seen under all its forms, noted in all its phases, starting from the principle that the social state so fits men to its needs and transforms them so thoroughly that nowhere are men like one another, and that it has created as many *species* as it has *professions;* that social humanity, in short, presents as many varieties as zoölogy does." . . .

This scientific principle once laid down, Balzac considers himself as the recorder of the facts which proceed from it. He would do for his own time what Walter Scott had done for the Middle Ages, and thus "give the novel its philosophical value of history." He would be simply a secretary of society, would take an inventory of its vices and virtues, would relate its deeds, paint its characters, making "types by means of the traits of several homogeneous characters," and thereby leave a history of the manners of his own time such as had never been bequeathed to posterity by any other writer of any epoch. And then when all these facts had been noted he would go beneath the surface and study their causes, find out the "social motor," dwell on "natural principles," and determine how closely society comes to "the eternal rule of the true and good." But already he can affirm that society does not harm man, as Rousseau argued. It improves him. He is "neither good nor bad; he is born with instincts and aptitudes," but "self-interest does develop his evil inclinations," which it is the province of the church to suppress. In other places he is even more explicit about individual development. He says that the social law affecting man is that of "each for himself," what we now term "the survival of the fittest." And necessarily in telling the truth about what he sees he narrates many things which are unpleasant, vicious, and criminal, the consequence of his secretaryship of society.

Balzac, as we see, lays down theoretically the two leading principles of French realism, the treatment of humanity from the physiological point of view, and the portrayal of society as a whole, the upper, middle, and lower strata. And he justifies his theory by his practice. Indeed, he justified it in practice long before he formulated it in words. With the exception of some notable works, all his stories and novels are based on the assumption that man is guided by "his instincts and aptitudes"; that he observes the law of "each one for himself"; or in other words, that he is governed by his appetites, physical or mental; that he seeks for luxury or power, that his goal is enjoyment, and his whole conception of life materialistic. The men who engage in these struggles, and the women also, represent all classes of society, but more especially the middle class, the Third Estate which planned the French Revolution, which profited again by the Revolution of 1830, and under Guizot's leadership came into its own with Louis Philippe, whose reign bounds Balzac's chief literary productiveness.   Science in fiction and democracy are his mottoes.   He rarely proves false to them.

Take, for instance, his heroes.   Who are the young men in his novels, whence do they come, and what do they want?   They are, as a rule, poor country lads, with respectable connections, who want social prominence at Paris.   They are ambitious.   They care for money, to be sure, but only as a means to an end—power.   Balzac has rung the changes on the greed for gain.   He has sketched misers, like Gobseck or old Grandet; he has portrayed the rage of relatives as they crowd to seize the property of the weak or the legacy of the dying or dead, as in "Ursule Mirouet" or "Cousin Pons"; he has shown the straits to which the need of money reduces aspirants to social honors, as in "Père Goriot."   But his heroes, it must be confessed, are not interested in money for itself. They wish it for what it will bring.   Apart from this distinction they are as unscrupulous in getting it as the misers are.   No pricks of conscience restrain them in their selfish desire.   And if they attain their goal they do so at the expense of others weaker than they, and sometimes better than they.   To these gladiators in the struggle for existence even love appeals only as a weapon with which they may hew their way to something material, higher up; and marriage is a business arrangement which, if well carried out, frees one from his creditors.   Still, in the majority of cases the assumed or real love of these men does not lead to marriage.   They pay their court to married women by whom they expect to be more quickly advanced.

And his heroines? With hardly an exception they are
the victims of man. Their love once won by the social
struggler is used to the full extent of its worth by him,
and then thrown aside when no further advantage is to
be derived from it. Whether married or not the story is
the same. Few of the married women are happy. They
look for consolation and affection outside of marriage, and
are easily beguiled by the first adventurer who presents
himself. Yet Balzac believed in these marriages *de con-
venance*, as the saying is, and opposed marriages for love.
In his "Memoirs of Two Young Brides" we trace the
happy—or phlegmatic—career of the one who married for
material reasons, and see it contrasted with the unhappy
career—because, forsooth, of financial troubles—of the
one who married for love. The material outcome dwarfs
all others in his eyes. Still his ideal, Madame de Mortsauf, who made the proper marriage ("The Lily in the
Valley") is anything but happy. Nor, on the other hand,
is Madame Claës, devoted to her husband, who in turn is all
wrapped up in the scientific pursuits which finally destroy
her ("La Recherche de l'Absolu"). The girls who fail
to marry the man they love are not happy ("Eugénie
Grandet"), nor are those who succeed in doing so
("Béatrix," "The Muse of the Department"). We are
puzzled to understand why with so many heroines who
are seeking for happiness through love so few succeed in
attaining it. But Balzac gives his own reasons. Women
are born to serve men. They are destined to sorrow and
to suffer. Their mission is to help the sterner sex, even
at the expense of their own hearts. The best among
them lead but a thankless life. As he says in "Eugénie
Grandet," where he sums up his theory on this point:

"To feel, to love, to suffer, to sacrifice themselves to others, will always be the text of women's lives."

The rascals are not Balzac's only heroes. His novels, even his leading ones, contain characters which he considers good or are really so. He evidently considers old Goriot good, who allows himself to be plundered by his self-seeking daughters, and who encourages them in all their immoral conduct, provided it will bring them happiness ("Père Goriot"). He seems to look upon the fond mother in "Béatrix" as good even in her desire to see her son gratify his passion. And he surely thinks the wife good in "La Recherche de l'Absolu," who allows her husband to ruin the family. All these are types of affection, and others might be included, as Cousin Pons. But there are good people in Balzac who prosper. In his longer stories a noteworthy instance is the Birotteau family ("César Birotteau"), and Daniel Darchon, the journalist, who appears now and then in the histories of Parisian life. And in many of his tales of manners outside of Paris, "The Country Doctor," "The Village Curate," "Modeste Mignon," and many others, we see good people at work who reach good results. Indeed, in these provincial scenes he is a more accurate observer. He gives a wider view of man. For one reason and another the moment Balzac catches a glimpse of Paris or Parisians his sense of observation is blunted, his judgment impaired, and his desires for luxury taking fire with the contact flame up in extravagant portrayals of an existence which is partly real, but which is mainly created by his own imaginative longings and by the theories of the corrupting influence of society he had inherited from Rousseau. An example of this literary legacy is the character of

Vautrin in "Père Goriot," as well as the demoralization which sets in on his provincials when they once tread the streets of the capital.

Balzac, the secretary of society, the painter of so many scenes and of so many people that are real, possessed other gifts as a novelist. As an omnivorous reader he had chanced on the books of the mystics, he had reveled in Dante's pictures of the unseen, he had imbibed notions of mesmerism, he had studied the tenets of Swedenborg. The result is a number of stories and novels which cannot be classed as realistic, but as romantic, imaginative. In them he never saw what he describes. Under this head comes "The Magic Skin" (1831), whose steady contraction reveals to his owner his waning life; "Louis Lambert" (1832), part of which is an autobiography of the author while at school at Vendôme, part the sketch of a romantic hero like Goethe's "Werther" or Chateaubriand's "René," epistolary in his habits and misunderstood by the world, and part Swedenborgian mysticism. But the crown of all this writing is "Séraphita" (1835), a presentation of the doctrines of Swedenborg, by means of fiction, where the hero shows himself as a man, Séraphitus, to Minna, the type of earthly love, and as a woman, Séraphita, to Wilfrid, who personifies worldly ambition. The teachings of this twofold being gradually wean the two mundanes from their material desires, and when in process of time the body of this being is wholly transformed by her soul, and she becomes transfigured, the two, ripe at last for heavenly love, are permitted to witness her transfiguration. Thus Balzac redeems his materialism by a poetical picture of the ideal state.

SELECTIONS FROM THE WORKS OF BALZAC

From the Preface to "The Human Comedy" (*1842*)

In giving to a work undertaken almost thirteen years ago the name of The Human Comedy it is necessary to say what its idea was, to tell its origin, explain its plan briefly, while trying to speak of these things as though I was not interested in them. . . . .

The idea of The Human Comedy was first like a dream in my mind, like one of those impossible projects which you cherish and allow to escape.

This idea came from a comparison between mankind and animals.

. . . . In reading again the extraordinary works of the mystics who have busied themselves with science in its relation to the infinite, such as Swedenborg, Saint-Martin, etc., and the writings of the best geniuses in natural history, such as Leibnitz, Buffon, Charles Bonnet, etc., we find in the monads of Leibnitz, the organic molecules of Buffon, the vegetating force of Needham, the *fitting together* of similar parts of Charles Bonnet, who was so daring as to write, in 1760, "The animal vegetates like the plant," we find, I say, the rudiments of that fine law of *self for self* on which *unity of composition* rests. There is but one animal. The Creator used but one and the same model for all organized beings. The animal is a principle which takes its external form, or speaking more exactly, the differences of its form from the surroundings in which it is called upon to develop itself. Zoölogical species result from these differences. . . . .

Imbued with this system long before the debates to which it gave rise, I saw that in this respect society resembled nature. Does not society make of man, according to the environment in which its action is exerted, as many different men as there are varieties in zoölogy? The differences between a soldier, a workman, an administrator, a lawyer, an idler, a scientist, a statesman, a trader, a sailor, a poet, a poor man, a priest are, though more difficult to grasp, as great as those which distinguish the wolf, the lion, the ass, the crow, the shark, the seal, the sheep, etc. Therefore social species have existed, will always exist, just as much as zoölogical species. If Buffon did a magnificent work in trying to represent in one book all of zoölogy, was there not a work of this kind to be done for society? But in the case of the animal varieties nature has placed limits which could not contain society. When Buffon painted the lion he finished the picture of the lioness in a few phrases; whereas in society woman is not always the female of man. There can be two completely unlike beings in one household. . . . . The description of the social species was, therefore, at least double that of the animal species, taking only the two sexes into consideration. Finally there are few dramas among animals, there is scarcely any confusion; they attack each other, that is all. Men also attack each other, but their greater or less degree of intelligence makes their conflict more complicated. . . . . Then Buffon found life among animals very simple. The animal has but little furniture, it has neither arts nor sciences; while man, by a law which is yet to be determined, tends to represent his manners, his thought, and his life in everything he appropriates to his needs. . . . . The habits of each animal are, in our eyes at least, constantly alike at all times; while the habits, the clothes, the words, the dwellings of a prince, a banker, an artist, a tradesman, a priest, and a poor man are wholly unlike and change with changing civilizations.

So the work to be done must have a threefold form: men, women, and things; that is to say, people and the material representation they make of their thought; in short, man and life. . . . .

But how make a drama of the three or four thousand characters which a society offers interesting? How please at the same time the poet, the philosopher, and the masses who wish poetry and philosophy in striking pictures? . . . . Walter Scott raised the romance to the philosophical value of history . . . . He put into it the spirit of olden times, combined in it drama, dialogue, portrait, landscape, description; he caused to enter into it the marvelous and the true. . . . . Though . . . . dazzled by the surprising fecundity of Walter Scott . . . . I did not despair, for I found the reason for this talent in the infinite variety of human nature. . . . . French society was to be the historian. I was to be the secretary only. By drawing up an inventory of vices and virtues, by collecting the principal deeds of the passions, by painting characters, by choosing the leading events of society, by forming types out of the union of the features of several homogeneous characters, perhaps I might succeed in writing the history which had been forgotten by so many historians, the history of manners.   With much patience and courage I might realize with France of the nineteenth century that book we all regret Rome, Athens, Tyre, Memphis, Persia, and India did not leave to us about their civilizations. . . . . As to the intimate sense, the soul of that work, here are the principles on which it is based.

Man is neither good nor evil; he is born with instincts and aptitudes; society, far from making him depraved, as Rousseau has claimed, perfects him, makes him better; but self-interest also develops his bad inclinations.   Christianity, and Roman Catholicism especially, being, as I have said in "The Country Doctor," a complete system of repression for the depraved tendencies of man, is the greatest element of social order. . . . .

In copying all society, grasping it in the immensity of its movements, it happens, it was bound to happen, that such and such a composition offered more evil than good, that such and such a section of the fresco represented a guilty group. . . . . In this respect I must call attention to the fact that the most conscientious moralists very much doubt whether society can offer as many good actions as it does bad ones, and in the picture I make of it there are more virtuous than blameworthy people. . . . . Obliged to conform to the ideas of an essentially hypocritical country, Walter Scott was humanly false in his portrayal of woman, because his models were dissenters.   The Protestant woman has no ideal.   She may be chaste, pure, virtuous, but her unemotional love will always be calm and composed like a duty done. . . . . In Protestantism there is nothing possible for woman after sin, while in the Catholic Church the hope of pardon makes her sublime.   So there is but one kind of woman for a Protestant writer, while the Catholic author finds a new woman in each new situation. . . . Passion is humanity entire.   Without it religion, history, fiction, art, would be useless.

In seeing me gather together so many facts and paint them as they are with passion for an element, some people have very wrongly imagined that I belonged to the sensualist and materialist school, two faces of the same thing, pantheism. But perhaps they might be, are bound to be, mistaken. I do not at all share the belief in the indefinite progress of society: I believe in the progress of the individual. Those who think they see in me an intention to consider man as a finite creature are strangely mistaken. "Séraphita," the doctrine of the Christian Buddha in action, seems to me a sufficient answer to that lightly advanced accusation. . . . . .

In noticing the sense of this work you will recognize that I grant to constant, daily facts, secret or manifest, to the acts of individual lives, their causes and their principles, as much importance as historians have hitherto attached to events in the public life of nations. The unknown battle waged in a valley of the Indre between Madame de Mortsauf and passion is perhaps as great as the most illustrious of known battles ("The Lily in the Valley"). In the latter the glory of a conqueror is at stake; in the other heaven. The misfortunes of the Birotteaus, the priest, and the perfumer are for me the misfortunes of humanity. La Fosseuse ("The Country Doctor") and Madame Graslin ("The Village Curate") represent almost complete types of women. We suffer in this way every day. I have had to do a hundred times what Richardson did but once. Lovelace has a thousand forms, for social corruption takes on the colors of all the surroundings in which it is developed.

The immensity of a plan which at the same time embraces history and the criticism of society, the analysis of its evils and the discussion of its principles, authorizes me, I think, to give my work the title under which it appears to-day, "The Human Comedy." Is this ambitious? Is it only just? That is what the public will decide when the work is ended.

SAINTE-BEUVE'S OPINION OF BALZAC IN 1834

[Article occasioned by "La Recherche de l'Absolu."]

It is time to come, in this gallery which without it would be incomplete, to the most productive, the most popular, of contemporary novelists, to the novelist of the moment *par excellence*, to that

one who unites in so great number the qualities or the defects of
speed, abundance, interest, chance, and prestige, which the title of
story-teller or novelist presupposes. M. de Balzac has become
celebrated in this way within four years only. His "Last
Chouan," in 1829, called attention to him for the first time, but
without raising him above the crowd; his "Physiology of Marriage" had won for him the reputation of a witty man, an exact
observer, ... but it is with "The Magic Skin" that M. de
Balzac first gained the ear of the public, which he has since, if
not entirely won over, at least stirred, furrowed in every direction,
astonished, surprised, shocked, or tickled in a thousand ways.
And we must admit that in this rapid success, aside from the
trumpeting at the beginning about the sale of "The Magic Skin,"
the press of Paris has been but a sorry ally of M. de Balzac's,
that he has himself created his vogue and favor with many people
by dint of activity, inventiveness, each new work serving, so to
speak, as an advertisement and aid to its predecessor. M. de
Balzac at the very start secured for himself one-half of the public,
which it is very essential to gain, and has made it his accomplice
by artfully flattering its secretly known fibers. "Woman is on
Balzac's side," M. Janin has somewhere said. "She belongs to
him in her finery, in her négligé, in the most minute things of her
heart; he dresses and undresses her." . . . . In order to insinu-
ate himself among women with his stories and novels, he hit on
the fortunate moment, when their imagination was most aroused,
after the July Revolution, by the pictures and the promises of
Saint-Simonism. . . . . Saint-Simonism, M. de Balzac on his
part, the illustrious writer called George Sand on hers, have been
the instruments and organs of that change which has come about,
not at all in manners, but in the expression of manners. In the
provinces especially, where the existence of some women is more
sorrowful, more stifled, more pallid, than in Parisian society,
where discord in the marriage relation is more compressing and
less easy to escape from, M. de Balzac has met with keen and
tender enthusiasm. The number of women from twenty-eight to
thirty-five, to whom he tells their secrets, who make a profession
of loving Balzac, who discuss his genius and try, pen in hand, to
embroider and vary in their turn the inexhaustible theme of these

charming stories, "The Woman of Thirty," "The Unhappy Woman," "The Abandoned Woman," is great there. . . . .

One of the reasons which further explains Balzac's rapid vogue throughout France is his skill in the successive choice of the places where he sets the scene of his tales. Travelers are shown in one of the streets of Saumur Eugénie Grandet's house; at Douai probably they are already pointing out the Claës house. With what mild pride the possessor of La Grenadière must have smiled, indolent Tourangean that he is! This flattery directed at each city where the author places his characters is as good as winning it. . . . . In Paris, on the contrary, his success has been less, though very considerable still; but he is denied several merits. As poet, as artist, as writer, his sentiment has often been decried, and his manner of composition. He has had difficulty in pushing himself, in ranking himself higher than his popularity, and in spite of his redoubtable talent, in spite of his marvelously delicate observation, he fails to rise to a certain serious position in the esteem of some people. . . . . To these reproaches, more or less well founded, to these dislikes or this disdain, too often justifiable, M. de Balzac has answered only by an increasing confidence in his imagination and an exuberance of novels, of which some have found favor in all eyes, and merit a triumph. The author of "Louis Lambert" and "Eugénie Grandet" is no longer a man whom we can reject and fail to recognize. . . . .

M. de Balzac has a very keen, deep feeling for private life, which often goes as far as minutiæ in detail, and as far as superstition. He knows how to move you and make you tremble at the very outset, merely by describing a garden walk, a dining-room, a set of furniture. He divines the mysteries of provincial life, he sometimes invents them. He most often fails to recognize the modest, quiet, concealed part of this style of life, and violates both it and the poetry it hides. He succeeds better in the parts that are less delicate from the moral standpoint. . . . . In the invention of his subject, as well as in the details of style, Balzac's pen is flowing, uneven, sensational. He goes, he starts at a gentle walk, he gallops wonderfully, and suddenly there he is down, but rises to fall again. Most of his beginnings are charming, but his endings degenerate or become excessive. There is a moment, a point, where he runs away in spite of himself. His coolness as an observer leaves him. . . . . Chance and accident play a great part even in his best productions. He has a manner, but it is uncertain, restless, often seeking to find itself. You feel you have a man who has written thirty volumes before acquiring a manner. When one has been so long in finding it, he is not very sure of always keeping it. . . . . We must, however, accept M. de Balzac as he is, and accept him according to his nature and habit. We must not advise him to make a selection, to repress himself, but to go on and continue constantly. He will make it up to us in quantity. He is a little like those generals who do not take the smallest position without lavishing the army's blood (it is ink only that he lavishes) and losing a great many soldiers. But although economy of means should count, the essential thing after all is to reach a result, and M. de Balzac on many an occasion is and remains victorious.

BIBLIOGRAPHY

A Memoir of Honoré de Balzac. Katharine Prescott Wormeley.
Balzac. W. P. Trent. In Warner's "Library of the World's Best Literature," Vol. III, or Warner's "Classics."
Articles in *The Atlantic*, Vol. LXXVIII, pp. 566 ff.; *Cosmopolitan*, Vol. XXVI, pp. 238 ff.; *The Chautauquan*, Vol. XXXIII, pp. 180 ff.

CHAPTER VIII

ZOLA

[ÉMILE ÉDOUARD CHARLES ANTOINE ZOLA, born at Paris, April 2, 1840; educated at the Aix lycée, and Lycée Saint Louis at Paris, 1852-1859; clerk at Hachette's, 1862-1866; journalism and hack writing, 1866-1869; novelist, 1869; the Dreyfus Affair, 1898; died at Paris, September 29, 1902. Chief works, in the Rougon-Macquart series: "L'Assommoir," 1877; "Germinal," 1885; "La Débâcle," 1892.]

The distinguishing characteristics of French realism, science and democracy, had been thoroughly established by Balzac's "Human Comedy." Subsequent adherents of the school had little to do but carry out the principles laid down in that work to their logical conclusion. And this is what was done. The generation which succeeded the master pushed the study of man, the animal, to an extreme, and chose its heroes and heroines from the petty *bourgeoisie* or the proletariat itself. In Balzac you can still find traces of moral responsibility with the people who play the parts in his dramas, while their social connections rarely fall below the reputable level of the Third Estate which owned the government of Louis Philippe. But with Flaubert, who had seen 1848 and the *coup d'état*, whose manhood was passed under the sway of that universal suffrage which buoyed up for a while the Second Empire, and whose mental training had been acquired through association with the students of experimental medicine and the expounders of positive science, the scen-

ÉMILE ÉDOUARD CHARLES ANTOINE ZOLA

ery changes and new actors mount the boards. His master-piece, "Madame Bovary" (1857), is the panegyric of the shallow, discontented woman, educated above her station in life, who knows no other guide than her emotions and appetites. Her surroundings are ordinary, her acquaintances superficial like herself, and like herself seeking each his own material gratification. And her story is told, her downfall traced, with a cold-bloodedness which was foreign to Balzac, and also in a language to which he rarely attained. For the motto of the new school of realists was an objectiveness which entirely ruled out the personality of the author and made him a mechanical recorder of the facts he saw. And united to this realism was a worship of style which made art an end in itself, not a means to an end. This school, which is first exemplified in "Madame Bovary," has since received the name of "naturalistic." It claimed to be more faithful to life, to nature, than the school of the earlier realists.

In the sixties Flaubert's impersonality of observation and desire for artistic composition won disciples in the persons of the De Goncourt brothers. But they indulged in theories, while Flaubert had merely practised. Accepting without reservation the Balzac view of physiological man, and the Flaubert example of objective reproduction of facts, they argued that novel writing had passed the stage of romancing, and had erected itself into a science, as exact as medicine, as unimpassioned as history. The first duty of the novelist, therefore, is to reproduce what he sees with the fidelity of a photograph, uncontaminated by reminiscences or by ideas obtained from books. He should also be comprehensive in his facts, and as the nineteenth century was the century of democracy, he should introduce the working classes into romance, and see whether there are misfortunes too low, too ignoble, to be given a literary setting. For the novel "is becoming by its analysis and psychological research, the moral history of contemporaneous society," and what it chronicles should be "true biography like modern historical biography." Nothing should appear in the book but what took place in the life of the individual represented in the book. No type should be formed by the fusion of homogeneous traits, as had been Balzac's custom, but each character should be some particular person who passed through the actual experiences narrated. And as the individuals who found their biographers in the De Goncourts were uneducated, for the most part, and unrefined, we have the story of cooks and unfortunate women, told us with an exactness of details which leaves nothing to be desired. Only they, the authors, abstained from the expressions suitable to the class they depicted. They chose their own words. This reservation was illogical. It contradicted the photographic exactness so loudly proclaimed. Each character should speak his own language, and not the author's. The De Goncourts' artistic temperament hesitated at this final step. Zola's did not, and with a courage which may or may not be attributed to a desire for notoriety he carried naturalism to its conclusion.

Zola was born at Paris in 1840. His mother was French, but his father came of mingled Greek and Italian stock, was somewhat of a rover, and followed the calling of a civil engineer. At the time of his son's birth he was engaged on a project of supplying the city of Aix, in South France, with water, and when the boy was three years old the family returned to that town, where the

father died, in 1847. The mother continued to live at
Aix, and aided by her parents gave young Zola the education which was at hand, a private school, followed, in
1852, by instruction at the Aix lycée. But the greater
part of his patrimony consisted in lawsuits against the
municipality. Money was lacking, and in 1858 his
mother moved to Paris, and entered her son at the Lycée
Saint Louis, near the Sorbonne. The transference of the
youth from the open life of Aix to the confinement of
Paris seems to have acted on his reserved and liberty-
loving nature much as Balzac's school-life had done on his.
He proved a poor student, failed to get his degree at the
end of the course, and failed again at Marseilles a few
months later, near the end of 1859.

During his school years Zola had shown some aptitude
for literary composition, and had written the usual plays
and verse of the French lycéen. He was fond of reading.
Of the moderns he had begun with Hugo, but soon passed
on to Alfred de Musset. Among the older French authors Rabelais and Montaigne were his chief delight, and
undoubtedly the example of the former incited him to his
later coarseness of expression. But he had no way of
earning a livelihood by writing, and took a clerkship in a
business house, which he held but a few weeks. Now
ensued a period of idleness and want. At night he would
write, by day he would stroll about the streets, dipping
into the second-hand books displayed in such abundance
in the Latin Quarter of Paris. Finally he fell into the
lowest kind of a lodging house, from which he emerged on
his engagement as clerk by the publishing firm of Hachette,
in January, 1862. This position relieved him of absolute
need, brought him into contact with the outside of books

at least, and at times into the presence of men of letters. He seems, however, to have derived little benefit from these surroundings, and made few acquaintances who could help him in his literary work. The stories written during this period, collected in 1864 in the "Stories to Ninon," are rather tiresome than otherwise. Still they afford a glimpse of the future Zola, in the close connection they assumed between inanimate nature and man, both products of the same creation, both loving and dying together.

This volume called some attention to its author, and seems to have opened to him the columns of Parisian and provincial newspapers. It also encouraged Zola in his literary career, and in 1865 he published a novel, "Claude's Confession," which appears to have attracted notice because of its coarseness only. A few weeks after its appearance Zola left Hachette's employ, and was at once engaged by De Villemessant, the proprietor of *Le Figaro*, to write book notices for a new journalistic venture, *L'Événement*. These notices proved such an attraction that their author was intrusted with the criticisms of the annual picture exhibition also, the "Salon," so called. Here was an excellent chance for self-advertising which Zola improved to the utmost. Attacks on the received canons of painting and the artists in vogue were accompanied by the exaltation of what is now named "impressionism." The scandal was great and the critic became notorious. But a serial story started in the same paper was a failure, and De Villemessant soon dropped Zola from his staff.

This dismissal took place in the first days of 1867. Once more Zola found himself reduced to a precarious livelihood. He managed to eke out a scanty subsistence by miscellaneous newspaper articles, and a serial which ran for many months in a Marseilles journal, and which was published in book form under the title of "The Mysteries of Marseilles." It was a compilation of police records, strung along a plot. It was all true, because it was based on legal documents, but its tone was entirely melodramatic—the virtuous rewarded, the vicious punished—and its animus against the upper social circles evident. Only certain of its phrases and the conception of nature, as an animate being close to man, remind one of the later Zola—or rather of the real Zola. In the same year he was slowly finishing a novel, begun in 1866, which does foreshadow his future work. This novel was "Thérèse Raquin." Its plot was suggested by a novel published in *Le Figaro* and reviewed by Zola, in which a husband is killed by his wife and her lover. He now renews the interest of the story by showing how the terror of their crime wrecked the nerves of the guilty pair and finally drove them to suicide.

In "Thérèse Raquin" we find the essential characteristics of the naturalist school, already exemplified by Flaubert and the De Goncourts. The people in the book belong to the lower classes of Parisian society, they have no other life than the life their appetites grant them. And they own no other law than the law of the flesh. They are animals, endowed with a finer nervous system than the beasts or birds, and this nervous system proves their ruin. In a preface in answer to his critics Zola admits this view of humanity. He is studying temperaments, not characters, he declares, and he is studying them from the standpoint of scientific analysis. His manner is also found in "Thérèse Raquin"—his sensual descriptions, his favorite phrases. The year 1868 saw another novel in print, "Madeleine Férat," which was the expansion of a play Zola had written in 1865, and which had been refused by the theaters. The success of "Thérèse Raquin" was not repeated, but certain ideas of heredity, in which Zola had long been interested, were here developed and prepared for later use.

Ten years had almost passed in this literary apprenticeship, and still Zola had not attained fame. Indeed, the talent he undoubtedly possessed had scarcely been recognized, obscured as it had been by his tendency towards coarseness and indecency. His direct use of the ignoble term to express what was low had shocked and offended the general public, accustomed to see vice pleasantly garbed. Force was conceded to him, and aggressiveness. Rebuffs had not daunted him. But that he occupied any respectable literary position in 1868 does not seem to have occurred to any one. Zola himself must have been aware of this very limited appreciation of his ability, for he now set to work to justify his ambition. He aimed high. He would be the Balzac of his generation, and paint for it the picture of its life and manners as Balzac had painted his contemporaries of the July Monarchy. And he makes a better plan than Balzac had done. Instead of connecting his various sketches of the society of his day by characters chosen somewhat at random, who reappear in different novels, Zola, acting under the influence of a more exact scientific environment, chooses his connecting links from the chain of heredity. His heroes and heroines will be bound to one another by the ties of blood relationship, a relationship not of brother and sister, as a rule, but of cousins in the third generation. In other words, he will write the history of a family, but will make that family representative of its neighbors also, and thus will chronicle the France of the Second Empire.

Zola's science is more exact than Balzac's, as the science of 1860 was more positive and experimental than the science of 1830. In other respects, however, he strongly resembles his great predecessor. He might be called a Balzac of the decadence. For with him physiological man is everything, man who differs from the plants and animals which surround him only by being a higher order of creation. From nature man came, to nature he shall return. While on this earth he follows the behests of nature only, his appetites of the body, his passions of the mind, which are gratified by the possession of power. When his race is run he dies as the dog dieth. There is no religion in Zola, not even the superficial religion of Balzac. He is an annihilationist, save as the race works out its own salvation by life following closely on the heels of death.

Zola differs from Balzac also in the social position of his characters. The Third Estate, which made the French Revolution, had found in Balzac its great apologist. Zola goes deeper. Like Flaubert and the De Goncourts he digs down even to the people, the workmen and the peasants, and it is the epic of the proletariat and its successful offshoots pushing their way through the upper strata of society which inspires his pen. So the field of observation is widened. Literature becomes still more democratic, keeping step with the social and political evolution of mankind. The influence of humanity on its individual members is described with greater precision, the effect of environment on man's development, as well as the effect on him of his race and epoch.   In 1864 Taine had applied these criteria of positivism to his study of English literature, and his example may have influenced Zola in his definiteness.   For in his novels strong natures assimilate their surroundings to themselves, weak ones yield to their degrading tendencies.

With these theories fully in mind, and with the ambition to force them upon the public only whetted by the partial successes already attained along like lines, Zola, in 1869, undertook his series of the Rougon-Macquart novels, names which represented by their sound—another trait of Balzac's—the strong and weak sides of the family, and defined the series by the sub-title of the "Natural and Social History of a Family Under the Second Empire." He contracted with a publisher to furnish two volumes a year, and started at once on the initial volume.   But various interruptions, including the catastrophe of the Franco-Prussian War, prevented the carrying out of the mechanical task he had set himself, and it was only in 1871 that the first of the series, "The Fortune of the Rougons," appeared.   The preface to this book summarizes what has been said: How a family under hereditary impulses, guided by its physical temperament and its environment, a temperament which has for its chief characteristic "overflowing appetites" and desires for self-gratification, starts at the bottom of the social ladder, mounts all its rungs, even to the top, and thus narrates in its various situations the story of the Second Empire "from the ambush of the *coup d'état* to the treason of Sedan."

But another point remains to be noticed.   This family is not any family whatsoever.   It has a flaw, a taint in its

blood, an "organic lesion," which produces certain disturb-
ances of the nerves and veins "which determine with the
individuals of this race, according to their environment,
the feelings, the desires, the passions, all the human
manifestations, natural and instinctive, whose products
are known under the conventional name of virtues and
vices." In other words, the grandmother of all the
Rougon-Macquart was an epileptic, who passed among
her acquaintances as mildly insane, and whose animal
instincts were not repressed by private misgivings or
regard for public appearances. One branch of her descendants looked back to a grandfather who was a hard-
headed, hard-working peasant, the other to an ancestor
whose trade was smuggling, a vagabond by nature, and
enslaved by drink. So by their blood the unhappy grand-
children of either pair were incited to wantonness and
bodily enjoyment, unrestrained by ethical considerations,
and in many of their number this vicious inclination was
coupled with a desire for license and a thirst for liquor.
In other words, by his very choice, Zola is consciously
limiting his picture of imperial society to exceptional characters, persons who do not represent the average of mankind, but rather its diseased minority, what we now term
the degenerate. It is necessary to keep this fact constantly in mind in order to reach a clear appreciation of
the author's work, and a just comprehension of the extent
to which the people of France are portrayed in his successive volumes.

For over twenty years, 1871–1893, this self-imposed
labor went on regularly, systematically, not so fast as Zola
had planned, for it required all that time to publish the
twenty books of the series, but quite fast enough for the

public demand. At first the sale of the successive biographies was small, the politician's, the real estate speculator's, the priest's, the tradesman's; and Zola was forced to earn his living by newspaper work of various kinds. Still he persevered, regularly, systematically, setting aside the morning hours for slow, patient composition, as he had once done in the case of "Thérèse Raquin," and giving up his afternoon and evening to the pursuit of a livelihood. If the adage *labor omnia vincit* was ever illustrated it was in the person of Zola. To hard and constant and regular work he not only owes his success, but seems to owe the development of his talent even. Inconsiderable at first, unremitting application seems to have developed it, fashioned it, and qualified its natural strength with breadth and picturesqueness. His imagination expanded under the stress, and finally illuminated the details his industry had accumulated.

His method of preparation was also uniform and regular. As he came to each occupation or profession he was to describe he would gather facts bearing on them, would visit the localities where they were exercised in order to procure the exact setting or scenery, would frequent the people engaged in them, acquire their ways of speech, their technical terms, notice their garb, their habits, their amusements. He would not disdain the use of books at this time, and would frequent libraries, reading descriptions, copying illustrations, or would search into criminal and civil records for instances of typical events, crimes committed by artisans, peasants, strikes organized by miners, financial panics engineered by operators. And when his preparation was complete, his mind impregnated with the surroundings, habits, speech of the people he was to paint, he would work out a rough sketch of their characters, their conversation, their connection with one another, the houses, streets, or localities they frequented, and all mechanically constructed, divided into parts, into scenes. Finally, with this full outline before him, he would settle down to the composition, always in the morning, always so many pages of print a day (four or three), no more no less, writing slowly, carefully, without corrections.

In this way he achieved his purpose. "L'Assommoir," which ran in serial form in a newspaper until popular clamor forced it into a review, was published in 1877, and Zola was famous. And what is "L'Assommoir"? It is the story of two of the Rougon-Macquarts, distant relatives, married to each other, who under the influence of the double pressure of temperaments inclined to sensuality and drink, and surroundings fostering the instinctive development of these temperaments, gradually fall from the position of diligent working men and women to the padded cell and the gutter. And the center of their life, the life of the quarter, is "The Assommoir," the saloon, the meeting-place of the working classes, their solace and their bane. The story is true. Its reality was attested by so many protests from the readers of the newspaper in which it began that they caused its withdrawal. All the events it describes can be proven by documents. But it is not typical. Working people who do not work are few in number. Someone must fashion the vast amount of material things which supply the demands of modern life.

"L'Assommoir" is not the only striking novel of the Rougon-Macquart series, though it is quite certainly its masterpiece. Zola continued on his way unmoved by criticism, compliments, or abuse. His next production was less sensational, "A Page of Love," and whatever his purpose, which he asserts was psychological, the book is mainly interesting for the variety of descriptions it contains of the city of Paris as seen from the high ground of Passy. Then came "Nana" (1880), devoted to the career of a wanton, with scenes from the boulevard theaters and horse races. Other volumes followed of less merit of description and force of plot, until in "Germinal" (1885), on miners and mining, Zola again reaches the strength of "L'Assommoir." In "Germinal" we see the beginning of those socialistic theories which were to occupy so large a part of Zola's later writings. "The Earth" (1887), on peasant existence, is powerful in its delineation of the overwhelming passion the agriculturist feels for the land he tills, but its episodes are little else than a succession of sensual and brutal crimes, which rob it of much of its intended merit. Certain scenes revolted many of his strongest admirers, and the appearance of the volume was followed by a public protest against its excesses, to which were appended the signatures of some of the best known writers of the younger generation. It was evident that the limits of "naturalism" had been reached.

Zola himself felt the sting of this protest, and at once betook himself to the composition of an idyl, "The Dream" (1888), which would show the world that he could treat other subjects than those which were furnished by vice and degradation. The young girl of "The Dream" who falls in love with the militant saint, pictured in the cathedral window, has sensuous longings, for she is one of the Rougon-Macquart race, but her soul is pure

and her passion ideal. "The Dream" is an idyl in fact,
but from it Zola turns to the crimes of a railroad engineer, possessed of the devil of homicide ("The Human
Beast," 1890), and the lubricities and swindles of a stock
speculator ("Money," 1891). Then came months of
preparation for the story of the soldier's life in that crisis
of the fatherland, the Franco-Prussian War ("La
Débâcle" "The Downfall," 1892), where the sacrifice
of the armies of France to the political necessities of the
Bonapartist dynasty is recited in tones which at times
exceed the epic elevation of "Germinal." Finally the
concluding volume of the series appears. We follow the
career of the philosopher of the family ("Doctor Pascal,"
1893), and his meditative review of the hereditary tendencies so fully displayed in the lives of his more worldly
kinsmen.

The Rougon-Macquart novels remain the great work
of Zola. They show his purpose and his manner. He
stands or falls with them. The first impression they
make as a whole is one of vulgarity and coarseness.
Accepting the premises from which they are derived, that
they are the history of the lower classes, or rather of a
portion of the populace which has inherited evil instincts,
that this history is almost wholly physiological, and merely
chronicles the doings of the human animal, we nevertheless cannot deny that the narrative is overcharged with
episodes of crime and sensuality. If it is necessary to tell
all the ignoble details of a degraded existence in order to
make it true to life, perhaps "L'Assommoir" is artis-
tically correct. But "Nana" is not, nor "Germinal,"
where the coarse episodes detract greatly from the real
import of the story; nor "The Earth," where these same

episodes overpower the excellent conception of the book; nor "La Débâcle," where they can be entirely passed over, erased, without affecting the narrative in the least. And it is quite useless for Zola to defend his superfluity of vulgarity with the threadbare argument that "everything should be said, that there are abominable words as necessary as a cauterizing iron," which he urges in his story of an artist's life ("L'Œuvre," "The Work," 1886). The excess of these scenes and expressions, disturbing as they often do the action of the plot, proves that the author's artistic sense is often overruled by a natural liking for them, which "Claude's Confession" had foreshadowed.

But there is one conception of Zola which he uses to justify this coarseness, a conception of "vast nature eternally in creation, life in short, total, universal life, which goes from one end of the animal kingdom to the other, neither high nor low, neither beautiful nor ugly," that commands our respect, though it entails at times a certain broadness of description. The conception is in essence pantheistic. Man and nature are one. They bloom, mature, and die together. The animal is man's brother. What matters it whether he or the animal is perpetuated, so long as the life of the world goes on from generation to generation? This idea, which lies at the bottom of Zola's best composition, is particularly elaborated in one of his earlier stories, "The Sin of Abbé Mouret" (1874), where that priest, wandering one day into a wildwood just expanding under the breath of spring, meets with a child of nature as shy as a bird, and as untrained, loves her amid the flowering of nature, and is reclaimed to duty as the grain yellows to the harvest.

And the woodland sprite, abandoned, dies, suffocated by the ripe perfume of those flowers whose buds had taught her love. Here is the elegy. Then comes the grotesque, but which only strengthens the author's argument. As the stricken maiden is lowered into the grave, in the neighboring stable a calf is born. So life continues on the earth. So nature is the mother of all, untiring, resistless, turning the dead into the living. The miners of "Germinal," radiating through the veins of the mine, are merely furrowing the land for a future generation of the just and good. Nature is also beneficent, fertile, providing food for man and beast.

This notion of nature approaches symbolism, and many of the Rougon-Macquart novels are illustrated by symbols. As Hugo had made the great cathedral the central point of his "Notre-Dame de Paris," so Zola expresses the idea of "L'Assommoir," by the saloon, of "Germinal" by the shaft, which daily swallows up and daily disgorges the population of the whole region, of "Le Ventre de Paris" (1873) by the fish market, of "The Work" by the painting which never satisfies. These symbols are evident. There are others more recondite. The idea of "Nana," for instance, is in Zola's mind the allegory of a beautiful flower growing on the dunghill of society, which poisons by its exhalations the whole social system. Therefore, if society allows its weaker section to fester in sin and want, it will perish by the miasma exhaled from the corruption. But it must be confessed that this moral application is not suggested by the reading of the novel in question.

When we look beyond the general conception of Zola's books to the details which form them we see that his power lies in his descriptions. His people are too often automatons. They are quite usually eccentricities. They have instincts instead of character. Consequently we are rarely attracted to them, though we may at times deplore their misfortunes. But his descriptions of things and places, of nature in its varying manifestations, of groups of men and the works of man, are not excelled by any writer of his generation. It is interesting to note how he produces his great descriptive effects. He begins with the smallest objects, coins a picturesque expression, the "black ants" of the German armies in "La Débâcle" for instance, which he repeats and repeats, enlarging steadily his circle of observation. Then, after one is almost weary of the constant, swelling repetition, after detail has been added to detail, and all the standpoints of view have been occupied, he finally proceeds to sum up the whole picture with a breadth of expression and a sweep of diction which bear us away in admiration. One can compare the process in some degree to the preparation for the crises in a Wagnerian opera. Famous among these descriptions are the fish market in "Le Ventre de Paris," the spring opening in the dry goods store of "Au Bonheur des Dames" (1883), the plains of Beauce rolling mile on mile to the distant horizon ("The Earth"), the Stock Exchange in "Money." The power of his driving style makes material things animate, and raises us at times to the notion of the supernatural, the deified forces of natural religion. And with this strength and vividness goes the poetical, the epic, where we meet with intangible things, the spirits of the invisible. This trait is especially noticeable in "La Débâcle." The French army, disorganized, disheartened, led hither and yon without reason, learns its doom from the shadows of night: "Hours must have passed, the whole camp black, motionless, seemed annihilated under the oppression of the vast evil night, where was weighing down that frightful thing, nameless as yet. Quick starts came from a lake of shade, a sudden death rattle was heard in an invisible tent."

Zola's entire strength between "L'Assommoir" and "Doctor Pascal" was, to be sure, not given to the Rougon-Macquart series. Having bought a place outside of Paris at Médan, he devoted considerable time to the entertainment of guests, the criticism of the works of younger authors. Out of such meetings came at least one book, "The Evenings of Médan," a collection of stories, published in 1880 by Zola and his intimates, which contains Guy de Maupassant's famous "Boule de Suif." For some years he was also correspondent of a Russian newspaper. The articles written for it were afterwards printed in book form in France under the titles of "The Experimental Novel" and "The Naturalist Novelists." He also tried the stage with indifferent success. His "Assommoir," when dramatized, became a genuine melodrama. Towards 1888 he began to aspire to a seat in the French Academy, and for years offered himself as a candidate for nearly every vacancy. But he was never elected.

Early in the eighties Zola had begun to tire of the inevitable end of his documented plots, of his human animals who died like the beasts, without hope of the future on earth or in heaven. Such a solution was becoming more and more unsatisfactory. It explained nothing, led to nothing. And besides, if man ends with the body, why disturb his natural course with considerations of immaterial things? In other words, Zola was looking for a religion which would take the place of the religion he had rejected. Renan had found it in science, Zola found it in work. Work will bring contentment, if not happiness, he argues. Therefore, work. This doctrine was preached at the end of "The Work." It became the text for the remainder of the series. And soon there was coupled with this glorification of work the eulogy of life, the life that goes on from one generation to another, the life by which the world will eventually be redeemed, by each generation improving on its predecessor. It is evolution expressed in Zola's terms.

After the Rougon-Macquart series was finished, Zola, then but fifty-three years of age, undertook to formulate this religion. He conceived the idea of substituting it for decadent Christianity, and with this object in view, he composed the trilogy of novels, known as "The Three Cities:" "Lourdes," "Rome," and "Paris." The hero of all three is a priest, who in the three successive volumes tries to revive his waning faith by pilgrimages to the Virgin's shrine at Lourdes, miraculous Christianity, the Holy See at Rome, historical Christianity, and finally by philanthropic work at Paris, private and organized charity. But his attempt is vain. Christianity can no longer work miracles; it has died in its own capital; it has failed in its mission to unfortunate man. The dispenser of private charity is swindled; organized charity, fashionable and complicated, reaches the recipient too late. Nor is socialism a substitute for Christianity. Those who try to reform society, especially those who wish to destroy it, the anarchists, injure the weak only. The strong escape their avenging arm. But after all there is a refuge from

the ills of this world. It is found in work and marriage.
And the unfrocked priest, united to a calm and serious
helpmeet, holding his child in his arms, looks out from
his workshop on Montmartre at the close of day on Paris.
"Paris was glowing, sown with light by the divine sun,
rolling in its glory the future harvest of truth and justice."

Zola had now come to consider himself the adviser and
guide for the France of the future, and he was planning
a new series, "The Four Gospels," which should preach
Fecundity, and a return to tilling the ground, Labor,
Truth, and Justice, when an unforeseen event threw him
suddenly into the midst of an unprecedented political agitation. The scandal occasioned by the Panama catastrophe had hardly died away in France before a new
question arose affecting the honor of the nation, and
dividing it into hostile camps. Late in 1894 a captain of
the army, Dreyfus, was accused of selling military secrets.
He was publicly degraded and sent into solitary confinement. Although the secrecy and haste with which the
matter had been managed seemed suspicious, the public
accepted the verdict without debate. But Dreyfus's
friends did not allow the matter to rest. New appointees
in military circles found evidences of fraud. It was clear
that injustice was being done some one. But nevertheless
the affair was being successfully stifled when Zola's attention was attracted to the subject. An investigation led
him to the conviction that Dreyfus was an innocent man,
and that he was being wronged. He determined to
reopen the case by forcing it into the courts, and with
that purpose in view, on January 13, 1898, he published
in the daily newspaper, *L'Aurore*, his famous letter of
accusation. All principals and agents in the trial and

condemnation of Dreyfus were cited by him before the bar of the public conscience. The letter accomplished its purpose. Zola was tried and convicted. He appealed, was tried again, fled to England in order to escape imprisonment, and remained there a year. Meanwhile new forgeries were being foisted on the French authorities, forgeries which were soon startlingly revealed by confessions and suicide. Dreyfus was brought back from his exile, and Zola returned to Paris.

His appearance in the political arena had interfered but little with his literary work. He brought back from England the manuscript of "Fécondité," the first of the Four Gospels, and had it published at once, in 1899. In 1901 "Travail" ("Labor") appeared, and in 1902 "Vérité" (Truth"). But its author did not live to see it in book form. Returning to Paris from Médan, late in September of that year, he had a coal fire made in order to warm his apartment. Gas escaped from a defective flue, and the next morning, September 29, 1902, he was found asphyxiated beyond resuscitation. His attitude in the Dreyfus affair, which had suggested the plot of "Vérité," made of his funeral a notable event, and in the eyes of many this act of patriotic courage has gone far to atone for the unwonted license of his works of fiction.

SELECTIONS FROM THE WORKS OF ZOLA

Preface to the Rougon-Macquart Series in "The Fortune of the Rougons"

I wish to explain how a family, a small group of beings, acts in a given society, expanding so as to give birth to ten, twenty individuals, who appear at first glance to be profoundly unlike, but whom an analysis shows closely bound to one another. Heredity has its laws, like gravitation.

I shall try to find and follow, in solving the double question of temperaments and environments, the thread which mathematically leads from one man to another. And when I hold all the threads, when I have a whole social group in my hands, I will show this group at work, an actor in an epoch of history, I will create it acting in the complexity of its efforts, I will analyze at the same time the amount of the will of each of its members and the general tendency of the whole.

The Rougon-Macquarts, the group, the family I propose to study, has as a characteristic the overflowing appetites, the broad upheaval of our age, which rushes towards enjoyment. Physiologically, they are the slow succession of variations in nerves and blood which show themselves in a race in consequence of a primary organic lesion; and which determine in each of the individuals of that race, according to his environment, the feelings, desires, passions, all the human manifestations, natural and instinctive, whose products take on the conventional names of virtues and vices. Historically they start with the populace, they spread into contemporaneous society in its entirety, they rise to all positions through that essentially modern impulse which the lower classes receive on their way through the social body, and thus they tell the story of the Second Empire, by means of their individual dramas, from the ambuscade of the *coup d'état* to the treason of Sedan.

For three years I had been collecting documents for this great work, and the present volume was even written when the fall of the Bonapartes, which as an artist I needed, and which I always found logically at the end of the drama, without daring to hope it was so near, came to give me the terrible and necessary solution to my work. This work is now complete. It moves in a rounded circle. It becomes the picture of a dead reign, of a strange era of madness and of shame.

This work, which will form several episodes, is then in my mind the Natural and Social History of a Family Under the Second Empire. And the first episode, "The Fortune of the Rougons," should be called by its scientific title, "The Origins."

The March of the Striking Miners, from "Germinal"

[The strikers on their way to close up mines which were still working, reach the house of the company's superintendent.]

Twilight was already filling the darkening room with gloom, it was five o'clock, when an uproar made M. Hennebeau start, dazed, motionless as he was, his elbows still buried in the midst of his papers. . . . . The tumult increased, a cry burst forth, a terrible cry, at the moment he drew near the window.

"Bread! Bread! Bread!"

. . . . The women had appeared, almost a thousand women, with streaming hair, disheveled by their march, with rags which showed their bare flesh, the nudities of women weary of bearing children to die of hunger. Some held their little ones in their arms, bore them aloft, waved them, like a flag of mourning and of vengeance. Others, younger, with Amazonian breasts, brandished clubs. While the old women, frightful, shrieked so fiercely that the cords of their skinny necks seemed to be breaking. And the men rolled down after them, two thousand mad workmen, ... a compact mass which rolled along in a single block, pressed together, commingled, to such an extent that you could not distinguish the faded trousers nor the ragged woolen jackets, blotted out in the same ashy uniformity. Their eyes burned, you only saw the holes of their black mouths singing the Marseillaise, whose stanzas were lost in a confused roar, accompanied by the clacking of wooden shoes on the hard earth. Above their heads, among the bristling iron bars, an axe stood up, carried high in air. And this solitary axe, which was like a standard for the band, had the sharp outline of a guillotine's knife in the bright sky.

. . . . Anger, hunger, those two months of suffering and this mad rush over and through the coal-pits had lengthened the placid faces of the Montsou miners into jaws like those of wild beasts. At this moment the sun was setting, its last rays reddened the plain with their dark purple blood-stain. Then the road seemed flowing with blood, women and men went on galloping, bloody as slaughtering butchers.

It was the red vision of the revolution which would sweep all away, beyond recovery, on some bloody evening of the century's wane. Yes, some evening the people, let loose, would gallop thus unrestrained along the highways. And it would drip with the blood of the burghers, it would carry their heads along with it, it would scatter the gold of their broken chests. The women would howl, the men would have those wolfish jaws open to bite. Yes, it would be the same rags, the same thunder of heavy shoes, the same fearful mob, with dirty skin and pestilential breath, sweeping away the old world under their overwhelming rush of barbarian hordes. Fires would flame up, not a stone of the cities would be left standing, all would return to wild woodland life after the great passion, the great revelry, in which the poor in a night would wear down the women and empty the cellars of the rich. There would be nothing left, not a sou of the fortunes, not a title of rank and office, until the day when perhaps a new earth would blossom forth again. Yes, it was these things which were going by, like a force of nature. . . . .

A great cry arose, sounded above the Marseillaise.

"Bread! Bread! Bread!"

The World's Future Belongs to the Working Class
(*From the Closing Pages of "Germinal"*)

[The strike has failed through violence and want. All the miners have gone back to work. Their leader takes leave of them as 'they enter the pit, and goes away, consoled for the future by his thoughts and reviving nature.]

Etienne took the Joiselle road to the left. He remembered he had prevented the marching miners from attacking Gaston-Marie. Far away in the bright sunshine he could see the belfrys of several coal-pits, Mirou on the right, Madeleine and Crèvecœur side by side. The work was everywhere rumbling on, the strokes of the miners' picks which he thought he could hear in the depths of the earth were now rapping from one end of the plain to the other. One stroke, and another stroke, and always strokes, under the fields, the roads, the villages laughing in the light, all the hidden work of these underground galleys, so crushed down by the enormous mass of rocks that you must know they were there underneath you in order to perceive their great dolorous sigh. And now he was thinking how violence did not perhaps advance things. Cut cables, torn up rails, broken lamps, what a useless task that was! Forsooth, they were well worth the trouble of galloping three thousand strong in a devastating band! Vaguely he was divining that some day legal forms might be more terrible. His reason was ripening; he had sowed the wild oats of his grudges. Yes, Maheude, with her good sense, had well said that this would be the thing to do: to enroll quietly, become acquainted with one another, get together in associations, when the law should allow. Then, the day when you felt your comrades close beside you, when you found yourself, working millions, face to face with a few thousand idlers, seize the power, become the masters. Ah! what an awakening of truth and justice! The satiated, unwieldy god would be done to his death at once, that monstrous idol, hidden in the depths of his tabernacle, in that far-off unknown, where wretches were feeding him on their flesh, without having ever seen him.

But Etienne, leaving the Vandame road, was coming out on the paved turnpike. To the right he could see Montsou straggling down its hillside, dying away from sight. Opposite were the mines of the Voreux shaft, the accursed hole at which three pumps were unceasingly working; then there were the other pits on the horizon, Victory, Saint Thomas, Feutry Cantel; while towards the north the lofty towers of the high furnaces and the files of coke ovens were smoking in the quiet air of the morning. If he didn't want to miss the eight o'clock train he should hurry, for he still had six kilometers to cover.

And under his feet the deep, obstinate strokes of the picks continued. His comrades were all there, he could hear them following him at every stride. Wasn't that Maheude under that bed of beets, her back bent double, and her breath ascending so hoarse, accompanied by the puff of the ventilator? To the left, to the right, farther on he thought he recognized others, under the grain, under the quickset hedges, under the young trees. Now the sun of April was streaming down in its glory from the high heaven, warming the earth in her travail. From her maternal flank life was gushing forth, the buds were bursting into leaf, the fields were quivering with the shooting stalks. On every side the seeds were swelling, reaching forth, cracking the plain, driven on by a need of warmth and light. Sap was flowing full with whispering voices, the noise of germs was rising in a great kiss. Again, again, more and more distinctly, as though they had come nearer to the upper soil, his comrades were tapping. In the blazing rays of the great star, on that morning of youth, this noise was filling the countryside. Men were pushing up from the earth, a black, avenging army, slowly sprouting in the furrows, growing for the harvests of the future ages, and their germination was soon to cleave the earth asunder.

BIBLIOGRAPHY

Émile Zola. R. H. Sherard.

Émile Zola. E. A. Vizetelly.

See also article on Zola and Dreyfus in *Atlantic Monthly*, Vol. LXXXI, pp. 589 ff.

CHAPTER IX

RENAN AND BIBLICAL CRITICISM

[JOSEPH ERNEST RENAN, born at Tréguier, Brittany, February 27, 1823; educated in seminaries at Tréguier (1830–1838) and Paris (1838–1845); tutor, 1845; mission to Italy, 1850; assistant in the National Library, 1851; mission to Palestine, 1860; professor of Hebrew at the Collège de France, 1862; elected to the Academy, 1878; administrator of the Collège de France, 1884; died at Paris, October 2, 1892. Chief works: "Averroës and Averroïsm," 1852; "General History and Comparative System of the Semitic Languages," 1855; "Life of Jesus," 1863; "Philosophical Dialogues and Fragments," 1876; "Recollections of Childhood and Youth," 1883; "History of the People of Israel," 1887–1894.]

The scientific spirit which the nineteenth century had inherited from the eighteenth gained impetus with its progressing decades. It had begun with the French disciples of Locke, philosophers and essayists. With them it rarely passed the bounds of speculation. Towards the French Revolution, however, it seems to have been on the point of extending itself, of leaving the domain of theory for the field of practical investigation. The physical sciences felt this extension, chemistry, botany, zoölogy, physiology. After the turmoil of the Empire had settled, and men were once more free to give themselves over to the vocations of peace, concrete application of the scientific idea became more and more evident. Under the influence of the great scholars of Germany this spirit invaded all branches of learning and renewed their method

JOSEPH ERNEST RENAN

and vitality.   Literature also recognized its sway.   We
have seen how Balzac based the plan of "The Human
Comedy" on the new zoölogical theories of his day.
Before him even, in 1827, the novelist Stendhal had
lamented the utilitarian tendency of the age.   In the preface to his story of "Armance," he had said: "We need
thrifty management, stubborn labor, solidity, and heads
from which every illusion is absent, in order to turn the
steam engine to account.   Such is the difference between
the century which ended in 1789 and the one which began
towards 1815."   And once again in the story itself:
"Since the steam engine has become the queen of the
world a title is an absurdity."   So Stendhal's hero, a
noble by birth, wishes he were a chemist.   And Stendhal's perception was correct.   His tentative prophecy was
borne out by subsequent facts.   The heroes of the nineteenth century were chemists, physicists, biologists.

Ernest Renan, too, belongs among the scientists,
though it is somewhat difficult to assign him his proper
category.   He was in turn a philologist, a historian, a
critic, an author.   He confesses to a fundamental faith
in mathematics and physical induction, and had he studied
the natural sciences thinks he might have reached some
of Darwin's conclusions.   There is, in fact, a curious
likeness between the English scholar and the French,
engaged though they were in wholly different occupations.
It is a likeness based on their mentality, the authority
which reason exercised over them both, and their passion
for objective truth.   Therefore, by whatever name Renan
may be designated as a writer, he was primarily a scientist.   The story of his life narrates to a considerable
extent the progress of pure science in France.

He was born at Tréguier, in the old province of Brittany, on February 27, 1823. His father was a native of the country, a mariner and trader. His mother was of Gascon parentage, like D'Artagnan of "The Three Musketeers." This mixture of race is used by Renan to explain his twofold character—much as Hugo had made his parentage responsible for his political views. The Breton was sad, dreamy, the Gascon merry, gay. "This complex origin," he says, "is, I believe, the cause, to a great extent, of my apparent contradictions. I am double; sometimes one part of me laughs when the other is weeping. As there are two men in me there is always reason for one of them to be satisfied." His father was drowned when Ernest was but five years old, and an older sister, Henrietta, became the mainstay of the family. At the age of fifteen she set up a school in Tréguier, and earned enough by it to give her brother a steady subsistence. Through her and the local clergy he began his education in a religious seminary of the town, an education that was curiously behind the times, dating perhaps from the seventeenth century, but which gave him, notwithstanding, a thorough drill in mathematics. He studied well, absorbed himself in dreams and books, took many prizes, and finally was chosen to recruit a school newly established in Paris. Thither he went in September, 1838, and there he "saw things as new to me as if I had been suddenly thrown into France from Tahiti or Timbuctoo."

The transfer from Tréguier to Paris was vital in Renan's experience. He had left behind him simple-minded priests, whose lives were passed in training the middle and lower classes of a devout population—Brittany and its neighbor, the Vendée, have ever been the stronghold of French Catholicism. In his new seminary of Saint Nicholas du Chardonnet, just intrusted to the brilliant Abbé Dupanloup, a man of the world, devoted to his creed and party, but a clerical dilettante rather than a profound theologian, he was to meet students drawn from the most promising of the aspirants to Church orders in France, mingled with the aristocratic scions of the old nobility. The school was a fashionable one. On the clerical side it was destined to train future priests in good manners as well as piety. Renan's sensitive soul was at once aware of the change. "My coming to Paris was a passing from one religion to another. My Breton Christianity no more resembled the Christianity I found here than an old canvas hard as a plank resembles percale. . . . . It was the most serious crisis of my life. It is hard to transplant a young Breton. The keen moral repulsion I felt, complicated by an entire change in administration and habits, gave me a most terrible fit of homesickness." He fell ill from the confinement, which followed so close upon the open life at Tréguier. He poured out his loneliness in tender letters to his mother.

But this melancholy of the heart soon vanished with the illness it had caused. Renan's intellect was stimulated by the literary education of the seminary, where even the director talked romanticism and classicism. The course in history, which included selections from Michelet, fascinated his ear and brain. "Thus the century gained access to me through all the cracks of a broken cement. I had come to Paris morally formed, but as ignorant as possible. I had everything to learn. I found out with astonishment that there were serious and learned laymen. I saw that something existed outside of antiquity and the

Church, and especially that there was a contemporaneous literature worthy of some attention.'' The result of this training, in which the refinement of Virgil held quite as much place as the dogmas of Scripture, and where knowledge of the world was deemed of quite as much importance as familiarity with Church history, altered the purity of Renan's faith and aroused in his soul a rival to the Christianity which had wholly occupied it. Still he did not doubt.

In 1841, after three years' residence at Saint Nicholas, Renan entered the seminary of St. Sulpice as a candidate for priestly orders. The first two years of this novitiate were passed outside of Paris, at Issy. There he studied a little natural history, which gave him his first inkling of genuine science, and a great deal of philosophy of the rationalistic sort. Always of a shrinking, meditative disposition Renan now gave himself almost bodily to books, reading the philosophers, especially Descartes, his disciple Malebranche, Locke, Leibnitz. In this reading he lost all faith in abstract metaphysics: ''Positive science remained the sole source of truth for me. The scientific spirit was the basis of my nature.'' What he learned of physical science showed him the insufficiency of spiritual doctrines: ''An eternal *fieri*, an endless metamorphosis, seemed to me the law of the world.'' And yet he still was a believing Christian. The example of others, particularly of Malebranche, who made the physical world an attribute of God, known to the mind only through God in whom all things are, held him back from unbelief. But all at once the logical consequences of these views came to light. It was the custom to train the future priests in theological argument. This was an exercise Renan thoroughly enjoyed. His reasoning ability easily got the better of his adversaries. Church dogmas when assailed by him found but a moderate defense. One evening, after such a debate, he was reproached for his fondness for study by one of his instructors. Research was useless, he was told: "Everything essential has been found out. Science does not save souls. And becoming more and more excited, he exclaimed to me, with an accent full of passion, 'You are not a Christian!' " But this judgment, though a true one, had for the time being no other result than Renan's sincere distress.

After Issy it was the turn of the seminary in Paris, where the study of Hebrew was begun. The classes were conducted by a scholar well versed in German exegesis, and unaffected by its heterodoxy. This man found in Renan a most enthusiastic pupil. He taught him the other Semitic languages also, and put his library at his disposal. The lectures at the Collège de France were also open. Renan at once showed great aptitude for philology. The world of science revealed itself to him. He learned German with the intention of pushing his new studies further. It was another epoch in his life: "The peculiar intellectuality of Germany at the end of the last century and in the first half of this [nineteenth] made a vivid impression on me. I thought I was entering a temple. That was what I was seeking, the reconciliation of a highly religious with the critical spirit." But he could not justify this reconciliation to himself. He was too rigorously scientific. If the Bible was divine it must be infallible everywhere. But Renan saw in the Bible contradictions, blunders, errors, and his logic forced him to unbelief in the inspiration of the Scriptures. He had learned from his favorite philosopher, Malebranche, to subordinate everything to reason, and that "the duty of man is to put himself before the truth," and let himself follow wherever truth may lead. He went this way and soon found his reason pitted against his faith. The consequences, for his scientific temperament, were inevitable. He renounced the priesthood.

It was during the summer vacation of 1845, spent in Brittany, that he finally decided on this momentous course. His sister, whose sympathy had never failed him in all his experiences and emotions, came once more to his support with an offer to defray his expenses for further independent study at Paris. His masters of St. Sulpice were surprised at the revelation of his mind, but agreed with him in his purpose. His mother was grieved, for she could not understand his feelings. Her sorrow was her son's severest trial. After one or two experiments at a livelihood he settled down as a tutor in a private school attached to one of the Paris lycées. Here again he was to meet with a new inspiration. Among the pupils of the school was Marcellin Berthelot, the future chemist, but four years younger than Renan. A close and lifelong friendship joined the two together from the very outset. Berthelot, plunged in the study of natural sciences with all the ardor of a new disciple, overflowed with the spirit of scientific investigation, which sought for truth through physical induction. Renan was no less scientific in his pursuit of linguistic verities. Each reacted on the other, and but a few months were needed to finish the destruction of everything in their minds which implied faith. "The affirmation that everything in the world is of one and the same color, that there is nothing supernatural or revealed by a special revelation, forced itself on our minds in an absolute fashion. The clear scientific view of a universe, where there is no free will at work in any appreciable manner which is superior to the will of man, became, with the first months of 1846, an immovable anchor for us which has never dragged.''

But the strength of Renan's previous training was equally irresistible. Had he never entered St. Sulpice, had he given himself over to the study of natural science on leaving Issy, he thinks he might have made a reputation of like kind to Darwin's. But St. Sulpice had interested him in the history of the Christian religion. ''The studies I had begun at the seminary had so absorbed me that I thought of nothing else than to take them up again. One occupation only seemed worthy to me of filling up my life; it was the continuation of my critical researches on Christianity through the wider means which were placed at my disposal by secular learning.'' He was aware that his criticism of texts reflected his former belief. At first conservative it always remained Catholic, literary, temperate, in contradistinction to the Protestant criticism of the German universities. And for these qualities, and others of character and manner, he was ever grateful to his teachers of St. Sulpice.

With his change of vocation Renan had left his old friends. The years found him new ones. The distinguished scholars of the capital soon recognized his talent. In 1847 he competed for the Volney Prize for the best philological essay, and won it with the embryo of his future history of the Semitic languages. In 1848 he won another prize for an essay on Greek, and contributed to the periodical *La Liberté de Penser*, founded in that year, an article on "The Origin of Languages" which he afterward revised and published in book form (1858). He also began a treatise to be called "The Future of Science," which did not see the light till 1890, but which furnished a chapter to *La Liberté de Penser*, in 1849. More important perhaps for his career was a monograph on "The Critical Historians of Jesus," published in the same periodical, severely attacking Strauss's "Life of Jesus," and foreshadowing Renan's own famous biography. Other literary work and a short service as substitute professor of philosophy at the Versailles lycée increased his reputation in scientific circles. In 1850 he was given a commission to explore in behalf of the government the libraries of Italy. His particular duty was to report on any rare Syriac and Arabic manuscripts he might find or documents relating to mediæval French literature.

This trip to Italy, while unimportant in the history of Renan's thought, did not remain without influence on his literary expression. Italian art and civilization appealed to his naturally refined temperament and increased the value he had always set on outward form and style. The information gathered during the mission he also turned to good use. In order to attain the degree of Doctor of Letters in France, it is necessary to submit two dissertations, one in Latin and one in French. In 1852 Renan came forward as a candidate equipped with the proper literary baggage. His French dissertation, the volume published under the title of "Averroës and Averroïsm," a treatise on mediæval Moslem philosophy in its relations with the scholasticism of Europe, while abounding in facts and most learned in conception, was so simply and pleasantly written that it appealed to the literary world, as well as to the world of science. It extended its author's reputation as a scholar across the boundaries of France.

The Revolution of 1848 could not fail to interest a mind so alert and open to impressions as Renan's. He hailed it much as the republicans of 1789 had welcomed the dawn of the French Revolution. The people at last were to come into the possession of their own. Democracy was to triumph under the leadership of reason. Science was to inculcate truths which should lead all classes to a higher moral and mental plane, while manual labor and culture would go hand in hand. These were the utterances of Renan in the first enthusiasm of his new-found ideal. Wider experience with men and acquaintance with other peoples of different ethical views were afterwards to change his position regarding the best practical state, if not to modify his governmental ideal. To him as to many others of the best minds in France the *coup d'état* of December 2, 1851, was to prove a bitter grief.

In 1851 his subsistence was assured by an appointment to the department of Oriental manuscripts at the National Library. His sister Henrietta, who had been teaching abroad, had returned to France the year before, and was now keeping house for her brother in the Rue du Val de Grâce. The light duties required of him at the library left him abundant leisure for private work, and the results soon appeared in his dissertations already noticed, and his first great work, the "General History and Comparative System of the Semitic Languages," which appeared in 1855, an expansion of the Volney prize essay of 1847. Here Renan buttresses his illuminating theory of the fundamental difference between the Aryan and Semitic races, a difference not of language only, he claims, but also of religion. The peoples of the former race were polytheists, worshiping the powers of nature. The Semitic peoples were monotheists. They created Judaism, Christianity, and Mohammedanism, and forced these last two creeds on the Aryans. The Institute at once crowned this book and elected him to the Academy of Inscriptions and Belles Lettres. In the same year of this election (1856) he married the niece of Ary Scheffer, the distinguished painter, through whose personality and surroundings the poetic side of Renan's temperament, already aroused by his Italian mission, was further developed. A constant contributor to the *Journal des Débats* and the *Revue des Deux Mondes*, with articles and essays on all kinds of subjects, religious, historical, philological, his style had become perfected until it combined ease, simplicity, and grace with unusual flexibility of expression. Many of these essays were published in book form, in his "Studies of Religious History" (1857), and his "Ethical and Critical Essays" (1859). In 1858 he revised his journalistic article of ten years previous, and published it under the title "On the Origin of Language." In 1859 a translation of the book of Job saw the light, together with a discussion of its period and spirit. In 1860 the Song of Solomon was edited, arranged as a pastoral drama.

This year of 1860 was a notable one in Renan's career. Through the mediation of mutual friends he received a commission from the government to explore the territory once known as Phœnicia, collect its inscriptions, and investigate its monuments. It was October when he reached Beirut. He visited Palestine, saw the land once trod by the Savior's feet, looked on the hills and valleys, lakes and rivers, which had listened to his voice, and at last began the long-cherished project of telling the story of his life. Hardly had the first draft of this volume been written when he and his sister, who was with him, were stricken down with fever. She died in September, 1861. He lived to profit by her devotion and perpetuate his gratitude in a most tender and beautiful memorial, which was first published after his death. To her was dedicated also the "Life of Jesus," that appeared in 1863. Her influence on him had been early exerted, and proved lasting.

Election to a professorship followed close upon Renan's return to Paris. For some years the chair of Hebrew had been vacant at the Collège de France. It had been a post long coveted by Renan, ever since his attendance on courses there, while a student at St. Sulpice. When the government asked the nominating faculties of the Collège and Institute for candidates, they both placed Renan first on the list. In January, 1862, he was appointed. The government had taken a hazardous step. Renan's contributions to general literature, and his versions of Job and the Song of Solomon, had made his name and career familiar to all the educated public. And it was a career which was bound to meet with the disapproval of the orthodox in religion, especially of the dignitaries of the Church, one of the mainstays of the Second Empire. Caution, therefcre, was advisable for the new incumbent, who in a certain sense was a representative of the government and responsible for his words to the ruling powers who had given him his office. That caution was not exercised. His opening lecture in February was delivered before a large audience. He took for his subject his theory of the religious difference between the polytheistic Aryans and the monotheistic Semites, and the great debt owed by the former to the latter. They might even have forced Judaism on the western world, he said, had not Judaism been re-formed into Christianity at the critical moment by one who had reached the greatest religious height ever attained by man, so great that Renan would not "wish to contradict those . . . . who call him God." Later came the Moslem creed, hostile to science and civilization, which must disappear before the new religion Europe was to proclaim, the religion of science, which advocates liberty and human rights. At the close of this address the lecturer was led home in triumph by his sympathizers. But the clericals, aroused by the denial of the deity of Christ, and also by a passage which foretold of the separation of Church and State, carried their cause to the Tuileries, and Renan's course of lectures was quickly suspended. However, he continued to give instruction at his house to all students who desired it.

As may be supposed, the publication of the "Life of Jesus," a year afterwards, did nothing to allay the hostility excited by this lecture. For it was a decided affirmation of the statement already made that Christ was the greatest of men, the man nearest God, and yet a man. The book is the consummation of a purpose to reconstitute the life of this man, in his surroundings, his teachings, and his ways. The result is little short of wonderful. Through his visit to the places mentioned in the Gospels, his faculty of calling up before himself the scenes and people of Judea and Galilee, and his appreciation of the character of Christ's mission and its historical significance, Renan has succeeded in placing before us the living, breathing personality of the Great Teacher. The founder of Christianity passes from the realm of the abstract into the domain of the real, the tangible.

In the "Life of Jesus" Renan combines those qualities which have made him one of the most stimulating of historians. We see in its pages a profound erudition which searches into meanings of the texts which contain the historical material—in this case the Gospels, the Old Testament prophecies, Jewish records, early Christian traditions, and the like — a logical alertness which enables him to induce conclusions of actual scientific value, an imagination which, tempered by criticism, fills up the gaps in his narratives, paints portraits, interprets symbols, and a style, simple, expressive, luminous. There is little wonder that such a subject, treated by such a man, should have produced a work of unusual power and steadily widening influence. The demand for the "Life of Jesus" was immediate and great. It pleased, to be sure, neither the strictly orthodox nor the skeptics, yet it gave light to many believers who sought for a more real foundation for their faith, and by its reverential reasonableness held many back from the aridity of agnosticism.

These results, however, which obtained with the moderate, were only an offense to the extremists of either party. In 1864 the Church authorities procured Renan's dismissal from his professorship and he was left dependent on his own resources. These had profited by the popularity of his last volume, and were sufficient to enable him to continue his scientific pursuits. His intellectual activ-

ity was not in the least lessened, and an article which soon
appeared in the *Revue des Deux Mondes* on the ultimate
reign of science through progressive evolution, a reign in
which the good and true will forever annihilate the evil
and false, proved to many of his countrymen a new incentive to virtue and self-sacrifice.

The "Life of Jesus" was the first part of a general
treatise on the origins of Christianity, which Renan now
prepared to continue. As he had visited Palestine in view
of his initial volume he now followed the journeyings of
the apostles over the Mediterranean. The results of this
journey, added to his usual scientific research and text
criticism—this time on the Acts of the Apostles and St.
Paul's Epistles—appeared in 1866 in "The Apostles,"
and in 1869 in "St. Paul." The historical value of both
works does not fall beneath the worth of their predecessors in the series, and Renan's interpretation given to the
services of St. Paul in rescuing the new religion from the
constraints of Judaism constitutes an important chapter in
the history of the early Church.

At the same time other interests were appealing to
Renan. The practical bent of his disposition had long
before drawn his attention to the study of political and
social conditions. In a collection of articles published in
1868 under the title of "Questions of the Day" he goes
so far as to discuss the state of public affairs in France.
He opposes the temporal power of the pope, supported at
that time by French bayonets, and criticizes the foreign
policy of the government. In 1869 he offered himself as
a candidate for the Corps Législatif on a platform of
peace and progress, freedom of the press and a continuation of the Empire. He was defeated by both a republi-

can and a conservative imperialist, but continued to advocate a constitutional monarchy. He was strongly opposed to the war with Prussia. He knew the Germans were superior to the French in military affairs as well as in science, and besides he wished to cultivate a national friendship with the people whose scholarship had formed so large a part of his own inspiration.

The Commune he detested. While it was sinking in blood, in May, 1871, he penned at Versailles the larger part of his "Philosophical Dialogues and Fragments." During the short period of the Franco-Prussian War he had been engaged in a patriotic controversy with his former idol, Strauss, and after the treaty of peace was signed, in 1871, he appealed to France to profit by her misfortunes and rise to better things. His ideal state now was a king upheld by a devoted aristocracy, and aided by men of learning. For universal suffrage, the suffrage of the *plébiscites*, he had learned to have little regard. Socialistic experiments, accompanied as they had been by violence and civil strife, he would guard against by a series of colonizing expeditions which should employ this dangerous energy in the useful task of subjecting inferior races to the rule of the higher.

In 1873 Renan continued his history of the origins of Christianity with a fourth volume, "The Antichrist," which dealt with the visit of St. Paul to Rome, Nero's persecution of the Christians, the belief that the emperor had not died, but would soon return from the East to harry them again—the Antichrist of St. John's Revelation—and finally the destruction of the Temple at Jerusalem, the last tie which bound Christianity back to Judaism. In 1877 a fifth volume appeared, on the composition of the Gospels by the converts of the apostles, "The Gospels and the Second Generation of Christians," and in 1879 a sixth, "The Christian Church," a history of the heresies following the composition of the Gospel according to St. John and of the persecutions under the Antonines. In the meantime, in 1875, he had recruited his wavering health by a trip to Sicily, had published (in 1876) his "Dialogues," written during the Commune, and composed a philosophical drama on democracy protecting science ("Caliban," 1878). The "Dialogues" once more affirmed his belief in evolution, a progress in which physics and chemistry would be leading factors, and in the resurrection of all consciences that had ever existed at the end of the world. There runs, however, through all these writings an ever-widening vein of pessimism. Is the final goal of nature really good, after all? Is it worth while to try to elevate the mass of mankind? Much of this discouragement was no doubt due to the Franco-Prussian War, which transformed in Renan's mind the intellectual German into a brutal warrior, and to the Commune, which had defiled by its very touch the principles of liberty, equality, and fraternity, it had so loudly advocated.

In 1880 Renan crossed the Channel for the purpose of delivering the annual lectures of the Hibbert Foundation. His subject was taken from the pages of the "Origins of Christianity." Soon after his return to France he issued the concluding volume of this series, "Marcus Aurelius" (1882), in which the reforms and the philosophy of the great emperor, his persecution of the Christians, the final constitution of the Church on the basis of the authority of the bishops, and the history of that Church in outline, are discussed, together with a prophecy that the Church will become independent of the state, and finally unite its most progressive children with liberal Protestants and Jews in a common, pure, and true religion.   Though his years were increasing, and his health waning, evidences of his literary and scholarly activity became greater and greater.   In 1883, at the age of sixty, he wrote the story of his early life up to the years which followed his separation from the Church ("Recollections of Childhood and Youth"), an autobiography where he shows the reasons for his change of faith.   In 1878 he had been elected to the French Academy, and during the eighties was more than once called upon to welcome still younger members. Two of his discourses on these occasions are especially noteworthy, one in 1882, greeting Pasteur, whose life devotion to science so much resembled his own, and one in 1885, congratulating De Lesseps on the achievement of the Suez Canal—which, however, he did not admit to be a work of peace, but rather a fresh cause for the rivalry of nations, who would make it their objective point in case of war.   He continued his philosophical dramas, in an Epicurean spirit, it must be admitted, which disconcerted the more serious of his admirers, translated the pessimistic book of Ecclesiastes, published new collections of essays, and delivered addresses, official and private.   In 1884 he was elected administrator of the Collège de France, and took up his residence in that building, where his receptions gathered together the artists and scholars of the French capital.   With a revival of interest in his native soil he attended a celebration held the same year in his honor at Tréguier, and soon afterwards purchased a summer residence on the coast of Brittany.

In this secluded spot, far away from the bustle of Paris,

he found leisure to plan the great work of his closing days, the "History of the People of Israel," which appeared in five volumes, from 1887 to 1894. The undertaking was a greater one than his "Origins of Christianity," for it covered the whole period comprised by the books of the Old Testament and their sequels down to the birth of Christ. But German criticism proved a more efficient aid here than in the former work, and Renan brought to it the same marvelous erudition, the same philosophical argumentation, and the same wealth of imagination which had characterized the history of the early Church. He affirms again the monotheistic religion of the Semites as opposed to the polytheistic worship of their Aryan neighbors, dwells on the strife which existed for centuries between the adherents of the Elohim, the myriad manifestations of the one divine presence, a universal deity, and the partisans of Jehovah, the national deity of Israel, whose attributes encouraged self-seeking, race prejudice, war with the foreigner, and abhorrence of his contact. It was two talented authors, representatives of each of these factions, who, in the ninth century before Christ, united the legends of the people with the traditions of their conquests into separate narratives tinged with their partisanship, and it is their accounts, combined with each other under the reign of Hezekiah, two centuries later, which form the greater part of Old Testament history.

But these records would have proved of little importance and would have passed into merited oblivion had they not been supplemented by the utterances of a new school of prophets which appeared near the beginning of the eighth century with the prophet Amos. Amos proclaims Jehovah a universal God, not a tribal,

Hebrew deity, a God who created the world and guides it, whose attributes are justice and mercy. Subsequent reactions of national feeling reduced the boundaries of this deity's beneficence, but the spirit of the prophets survived among the few, breaking out now and again, and culminating in the world-wide morality and religion of the last of their succession, the Messiah, the Prince of Peace. With him narrow Judaism was finally merged in the broader Christianity, which in turn will fade away before its descendant, Socialism. Liberty of the individual, which Jesus proclaimed, will remain, an acquired good, but its continuance will be bought by concessions granted by it to the rights of the community. In the future political and national questions will occupy less and less attention, social questions more and more.

It is significant of Renan's real nature that his great works end with a forecast of humanity's future. Like the great prophets of Israel, whom he so admired, his soul was only temporarily bowed down by sorrow and discouragement. In the preface to his ''Recollections of Childhood and Youth'' he had regretfully admitted the advent of the rule of the multitude, the ''Americanization,'' as he termed it, of the nations, but universal vulgarity once allowed he found in it a hope for the continuance of scientific investigation, of research after the truth, under better conditions than in the more aristocratic administrations of the past. In the body of the book, indeed, he had rather disclaimed any liberal views of government: ''I would willingly resign myself,'' he says, ''if the occasion should offer (and I must say that it grows more and more distant each day), to serve for the greater benefit of poor humanity, so wrecked at the present time, a tyrant who would be philanthropic, learned, intelligent, and liberal." And in the last year of his life, in an essay on God and the visible universe, while reaffirming that nothing within our finite comprehension reveals the intervention of a superior power into nature, he admits that there may be an infinite universe to which ours is subordinated, and in which the intervention of a God may be the rule. The "kingdom of God," foretold by Christianity, may become some day a reality, and the world now ruled by blind unconsciousness may in the future be governed by a consciousness which is supremely good and supremely just. Then wrong will be suppressed, and "every tear be dried. 'And God shall wipe away all tears from their eyes.' " Thus with hope for a future state in which he could not rightly believe, amid severe physical pains, but preserving the lucidity of his mental faculties to the last, Renan passed away in the Collège de France on October 2, 1892. A state funeral was accorded his remains, which were finally deposited in the Pantheon.

SELECTIONS FROM THE WRITINGS OF RENAN

Translations from "Recollections of Childhood and Youth"

[He is about to leave Issy for St. Sulpice. History and natural science studies.]

It was decided, therefore, that after my two years of "philosophy" I should enter the seminary of Saint Sulpice in order to study theology. The flash which had lighted up for a moment M. Gottofrey's mind [that Renan was no longer a Christian] had failed to produce any results. But to-day, at thirty-eight years of distance, I recognize the great penetration he showed. He alone was clear sighted, for he was a genuine saint. I surely regret now that I did not follow his admonition. I should have left the seminary without having studied Hebrew or theology. Physiology and the natural sciences would have attracted me. But—I can safely say it—the extreme ardor which those vital sciences excited in my mind makes me believe that had I cultivated them regularly I should have reached several of Darwin's results, of which I had a glimpse. I went to Saint Sulpice, I learned German and Hebrew; that changed everything. I was drawn towards the historical sciences, petty conjectural sciences which are undone as soon as formed, and which will be neglected in a hundred years. Indeed, we are witnessing the dawn of an age in which man will no longer accord much interest to his past. I am very much afraid that our exact contributions of the Academy of Inscriptions and Belles Lettres, destined to give a certain definiteness to history, will decay before they are read. It is through chemistry at one end of the ladder, through astronomy at the other, it is through general physiology especially that we really attain the secret of being, of the world, of God, as they wish to call him. My lifelong regret is that I chose for my studies a kind of research which will never reach conclusions, but will always remain in a state of interesting considerations about a reality gone forevermore. But so far as the exercise and pleasure of my thought were concerned, I certainly chose the better part. At Saint Sulpice, in fact, I was placed face to face with the Bible and the sources of Christianity. In the following account I will tell with what ardor I set about this study, and how by a series of critical deductions, which forced themselves onto my mind, the foundations of my life, such as I had understood it to be up to that time, were wholly overthrown.

From the Preface to the "Recollections of Childhood and Youth." On the Americanization of Europe and the Future of the Universe

On the whole, it is quite possible that the American kind of society, towards which we are advancing, whatever our form of government may be, will not be more unendurable for intellectual people than the social conditions we have passed through, which offered better guaranties. We will be able to make quite calm retreats for ourselves in such a world. "The era of mediocrity is beginning in all things," said recently a talented thinker (Amiel). "Equality engenders uniformity, and it is by sacrificing the excellent, the remarkable, the extraordinary that we get rid of the bad. Everything becomes less uncouth; but everything is more vulgar." At least we may hope that vulgarity will not turn persecutor of free thought so quickly. Descartes, in that brilliant seventeenth century, found himself nowhere so well off as at Amsterdam, because "everybody there being engrossed in trade" no one bothered about him. Perhaps general vulgarity will some day be the condition of the happiness of the elect. American vulgarity would not burn Giordano Bruno, would not persecute Galileo. We have no right to be very hard to suit. In the past, in the best of times, we have been no more than tolerated. We shall surely obtain this tolerance at least from the future. A limited democratic government is, as we know, prone to be vexatious. Still intellectual people live in America, provided they do not exact too much. "Touch me not," is all we must ask of democracy. We shall yet pass through many alternatives of anarchy and despotism before we find repose in that golden mean. But liberty is like truth. Almost no one cares for it for itself, and yet, on account of the impossibility of extremes, we always return to it.

Let us, then, without being disturbed, allow the destinies of the planet to be fulfilled. Our cries won't do any good; our ill humor would be out of place. It isn't certain that the earth will not fail of its destiny, as innumerable worlds have probably done. It is even possible that our times may be an epoch which is considered to be the highest point, beyond which humanity will only decline. But the universe does not know discouragement. It will begin again, and endlessly again, the ill-fated task. Each failure leaves it young, alert, full of illusions. Courage, courage, nature! Like the deaf and blind starfish, which vegetates at the bottom of the ocean, pursue thy obscure life labor. Be persistent. Repair for the millionth time the broken mesh of the net, make over the auger which bores to the last limits of the attainable the well whence living water will gush forth. Aim and aim again at the mark thou hast missed since eternity began. Try to steal into the imperceptible hole of the orifice which leads to another sky.

Thou hast infinite space and infinite time for thy experiment. When one has the right to make mistakes with impunity, success is always sure.

"*The Life of Jesus*"

(Dedication.)

To the pure soul of my sister Henrietta, dead at Byblos, September 24, 1861.

Do you remember, in the bosom of God, where you are resting, those long days at Ghazir, where alone with you, I wrote these pages inspired by the places we had visited together? Silent by my side you read over each page and copied it as soon as it was written, while sea, villages, ravines, mountains, unrolled themselves at our feet. When the blinding light had given way to the innumerable army of stars, your keen and subtle questions, your prudent doubts, would lead me back to the sublime object of our common thought. One day you told me you would love this book, in the first place because you had helped make it, and also because it pleased you. If you sometimes feared the narrow judgments of frivolous people on it, you were always sure that the souls of the truly religious would finally like it. In the midst of these sweet communings death struck both of us with his wing. The sleep of fever seized us both at the same hour. I awoke alone! . . . . You are sleeping now in Adonis's land, near holy Byblos, by the sacred waters where the women of the ancient mysteries came to mingle their tears. Reveal, good genius, to me whom you loved those truths which rule over death, prevent our fearing it, and almost make us love it.

From the Last Chapter of the "Life of Jesus." The Essential Character of Jesus' Work

Jesus' activity, as we have seen, was never exerted outside the circle of the Jews. Although his sympathy for all those scorned by the orthodox inclined him to admit pagans into the kingdom of God, although he resided more than once in pagan territory, and once or twice we find him in kindly relations with unbelievers, we may say that his entire life was passed in the little shut-up world where he was born. Greek and Roman countries did not hear of him. His name is not found in profane writers until a century later, and then in an indirect way, in connection with seditious movements provoked by his teaching, or persecutions of which his disciples were the object. In the bosom of Judaism even Jesus did not make a very lasting impression. Philo, who died towards 50 A.D., has no suspicion of him. Josephus, born in 37, and writing in the last years of the century, mentions his execution in a few lines, as an event of secondary importance. In the enumeration of the sects of his day he omits the Christians. . . . . The essential work of Jesus was to create a circle of disciples around him, in whom he inspired a limitless attachment, and in whose bosom he placed the germ of his doctrine. To have made himself loved "to such a degree that they did not cease to love him after his death," this is the master work of Jesus and the thing which struck his contemporaries the most. His doctrine was something so lacking in dogmatism that he never thought of writing it down or having it written down. Men became his disciples, not by believing this or that, but by attaching themselves to his person and loving him. Some sentences soon taken down from memory, and especially his moral type and the impression he had left were what remained of him. Jesus is not a founder of dogmas, a maker of symbols; he is the one who initiates the world into a new spirit. . . . . To cling to Jesus in view of the kingdom of God, that was what was first called being a Christian.

In this way we understand how pure Christianity, by an exceptional destiny, still presents itself at the end of eighteen centuries with the character of a universal and eternal religion. It is because in fact the religion of Jesus is in some respects the definitive religion. The product of a perfectly spontaneous movement of souls, freed at its birth from all dogmatic constraint, having struggled three hundred years for liberty of conscience, Christianity, in spite of the relapses which have followed, still reaps the fruits of this excellent origin. To be renewed it has only to revert to the Gospel. The kingdom of God, as we conceive it, differs notably from the supernatural apparition which the first Christians hoped to see burst forth in the clouds of heaven. But the sentiment which Jesus introduced into the world is truly ours. His perfect idealism is the highest rule for a self-renunciating and vir-

tuous life. He has created the heaven of pure souls where is
found what we in vain ask for from the earth, perfect nobility of
God's children, absolute purity, total separation from the world's
uncleanness, liberty finally which actual society excludes as an
impossible thing and which reaches its whole amplitude only in
the domain of thought.   The great master of those who take refuge
in this ideal kingdom of God is Jesus still.   He first proclaimed
the royalty of the mind.   He first said, by his acts at least, "My
kingdom is not of this world."   The foundation of true religion
is indeed his work.   After him nothing remains to be done but
develop and fructify.

The Final Paragraphs in "Marcus Aurelius."   On the World's Future

What is beyond all doubt is that whatever be the religious
future of mankind, Jesus' place in it will be very great.   He was
the founder of Christianity, and Christianity remains the bed of
the great religious stream of humanity.   Tributaries coming from
the most opposite points of the horizon have mingled there.   In
this meeting of waters no one source can now say, "This is my
tide."   But let us not forget the primitive brook of the origins, the
mountain spring, the headwaters, where a river which afterwards
became broad as the Amazon, at first ran along in a fold of
ground no wider than a step.   It is the picture of this head
stream that I have wished to draw, fortunate if I presented in its
truth the sap and the vigor there was on those high peaks, the
sensations, now warm, now icy, the life divine, the intercourse with
heaven!   The creators of Christianity rightly occupy the first rank
in the homage of humanity.   These men were very inferior to us
in their knowledge of the real, but they had no equals in conviction, in devotion.   And yet this is what founds things.   The
solidity of a structure is in proportion to the amount of virtue—
that is to say, of sacrifice—which has been placed in its foundations.   In this edifice which has been ruined by time what excellent
stones, moreover, which might be employed again just as they
are to the profit of our modern buildings!   What will teach us an
unshaken hope in a fortunate future better than messianic Judaism,

faith in a brilliant destiny for humanity, under the government of an aristocracy of just men? Is not the kingdom of God the complete expression of the final end which the idealist pursues? The Sermon on the Mount remains its finished code. Reciprocal love, gentleness, goodness, disinterestedness, will always be the essential laws of the perfect life. The association of the weak is the legitimate solution of the greater part of the problems which the organization of humanity raises. On this point Christianity can give lessons to all the ages. The Christian martyr will remain to the end of time the typical defender of the rights of the conscience. In short, the difficult and dangerous art of governing souls, if it is taken up some day, will be taken up on the basis of models furnished by the first Christian doctors. They possessed secrets which we shall learn in their school only. There have been more austere professors of virtue, more unyielding perhaps, but there have never been such masters of the science of happiness as they. The soul's delight is the great Christian art, to such a degree that civil government has been obliged to take precautions that men may not bury themselves in it. Fatherland and family are the two great natural forms of human association. Both of them are necessary, but they could not suffice. We must maintain by their side the place of an institution where one may receive nourishment for the soul, consolation, advice, where charity may be organized, where spiritual teachers may be found, a spiritual guide. This is called the Church. We shall never get rid of it, unless we wish to reduce life to a despairing aridity, especially for women. What we are concerned about is that ecclesiastical society may not weaken civil society, that liberty be one and undivided, that the Church does not wield temporal power, that the state pay no attention to it, either to control it or foster it. During two hundred and fifty years Christianity gave perfect models of these small and free associations.

BIBLIOGRAPHY

Ernest Renan. Sir M. E. Grant Duff.

Life of Ernest Renan. F. Espinasse.

Renan. F. Brunetière, in Warner's "Library of the World's Best Literature," Vol. XXI.

CHAPTER X

PASTEUR AND THE GERM THEORY

[Louis Pasteur, born at Dôle, December 27, 1822; educated at
Arbois (1829), Besançon (1839), and the École Normale
at Paris (1843); assistant professor of Chemistry in the University of Strassburg, 1849; full professor, 1852; dean of the
Faculty of Sciences at Lille, 1854; director of sciences at the
École Normale, 1857; professor of Geology and Chemistry at
the École des Beaux-Arts, 1863; professor of Chemistry at
the Sorbonne, 1867; pensioned by the government, 1875;
elected to the French Academy, 1881; Pasteur Institute
founded, 1888; died at Villeneuve l'Étang, September 28,
1895. Chief discoveries: Molecular dissymmetry of crystals,
1848; fermentations, 1857; spontaneous generations, 1862;
diseases of wine, 1865; silkworm disease, 1868; studies on
beer, 1876; vaccine virus, 1881; prophylactic for hydrophobia, 1885.]

While the nineteenth century witnessed the rapid
strides of the natural sciences the one nearest the heart
of humanity, the science of medicine, was advancing with
faltering steps. The reason for this lagging is now clearly
seen. For many centuries disease had been treated theoretically, with remedies prepared beforehand and applica-
ble to nearly all forms of illness. With the discovery of
the circulation of blood by William Harvey in the seventeenth century, observation began to be substituted for
theory. So fast as the minds of practitioners could be
freed from prejudice the symptoms of different kinds of
maladies were noted, and experiments tried to meet their

peculiar conditions. Though much good was accomplished in this way, by discontinuing the use of harmful prescriptions and allowing nature to follow her own course, though the patient in many cases was relieved from unnecessary torture and his vitality given a fair chance to assert itself, yet the disease was not stopped, nor even scotched in its first stages. In other words, the mere observation of the phenomena of disease and the deductions made from them produced really negative results. Something which should go behind the symptoms and reach their hidden causes was essential to any forward movement. So medicine was forced to wait on the progress of the other sciences, chemistry, biology, physiology, even physics, and it was only in the last half of the nineteenth century that these allies were ready to come to its aid.

In the light of these facts it should be no matter of surprise to us, that one of those investigators, who have most contributed to the advancement of medical knowledge in the past thirty years, should begin his career as a devotee of the natural sciences and always hold the official title of professor of chemistry, and that the discoveries and inventions which have entered into the daily life of nearly every household in Christendom should be made by a student whose researches were first directed towards problems of a purely theoretical nature. It is not necessary to name Louis Pasteur.

Pasteur was born in 1822 at Dôle, in the Jura Mountains, the son of a Napoleonic veteran, decorated on the battle-field, who had retired to the homely vocation of a tanner. When the child was two years old the family moved to Arbois, and it was there that he first attended school. For a while his father was more ambitious than he. He desired to see his son a teacher in this petty institution, but young Pasteur seemed to prefer an outdoor existence and the drawing pencil to the use of books. However, as he grew older his interest became awakened. When he reached the limit of instruction at Arbois he was sent to Besançon, where he took his baccalaureate in 1840. Appointed tutor in the school on graduation, he began to devote himself to mathematics, got all the chemistry which the teacher and the town apothecary could give him, and prepared for the examination in science at the École Normale at Paris. Failing in 1842 to pass with as high a grade as he wished he went to Paris, entered a private school, and in October, 1843, entered the École Normale with improved standing. His taste for chemistry had grown. The courses at the school and the Sorbonne were open to him. His toil was unremitting, his progress rapid.

One of the lecturers at the École Normale was devoted to the study of molecular physics, and communicated this enthusiasm to his pupil. With a mind full of the subject, the announcement in 1844 by the German chemist, Mitscherlich, of an unexplained difference in regard to the polarization of light between two apparently like substances, the paratartrate and the tartrate of soda and ammonia, attracted Pasteur to the investigation of crystals. Availing himself of experiments made on rockcrystal years before, he entered on a series of tests, and after long months of patient effort, discovered that the substances mentioned by Mitscherlich were not alike in the disposition of the atoms in their molecules. This discovery, which affirmed the theory of molecular dissymmetry, has proved of great value to chemical science, and a quarter of a century later led to the foundation of what is now called stereo-chemistry. Pasteur's results were made known in 1848. His three years at the École Normale had expired in 1846, but he had remained as assistant in the laboratory.

In 1848 he was appointed professor of physics at the Dijon lycée, but after three months' service was transferred to the University of Strassburg as assistant professor of chemistry. Here he continued his work on molecular dissymmetry, verifying with other substances the results already reached with soda and ammonia. All this study lay in the domain of theoretical science. But Pasteur's mind was such that practical results were quite sure to follow in the steps of theory. They came about in this way. A firm of chemists had noticed that impure tartrate of lime in contact with organic matter fermented in warm weather. Pasteur's attention being attracted to this fact, he began experimenting with one of the ammonia tartrates, and produced fermentation by mixing it with albumen. An examination of the mixture revealed the presence of a microscopic organism, small living cells, which were afterwards shown to produce the fermentation. Following up this test with a similar one on the paratartrate of ammonia, he discovered that the organism destroyed some of the crystals and did not affect others. This discovery has proved of great importance to the science of bacteriology, proving as it does that substances which are chemically alike may be very different physiologically.

Pasteur's practical bent was further stimulated by a change of residence. After being made full professor at

Strassburg in 1852, he was appointed, in 1854, dean of the Faculty of Sciences in a new institution at Lille, with the commission to organize the work. Lille is a manufacturing center, and Pasteur saw the advisability of bringing his school into touch with local industries. Among these latter was the manufacture of alcohol from beet root and grain. Pasteur at once offered a course of lectures on fermentation. He had already convinced himself that ferments, contrary to the generally received opinion, are living things, and the so-called ferments, as yeast, are really the especial food of ferments. The changes they produce in a substance, which often is apparently putrefying, are therefore not chemical but physiological. They are replete with life, not with death. Various investigations confirmed these opinions, especially one connected with the souring of milk. For in the solid matter which is deposited during this process, Pasteur found minute rod-like corpuscles, wholly unlike the yeast cells of alcoholic fermentation. Taking some of these corpuscles and placing them in a mixture of dissolved sugar, yeast, and chalk, he found that they multiplied and produced fermentation. Carrying on this process from one substance to another, but always providing the chemical element which gave the corpuscles food, he finally showed that brewer's yeast is a living organism, whose growth is accompanied by the conversion of sugar into alcohol and carbonic anhydrid. These conclusions on the fermentation of milk and alcoholic fermentation were published in 1860, and mark the first step in the science of bacteriology.

Meanwhile he had left Lille, in 1857, for his old institution, the École Normale, where he was made director of sciences, and where we have seen Thiers among his pupils. In one of the garrets of the school he had set up an apology for a laboratory. Pursuing his studies in fermentation, he had not only reached the results already noted, but had further demonstrated, by experiments on butyric acid, that exposure to the air, to a large supply of oxygen, stops the fermenting process in certain substances. The conclusion was at once drawn, that besides the living beings which need free oxygen in order to live, there are other beings whose power of respiration is such that they can live by robbing certain compounds of their oxygen, thus decomposing them. This class would be represented by the ferments, and the most active ferments are those which can live without free air. The tremendous part played by these micro-organisms, "microbes" as we now call them, was at once manifest. They destroy the old and produce the new, preserving the world from decay and death.

But Pasteur was now turned aside from following out the consequences of these great discoveries by matters of a minor though pressing importance. In the first place, he had to combat a revival of the theory of "spontaneous generation," which claimed that life could originate spontaneously. In 1860 the Academy of Sciences had offered this question as a subject for a prize competition. Pasteur set about the task of reaching a definite solution, and in 1862 demonstrated in the presence of the Academy itself that the theory was not tenable, and that substances subjected to certain temperatures come to show entire lack of life.

The same year of 1862 saw Pasteur once more occupied with the problem of fermentation, the vinegar vats of the manufactories at Orleans furnishing him the material for his researches.   He showed the vinegar-makers that the conversion of wine into vinegar was caused by a minute organism requiring free oxygen, which could be cultivated, and by its cultivation greatly reduce the time required for vinegar fermentation.   From experiments with vinegar he was naturally led to a consideration of the diseases which affect the production of its "raw material," wine.   The wine growers were having much difficulty with their vineyards.   The wine in many cases spoiled on their hands. Pasteur discovered in some wines, in addition to the regular yeast cells of fermentation, a microscopic organism which was absent from the good wines.   He suggested raising the wines thus affected to a certain temperature, which should be sufficient to stop the growth of the bacteria and yet preserve the native flavor of the wine.   This process of partial sterilization, now known by the term "Pasteurization," has already proved of the greatest benefit to humanity, notably in the case of milk.   And its application to provisions of a perishable nature may be said to be still in its infancy.

In 1863 Pasteur added to his position at the Ecole Normale the professorship of geology and chemistry at the School of Fine Arts.   The new post in no way interfered with his assiduous daily attendance at his laboratory, nor in the prosecution of his favorite studies.   But in 1865 he was called upon to give them up for the time being and begin another line of work.   The silkworm disease had attained the proportions of a national calamity in France.   The regions given over to the cultivation of raw silk had been practically ruined.   As long before as 1857 the government had sent Pasteur's old teacher at the Sorbonne, Dumas, to the stricken localities to examine into the situation. But he had been unable to suggest remedies. In 1865 the question again became urgent. Dumas had done his best. He fell back on Pasteur. The latter objected to abandoning his experiments on fermentation, but finally yielded to pressure, and once more shifted his specialty, this time to the field of entomology. He knew nothing at all about the subject, but profiting by the reports of predecessors and his own observation on the spot, he decided that the root of the trouble lay in minute corpuscles which were present in large numbers in the bodies of the diseased worms. How they came there was the question. Unexpected obstacles baffled for a while the investigator, and even turned him into the wrong way, but finally his persistent toil and concentration of purpose won the victory. He reached the conclusion that the disease was due to a parasite, that this parasite first existed in the moth which laid the eggs which hatched into worms. By pounding the body of the moth in a mortar, mixing the dust with water, and examining the liquid thus formed under a microscope he discovered the same organism which had been noticed in the worms. It was absent from healthy moths. All that was necessary, therefore, was to persuade the silkworm growers to examine the moths under a microscope and separate the healthy ones from the diseased. This is what is done to-day. In ferreting out the origin of this disease Pasteur discovered the existence of another, which attacks the worms after they have grown. For this also he suggested remedies.

Rewards followed the success of this work. In 1868 the University of Bonn conferred on him the honorary degree of Doctor of Medicine. The same year the Austrian government awarded him a prize which had been offered for the extermination of the disease among silk-worms, and in 1869 he was elected a foreign member of the Royal Society of London.   Napoleon III offered him the Prince Imperial's estate near Trieste for further experimentation with the worms, and in July, 1870, nominated him to the Senate of the Empire.   His book on "Silkworm Diseases," published in 1870, was dedicated to Empress Eugénie.

But such results had not been reached without much self-sacrifice.   In 1866 his wife and daughters had joined him at Alais, in southern France, near which town he was experimenting.   One of the children developed typhoid fever there and died.   In the autumn of 1868 anxiety over the outcome of the investigations, coupled with over-work, brought on an attack of paralysis, from the effects of which his body never fully recovered.   But his mind remained clear, and as soon as he could be moved, he insisted on returning to the field of action, where he directed his humanitarian campaign from his arm-chair. During the Franco-Prussian War, a war which inflicted such wounds on his patriotism that he formally requested the University of Bonn to take back the degree conferred on him in 1868, he was forced to remain inactive.   But his energy was only heightened by his involuntary vacation, and in the spring of 1871 he returned to his researches into fermentation.   The Commune held Paris.   He took refuge with an old pupil in the latter's laboratory at Clermont-Ferrand.   Partly actuated by a desire to contribute to the restoration of France, he now took up the subject of beer, and found out how to preserve its yeast pure and uncontaminated.   Further experiments in sterilization accompanied these studies, while the phenomena of fermentation were reviewed and explained, particularly in regard to the varying amounts of oxygen required in the fermentation of different substances.

We have reached the time when Pasteur was to give himself up to studies even more closely related to the health of man. It was evident that what had happened in the case of silkworms, a disease cured by the removal of the germ which caused the disease, could also happen in the case of mammals. That this deduction had long suggested itself to Pasteur's mind is proven by various allusions in his publications to the possibility of destroying infectious diseases. His studies on fermentation had aroused universal interest, and had led to many investigations and successful experiments, among which should be mentioned the antiseptic treatment of wounds in surgery, by which the harmful bacteria are made innocuous. He had also cultivated germs and transplanted them from one medium to another, as we have seen. Furthermore, during his long years of laboratory work he had come into the possession of apparatus of unusual efficiency and variety. So that when, in 1876, his attention was called to the prevalence of splenic fever in cattle by a monograph on the subject by the now famous German, Doctor Koch, he was quite prepared to push on the discoveries made by this younger student and his older predecessors.

For over twenty years it had been asserted that splenic fever was contagious, and that the seat of the contagion undoubtedly lay in small, rod-like bodies to be found in the blood of the infected animals. But these views were not generally accepted, and part of Pasteur's service was to lie in the way of proving them beyond a doubt. He does this by cultivating the bacillus of the fever and inoculating successive flasks of sterilized liquid with it. Traces of the microbe could be found even in the last and weakest of the inoculations. He then proceeded to further tests, which finally revealed in the blood of animals that had died of the fever another and more virulent bacillus. This newcomer would declare itself only a few hours after death, and would destroy the first bacillus. He also noted that this bacillus, while destroyed in turn by the oxygen of the air, could put out spores which resist the air's action. The report of these experiments was first given to the Institute in 1877, on which occasion Pasteur particularly emphasized the annihilation of one bacillus by another, a new step won in the domain of bacteriology. It is the bacillus which can do without free oxygen that triumphs. Pasteur had also noticed that the regular bacillus of the fever when inoculated into rabbits, sheep, and other animals invariably proved fatal, but had no effect on fowls. This peculiarity led him to the idea that this failure was due to the higher temperature of the blood of bipeds. He lowered this temperature artificially, and succeeded in proving that his conception was correct. The fowl died if left at low temperature, or recovered if gradually warmed to its normal.

Filled with these ideas, advancing from one step to another, Pasteur discovered the germ of puerperal fever. Koch's introduction of gelatine plates for the purpose not only of studying bacteria in a transparent medium, as had already been done, but also with the intention of isolating the microbes rendered all such experiments much easier of prosecution and gave them a great extension. Pasteur, however, was now deeply engrossed in the corollary of his theory, how to produce immunity from the virulence of these unwholesome organisms. Turning to fowl cholera he discovered the microbe which caused it, inoculated rabbits with it with fatal results, guinea pigs without harming them, but on reintroducing it from the pigs into the fowls found it had lost none of its activity. No progress had been made evidently. Vacation had come —it was the summer of 1880—and the laboratory was abandoned for a while. On Pasteur's return, some weeks later, it was found that many of his cultures were dead. Those which still lived he transplanted, but with poor results. The fowls remained healthy. It then occurred to him to inoculate the same fowls with new bacteria. They were not affected by them, while other fowls not previously inoculated, died of the disease. Here was a discovery, of which it remained to test the circumstances. The experiments which followed showed that the virus, if kept at a fairly high temperature, and exposed to the action of air, lost the malignity it retained away from free oxygen. Here was vaccine matter which possessed the power to transmit its weakened character. Fowls inoculated with it were but slightly affected, and proved immune to the attacks of the unmodified germ.

Encouraged by these results, Pasteur returned to his original proposition, the discovery of a vaccine for the cattle disease. This was a more difficult problem, for the spores put out by the splenic fever bacillus resisted the action of free oxygen. It was necessary to prevent this production of spores. Various tests were made. Experiment followed experiment. The "Master," as his assistants delighted to call him, became more and more preoccupied, more and more concentrated. Finally it was found that the virus did not form spores at a certain high temperature, that after a lapse of time it lost some of its power and transmitted this lower activity to other generations. Here was the vaccine. In February, 1881, the report was given to the Institute, and in May of that year the test was made on a large scale—with fifty sheep—near Melun. The verification was absolute, and the vaccination of cattle and sheep for splenic fever has since this date been extensively performed in France. Soon afterwards a vaccine for swine measles was obtained by passing its virus through rabbits, from one to another until its activity was lessened and it could be used on swine again for inoculation. On the other hand, if the same virus be passed through the bodies of successive pigeons it increases in virulence. It must be remembered that a great share of the actual labor of these experiments devolved on the "Master's" devoted assistants, among whom were counted some of the foremost scholars of the present generation in France.

From the disease of animals Pasteur rose, in 1881, to the diseases of man, or rather to a disease of both animals and men. He now possessed abundant leisure and means for prosecuting these more complicated researches. Already, in 1875, he had resigned his Sorbonne professorship, conferred on him in 1867, and was thus rid of even the somewhat perfunctory instruction the position had required. At the same time the National Assembly had recognized the value of his private work by granting him an annual pension of twelve thousand francs. In 1883 this sum was increased to twenty-five thousand, and its provisions extended to cover the lifetime of his wife and children. On the financial side, therefore, he had no cares, and it was with undivided attention that he now gave himself up to the study of hydrophobia. His choice of this somewhat unimportant malady was probably determined by the consideration that its causes could be discovered through experiments made on animals.

Various attempts to inoculate dogs with the disease met with but slight success. It was recognized that the seat of hydrophobia is located in the nervous system. Now, the center of the nervous system lies in the brain, and the best test of rabies cultivation would be to introduce the virus into the brain, an operation which would require trepanning. Out of dislike to cause suffering Pasteur hesitated before this act, and finally it was performed by his assistant, Doctor Roux, during his absence. Subsequent experiments showed that exposure to free oxygen, to a dry atmosphere, diminished the power of the virus, and that animals inoculated three times in daily succession with the virus, weakened in varying degrees, became immune to the disease. It was also proven that the vaccine process takes two weeks, and as hydrophobia in man requires a month or more for its development, there was no reason why prompt attention to the bites of rabid animals should not save the victims from serious consequences. In July, 1885, this conclusion was first verified in the person of a young Alsatian, who had come to Paris to be treated, and in October of the same year Pasteur felt authorized to make an official report to the Institute on the subject. Since that date patients have not been lacking, and the statistics show that immunity has been brought about in all but five per cent of the individuals thus treated.

The vaccine for hydrophobia was the last of the great

discoveries made by Pasteur himself. Though still comparatively young in years—he had but just passed his
sixty-second birthday—his constitution had been weakened by the arduous toil he had forced upon it, and his
nerves shaken by the anxieties attendant on the solution
and promulgation of his results. For his life had been
one of almost unceasing warfare. His conclusions had
been attacked again and again, each in turn as they appeared, by many of the most competent scholars of the
day. And this last battle was not the least severe. For
the solicitude with which he watched over each human
patient destroyed his rest, and caused disorders which
necessitated a journey to Italy for relief. Besides, in his
anxiety to relieve all victims of the fearful madness he
attempted cures which were hopeless from the outset,
failures that were magnified by his opponents in an
endeavor to hide his triumphs. Hugo's dictum that
"Old age has no hold on geniuses of the ideal" leaves
the nerves out of account. Pasteur returned indeed from
Italy, but his work as an experimenter was ended. Henceforth he must content himself as a scientist with the
wonderful researches in pathology and bacteriology which
his devoted career had done so much to set in motion.

Yet he had his reward. Not only did he live to see all
criticism confounded, but he knew the joys of popularity
and hero-worship. His investigations tended in such a
large degree towards practical and beneficial results that
all classes of society and all civilized peoples united in his
praise. Foreign nations vied with one another in bestow-
ing honors and dignities on him. Nor did his countrymen
lag behind. In 1881 he had been elected to the French
Academy, and his reception into that body in 1882 had

been signalized quite as much by his assertion of a belief in the supernatural, which his predecessor, the positivist Littré, had denied, as by the eloquent eulogy which Renan had pronounced on his work. A decade later, in 1892, on the occasion of his seventieth birthday, a jubilee celebration was held at Paris, which was attended by the President of the Republic and high state officials, the Institute of France in a body, deputations from the scientific societies and universities of France and Europe, and admirers of all ranks, who in the name of their constituent bodies presented to the distinguished Frenchman a medal provided by international subscriptions. But the greatest testimonial to his worth had already taken shape at Paris in the buildings of the Pasteur Institute.

The idea of this famous structure seems to have been suggested by the overcrowding of Pasteur's laboratory by patients attracted by the knowledge of the cure for hydrophobia. In 1886 a popular subscription to furnish more commodious quarters was planned, and was carried out in France and elsewhere with the greatest enthusiasm. Some three million francs were thus raised, of which some two million were used in construction. On November 14, 1888, the Institute was formally opened in the presence of a distinguished assembly. It is here that the bacteriological and pathological work of the nation now centers, directed by eminent specialists who have received their training from the master hand. It has a practical purpose also to prevent diseases by discovering the germs and the antidotes for them. The anti-toxin for diphtheria is one of the results already reached. Hydrophobia patients continue to be treated at the Institute, vaccine matter for the inoculation of cattle and hogs is prepared there, and Pasteur's studies on fermentations are carried on. The Institute also supports a journal, which contains reports of the experiments made by its officers and attendants.

All this preparation to extend the scope of his discoveries and the field of his influence Pasteur lived to see. His mind continued active and his interest in laboratory work unabated. But his bodily weakness grew. His jubilee answer to the addresses of congratulation was his last public utterance, and even this had to be read in his presence by his son. He lingered still for nearly three years. In September, 1895, paralysis reappeared. He died on the 28th of that month at Villeneuve l'Étang, an estate which had been assigned to him for experimental purposes by the French government. His remains were given a public funeral at Notre Dame in Paris. They have found an abiding resting-place at the end of a corridor in the Institute called after his name.

SELECTIONS

From the Discours de Réception, before the French Academy

[Pasteur affirms his belief in the supernatural.]

Science begets wonders every day. You have wished to bear witness once again to the deep impression which society, the habits of life, literature, receive in turn from so many accumulated discoveries. If you deigned to cast your glance on me the nature of my work doubtless spoke in my favor. In several places it is concerned with the manifestations of life.

By proving that up to the present time life has never been shown to man as a product of the forces which rule matter, I have been of service to the doctrine of spirituality, much neglected elsewhere, but assured at least of finding in your ranks a glorious refuge.

Perhaps you have also been well disposed toward me for having carried into this arduous question of the origin of the infinitely small an experimental rigor which has finally tired out contradiction. Let us, however, refer the merit of this to the severe application of the rules of the method which the great experimenters Galileo, Pascal, Newton, and their rivals have bequeathed to us for two centuries. Admirable and sovereign method which has, as constant guide and director, observation and experience, freed from all metaphysical prejudice, like the reason which sets them at work, a method so fruitful that superior minds, dazzled by the conquests which the human intelligence owes it, have thought it could solve all problems. . . . .

What is there beyond this starry vault? Other starry heavens. Well, and beyond? The human mind, urged by an invincible force, will never cease to ask itself: What is there beyond? Suppose the mind stops somewhere in time or space? As the point where it stops is only of a finite greatness, greater only than all those which have come before it, the mind hardly begins to contemplate it before the implacable question returns, and returns again, without the mind being able to make its cry of curiosity cease. It is of no use to answer: Beyond are spaces, times, or limitless greatnesses. No one understands these words. He who proclaims the existence of the infinite—and no one can escape from it—accumulates in this affirmation more of the supernatural than exists in all the miracles of all religions. For the notion of the infinite has this double character, it forces itself upon our mind and yet is incomprehensible. When this notion takes possession of the understanding we have only to bow before it. At this moment of keen anguish we must ask our reason to pardon us. All the springs of intellectual life threaten to relax. We feel ourselves on the point of being seized by Pascal's "sublime madness." This notion, which is positive and primordial, positivism gratuitously puts aside, together with all its consequences on the life of society.

Reply of Renan to Pasteur on the Same Occasion

We are quite incompetent, sir, to praise what makes your true glory, those admirable experiments by which you attain even the limits of life, that ingenious way of questioning nature which has availed you so many times the clearest answers from her, those precious discoveries which are every day transformed into 'conquests of primal importance for humanity. You would repudiate our eulogies, accustomed as you are to value the judgments of your peers alone, and in the scientific debates which so many new ideas excite, you would not wish to see literary appreciations come to mingle with the suffrages of the scientists whom the fraternity of glory and labor brings near to you. Between you and your learned rivals we may not intervene. But outside the substance of the doctrine, which is not in our province, there is a school, sir, where our acquaintance with the human mind gives us the right to express an opinion. There is something which we can recognize in the most diverse applications, something which belongs in the same degree to Galileo, Pascal, Michael Angelo, Molière, something which causes the poet's sublimity, the philosopher's profundity, the fascination of the orator, the divination of the scientist. That common base of all beautiful and true works, that divine flame, that indefinable spirit which inspires science, literature, and art we have found, sir, in you. It is genius. No one has traversed with so sure a step the circles of elementary nature. Your scientific career is like a luminous trail in the great night of the infinitely small, in those outermost abysses of being where life is born.

How fortunate you are, sir, to thus reach through your art to the very sources of life! Yours are admirable sciences! Nothing is lost in them. You will have set a valuable stone in the foundation of the eternal edifice of truth. Among those who give themselves up to the other departments of mental work, who can have the same assurance? M. de Maistre somewhere paints modern science "under the scanty garb of the North, ... its arms laden with books and instruments, pale with vigil and labor, dragging itself, stained with ink and panting, along the road of truth, always bending towards the ground its forehead furrowed with algebra." How well you have acted, sir, not to stop short at this preoccupation of a nobleman! Nature is plebeian. She wishes us to work. She likes callous hands, and reveals herself to anxious brows only.

Your austere life, wholly consecrated to disinterested research, is the best answer to those who consider our century cut off, as it were, from the great gifts of the soul. Your laborious assiduity would not know diversion or repose. Receive the reward for this in the respect that surrounds you, in that sympathy, the manifestations of which appear to-day in such great numbers about you, and above all in the joy of having done your work well, of having taken your place in the first rank of that chosen company, which assures itself against oblivion by a very simple means, by creating works which last.

BIBLIOGRAPHY

Louis Pasteur, his Life and Labors. By his Son-in-law. Translated by Lady Claude Hamilton, with Introduction by John Tyndall.

Pasteur. Percy Frankland and Mrs. Percy Frankland (Century Science Series).

The Life of Pasteur. R. Vallery-Radot. Translated by Mrs. R. L. Devonshire.

FERDINAND MARIE DE LESSEPS

CHAPTER XI

DE LESSEPS AND INTER—OCEANIC CANALS

[FERDINAND MARIE DE LESSEPS, born at Versailles, November
19, 1805; educated at Paris; entered public service, 1823;
vice-consul at Alexandria and Cairo, 1832–1837; consul at
Malaga and Barcelona, 1839–1848; minister to Spain, 1848;
retired, 1849; efforts to build Suez Canal, 1854–1859; construction of the canal, 1859–1869; freedom of the city of London, 1870; Panama Canal Company, 1879; construction of
the Panama Canal, 1881; elected to the French Academy,
1884; failure of the Panama Canal Company, 1888; died at
La Chesnaie, December 7, 1894.]

Perhaps the most striking result of the practical applications of science in the nineteenth century is seen in the
inventions which shorten distance. The steam engine,
the electric telegraph, the telephone, all tend to a common
purpose, to put men living in different localities into rapid
communication with one another. In the twentieth century this movement is continuing with ever-increasing
intensity. Faster trains, faster steamboats, faster street
cars, more speedy electrical transmissions, are demanded
and supplied. Humanity would seem to be engaged in
one absorbing endeavor to annihilate time and space.
This purpose has always prevailed. Succeeding generations throughout time have been coming more and more
into closer relations among themselves. But while once
such quickening of speed was arithmetical, it now might
be fairly termed geometrical. And one of the most evi-

dent proofs of this heightened acceleration is offered by the building of isthmian canals.

The idea of piercing necks of land which separate navigable bodies of water is not a new one. Indeed, it is quite probable that it presented itself quite as forcibly to the peoples of the most remote civilizations as it does to our own. More forcibly perhaps, for the perils of navigation were much greater in the distant past, and capes were not doubled with impunity. So the Greeks looked with longing eyes at the narrow ledge of rock which separated the Ægean Sea from the Gulf of Corinth, and the conquerors of the East at the stretch of sand between the Red Sea and the Mediterranean. This latter obstacle was indeed overcome. Rameses II of Egypt, the probable Pharaoh of the Jewish oppression, is credited with a waterway dug from the delta of the Nile to the Red Sea. Centuries later, when the sands of the desert had partially choked its channel, it is said that Darius I of Persia cleared and used it. Then, in the Christian era, after the death of Mohammed, when Moslem invaders attacked Egypt, its bed was once again restored. But afterwards one of the rulers of the land wilfully filled it up, and it remained abandoned for more than a thousand years. The eighteenth century saw the birth of a short-lived project to utilize it again. And finally, when western enterprise reached the East, in the person of Napoleon Bonaparte, a French engineer, Lepère, was asked to report on the feasibility of reviving the old canal. He claimed that either this could be done or that a new passage could be cut from sea to sea. Nothing, however, came of this report. Later engineers studied the question at various times without tangible results, until at last it came to the attention of Ferdinand de Lesseps.

This future canal-builder came of enterprising blood. His father was in the diplomatic service of France, and had been consul in Egypt. His uncle was a sailor, had visited the northern coast of Asia, and returned to France through Siberia. His mother was of Spanish origin, a great-aunt of the future Empress Eugénie. Ferdinand himself was born at Versailles in 1805, followed as a child his father to an Italian consulate (at Leghorn), but returned to study at the College of Henry IV, in Paris. At the age of eighteen he was ready to begin life, and entered government employ in the commissary department of the army. Two years later, in 1825, he was attached to the French consulate at Lisbon, where his uncle was in charge. In 1828 he was again at Paris, in the department of foreign affairs. In 1829 he was made assistant to the vice-consul at Tunis, under his father, who was consul general. In 1832 he was transferred to Alexandria as vice-consul, and for the next five years occupied this post or a similar one at Cairo, distinguishing himself for his energy and alertness, and the excellent administration of his office during a severe pestilence. During this residence he had become acquainted with the views of Napoleon's engineer, Lepère, and had contracted a firm friendship with the young prince, Said Pasha, whose father had profited by the good offices of the elder De Lesseps when he was consul at Cairo in 1803.

Returning to France at the end of 1837, De Lesseps was appointed consul at Rotterdam, Malaga, and Barcelona, in succession. At the last named place he gave new proofs of his activity and courage in protecting during a civil war all who put themselves in his care. For this praiseworthy conduct he was publicly thanked by the city of Barcelona, his own and foreign governments, who conferred various orders on him as tokens of their regard. In 1848, in the first months of that Republic which had displaced Louis Philippe, De Lesseps became minister to Spain. One of his official acts in this new post was to intercede for some friends of Eugénie de Montijo (later Empress Eugénie), who had been sentenced to death for mutiny. Recalled at the end of the year, he was intrusted with a mission to the Roman republic, just established. Louis Napoleon, then President of France, expected duplicity on the part of his agent. But De Lesseps proceeded according to the letter of his instructions, and tried to induce the Italian republicans to consent to the presence of the French troops which had been sent to protect the person of the pope. His acts, however, were neutralized by the French general in command, who was following secret instructions from Louis Napoleon, and De Lesseps asked to be relieved of his mission. On his arrival at Paris his management was made the subject of an official inquiry, which resulted in his condemnation. He retired at once from the service of the state and began to occupy his leisure with studies on agriculture. It was during this period of retirement that his plan of piercing the Isthmus of Suez was matured.

The general trend of De Lesseps's official career—so suddenly terminated—shows a character which was unusually open, straightforward, and self-sacrificing. Several times during his consular residences, particularly in Egypt and Spain, he had exposed his health and reputation to rescue others from disease or violence. He was a man who seems to have always acted on the principle of service to his fellows, whatever the consequences to himself, and as we have seen in the instance of the double dealing of the French government with the people of Rome, he could not be brought to deception, even though his own future were at stake. He began his real life as a builder of canals with clean hands and an honest purpose.

The five years (1849–1854) which he passed on his farm in the old province of Berry were employed in acquiring information regarding commerce and transportation. Excited by Lepère's report, instigated by other developments, as Fourier's writings, the engineers' experiments, and a project advocated in the late forties by the followers of Saint Simon, the socialist, he became fully possessed of the idea that a canal should be cut through the Isthmus of Suez; that it should be a maritime canal, from sea to sea, and that it should be level, without locks. These points are important because their justification when put into execution at Suez involved the later failure at Panama. Furthermore, at the rate at which traffic was increasing the canal would prove a financial success almost at the start. These views he submitted to the Sultan of Turkey in 1852, who returned them after a courteous examination. But in 1854 the way was opened. The Viceroy of Egypt died, and Said Pasha, De Lesseps's young friend of the thirties, ruled in his stead. In answer to a letter of congratulation the new Viceroy invited De Lesseps to visit him. The visit was paid. Royally welcomed, the visitor did not delay in laying his plan of a canal before the new sovereign. The latter called his generals into consultation, and as they were already favorably disposed towards the foreigner because of his feats at horsemanship—so De Lesseps himself says—they agreed in advising the concession to dig the canal. It was officially granted on November 30, 1854.

It was now in order to survey the route and raise money for the undertaking. De Lesseps and his friends provided for the preliminary work, and when this fund was exhausted the Egyptian government came to the rescue. But the sanction of Turkey, Egypt's over-lord, was necessary, and owing to the opposition of England, then all-powerful at Stamboul, some time elapsed before a tacit permission could be secured. De Lesseps was everywhere, at Constantinople, Paris, London, where he argued long and eloquently with Lord Palmerston, appealed to the British public, and formed an international commission to look into the matter, returned to France, to England again, saw the Queen and Prince Albert, made addresses, wrote letters, interviewed statesmen and rulers until all Europe but Great Britain was on his side. Yet this attitude of the insular power now began to work in his favor. The enterprise came to be regarded in France as a patriotic one. Subscriptions to the company flowed in. Nearly twenty million dollars were raised there and elsewhere on the Continent, while the Khedive of Egypt advanced one-half that sum, and a like amount was placed in the other markets of Europe and in the United States, which had supported the project from its inception. In all, four hundred thousand shares of stock were issued at one hundred dollars a share, including the original shares of the preliminary survey. Actual work was begun without receiving the Sultan's permission, which came several months later, and on April 25, 1859, De Lesseps himself, in the presence of engineers and workmen, gave the first blow with the pick and turned the first shovelful of earth on the Mediterranean side of the canal, at a spot now called after the Viceroy, Port Said.

Thousands of laborers were soon swarming along the route. In 1862 a canal was completed, which brought Nile water to the middle of the isthmus, and in November of that year the Mediterranean was allowed to flow along the newly dug bed to Lake Timsah. Dredging machines had been invented for the undertaking. All was going well, when the friendly Khedive died, in January, 1863. Under his successor, Ismail Pasha, also well disposed, it was argued by Turkey that the work was being done by forced labor, contrary to the law of the land, and a demand was made for this compulsion to cease, and a concession of the land bordering the canal to be made by the company. The whole matter was finally submitted to Napoleon III to arbitrate. In 1864 a decision was reached which compromised all the points involved, and the permission for the construction of the waterway was embodied in a firman of the Sultan, issued March 19, 1866. But from 1864 on the work had been vigorously pushed, and on November 17, 1869, in the presence of many European sovereigns and diplomats and a large concourse of visitors from all parts of the world, the imperial yacht of France bearing the Empress Eugénie, long bound to De Lesseps by ties of gratitude for his mediation while minister to Spain, steamed into the cut at Port Said, and escorted by other royal yachts and men of war, proceeded by slow stages to Suez.

De Lesseps's success, his triumph over so much political opposition—for the obstacles raised by nature were few—made him the hero of the day. It also brought him many honors and decorations, including one even from England. A visit paid to that country in 1870 was turned into a popular ovation, and on July 30 he was awarded the unsuual distinction of the freedom of the city of London. But in one respect his plans had lacked exactness, the expense. The canal had cost fifteen million dollars more than the estimates—a sum which had been raised by issuing bonds. The receipts for the first few years of operation proved unequal to meeting the interest thus pledged, and in 1874 the sum in arrears was added to the capital stock. In November, 1875, the British government bought the Khedive's shares for twenty million dollars, which, however, represented but a fraction of the eighty millions and over the canal is supposed to have cost Egypt. Political susceptibilities were aroused by this transaction, in Russia as well as in France. But nothing of a serious nature followed.

In 1882, on the occasion of Arabi's rebellion, England felt called upon to insure navigation through the canal for herself, bombarded Alexandria, and occupied Egypt. France unfortunately declined to share in the responsibilities which the pacification of the country would incur, and taking advantage of the poor management of the company, a meeting of English merchants was held in May, 1883, to consider the construction of another waterway through Egypt. But De Lesseps was enabled to come to an understanding with the English government, and in 1884 improvements were begun on the bed of the canal which resulted in widening and deepening it, and the reduction of the time of transit to less than twenty hours. In

December, 1888, after six years of negotiations, the neutrality of the canal and its outlets was guaranteed by the powers of Europe. Since 1880 traffic has increased to such an extent that large dividends have been paid, and the market value of the stock has risen to eight times its face value.

Meanwhile De Lesseps's activity had not been restricted to his duties of the presidency of the Suez Canal Company. In 1873 he was working upon the project of a railroad through Central Asia, which was submitted to Russia, but declined. He also interested himself in the scheme of turning part of the Desert of Sahara into an inland sea, which later surveys have shown impracticable, and gave his influence to the opening up of the Congo under the leadership of the King of Belgium. But another idea was nearer to his heart. He had joined the Mediterranean to the Red Sea and opened a pathway between West and East. He aspired to connect the Atlantic with the Pacific, and complete his cutting of the globe in half.

The idea of piercing the Isthmus of Panama had haunted mariners and idealists ever since the voyages of Balboa in discovery of the Pacific Ocean. Routes by Darien, Nicaragua, and Tehuantepec were planned on paper time and again during the sixteenth and seventeenth centuries. In the nineteenth the notion was vigorously revived. A canal through Nicaragua was seriously considered in 1850, so much so that when Said Pasha announced the Suez concession to the foreign representatives at Cairo, on his accession to power in 1854, he said to the American consul: "We are going to start an opposition to the Isthmus of Panama, and we shall be done before you." He was right. Work had not been even begun at Panama when Suez was already an accomplished fact. In 1870 a report had been presented to the American government favoring a canal with locks at Panama. In 1875 and 1876 successive international congresses had sanctioned engineering expeditions to Central America, and on May 15, 1879, at a new session of the congress, presided over by De Lesseps, and attended by many Americans from the north and south, the whole matter was taken up afresh, the different routes discussed at length, and the report of the French engineer, Bonaparte Wyse, which outlined a canal at Panama, was adopted. Wyse's scheme utilized the Chagres River, tunneled the Cordilleras, and reached the Pacific by the valley of the Rio Grande. This route had been favored by De Lesseps because it was shorter, because the Nicaragua route was exposed to earthquakes, and also because the latter route required locks, which in the opinion of De Lesseps the Panama did not. In other words, without personal inspection, guided simply by logic, he decided that what had been done at Suez could be done elsewhere, whatever the physical differences, and his prestige decided the votes of the congress.

It must be remembered that at the time of this decision "The Great Frenchman," as he was now dubbed by Gambetta, had more than passed his threescore and ten. His physical strength, developed so well by the athletic pursuits of his early years, and preserved by his open-air life, had fortified that self-confidence which the opening of Suez in the face of ill-boding prophecies and opposition had abundantly justified. He had always been right. He could not conceive at the age of seventy-three that he could err.   A glamour surrounded him.   He was looked upon very much as a wizard, capable of overcoming nature.   No doubt the touch of his wand would subdue the Chagres and open the rocks of the Cordilleras. And so the congress, charmed by him, adopted his views. A Universal Inter-Oceanic Canal Company was incorporated on October 20, 1879, which took over concessions granted by the United States of Colombia to Wyse.   No time was lost.   Subscriptions to stock were immediately opened.   But the public was as yet uninformed about the project, and failed to respond.

De Lesseps started for the American isthmus.   His young daughter formally gave the first blow on the excavation on January 1, 1880.   After a hasty inspection he estimated that the cost would be some one hundred and seventy million dollars, and hurried back to France by the way of the United States, where he was given the opportunity to appeal to the good will of Americans, and their financial assistance at dinners held in his honor.   Reaching home after this somewhat spectacular journey he again called on the savings of France to the extent of one hundred million dollars.   His name was one to conjure by.   The profits from Suez were now becoming evident. The loan was covered several times, and on February 1, 1881, work was actually begun on the isthmus.

The difficulties of the enterprise soon became manifest. The estimates proved far below the actual expenses, and in September, 1882, an issue of bonds was made which realized some twenty-two million dollars.   The same month a severe earthquake threw doubts on the availability of this route too, and later in the season the contractors canceled their contract.   New contracts were let, a new issue of bonds followed, in 1883, and work was vigorously pushed. Still the expenses grew. Not only was the nature of the soil and the climate of the locality hostile to invasion, but moderation was lacking in the supply of incidentals and accessories, such as luxurious quarters for the engineers, staffs of useless officials, and even private grounds constructed out of the company's treasury. In 1885 another loan was made. In 1886 the French government sent a special agent to the isthmus to inspect the condition of affairs. His report was so unfavorable, particularly in its condemnation of the waste everywhere visible, that the Assembly refused its permission to raise more money by a lottery scheme.

In November, 1887, De Lesseps at last renounced the idea of a canal at tide level, and contracted with the celebrated engineer, Eiffel, for the construction of several locks. Money, however, was not forthcoming, and disaster seemed inevitable. To avert it a regular campaign was planned at home. Newspapers were heavily subsidized or menaced—for the number of stock and bond holders in France was very large—deputies were influenced by every means that could be devised, and under this pressure the Assembly, in 1888, passed a bill which authorized the company to place a lottery loan. But the loan, when issued, was not covered, and in December, 1888, the company suspended payments. In February, 1889, a receiver was appointed to take charge of its affairs. Work now ceased. Distress ensued among the workmen on the isthmus, and accusations against the management began to be heard in France. Finally, after many months of debate and petitioning, the Assembly took up the matter in January, 1892. In Sep-

tember of that year some of the deputies who had voted for
the lottery loan of 1888 were alleged to have been bribed.
In November De Lesseps and his fellow directors were
cited to appear before the civil authorities for malversa-
tion, and in February, 1893, he was judged guilty of the
charge.

The condemnation struck a defenseless head. The
aged engineer had never rallied from the shock of the
company's failure, and early in 1892 had fallen into a
state of numb senility, of somnolence, from which it was
almost impossible to arouse him. He had been taken
from Paris to his country-seat of La Chesnaie, and was
not present at the court either during the trial or on the
day of sentence. Nor is it believed that he knew anything about the criminal proceedings which were carried
on against him. His son Charles exposed himself on all
occasions to save his father, and perhaps assumed responsibilities which should have been borne by the latter. The
whole family keenly felt the disgrace of its position, but
did not relax in its devotion to its head. Another year
and more passed. The Great Frenchman's vigorous
frame yielded slowly to the attacks of time, and it was
only on December 7, 1894, at the age of nearly fourscore
years and ten, that he breathed his last, far away from the
scenes of his triumphs and defeat.

But the last decade of his life had not been one of constant disappointment. Though it must have been plain as
early as 1882 that the Isthmus of Pánama was not to be
conquered as easily as Suez, yet De Lesseps's optimism
was such, and his physical condition so sound, that he
apparently felt few misgivings. The public still adored
him. In 1884 the popular voice had voted him into the

French Academy, in spite of his entire lack of literary work, and his reception in 1885 had been an event, marked by the eloquence of Renan, who officially welcomed him. In 1887 the French government had even intrusted him with a secret mission to Berlin. Always his figure had been one of the prominent ones at Paris. At the age of eighty and more it was one of the morning sights, at the Place de la Concorde, to see De Lesseps on horseback leading a bevy of his children, mounted on ponies and fillies of different sizes, on a canter towards the Bois de Boulogne. And when the evil days came, though technically a criminal, few believed he had consciously done wrong. He was sanguine, absolutely self-confident, impatient of opposition. It is quite certain also that he was averse to the consideration of details. His vague estimates and hurried inspection show this. And then he was old, and had a right to lean on younger shoulders. But he risked his fortune as well as the savings of his compatriots. All he possessed seems to have gone into the enterprise. Panama swallowed Suez, and it was the latter company which came to the aid of his impoverished family.

Now it is apparent that his eclipse was only temporary. His failure is dead. It may be even changed to victory by the completion of the undertaking which caused it. His success lives. His statue cast in bronze and erected in 1899 near Port Said perpetuates the good he accomplished in the Old World. And it may be that in the New those prophetic words will some day come true which were uttered in 1896, at the reception of his successor into the French Academy: "Yes, the interrupted work will be begun again and finished. By whom and for whom? Political interests and passions will perhaps decide. But the day when the first flags shall cross the space which separates the two oceans—forgetting the failings of age and the slights of fortune, misfortunes, and faults, the entire world will remember that the man who had taken up the idea of Leibnitz and Goethe, in order to accomplish it for the profit of mankind, was he whom a popularity that was universal had named 'The Great Frenchman.' "

SELECTIONS

From the Speech of Anatole France on his Reception into the French Academy as the Successor of De Lesseps.
His Character

I must finish my purpose and follow M. Ferdinand de Lesseps in the last years of his life. When he was near to death he was smitten by a misfortune which had the extent of a public misfortune. The disaster was great, like the dream which had preceded it. The enterprise of the inter-oceanic canal crumbled to dust; its ruins still breathe forth groans. Here is neither the place nor the time to consider them. You do not expect me to search into their causes. Scarcely am I allowed to point out the most general among them, and to say that in France the slow, concealed, sometimes obscure, but constant and sovereign, will which sustained the work of Suez was no longer there to withstand the violent blows of passion, instinct, and chance in order to defend a new enterprise, more adventurous than the first, against itself, and give it moderation; and that in the weak, diffuse, and changing management of public affairs nothing was left which was henceforth capable of restraining the covetousness of a crowd of financiers, adventurers, and political robbers, nor of stopping that instinctive panic of the mob which upsets everything in a moment. Everything gave way. Conquered by age, overwhelmed by the blow which struck him, but retaining (I think I know this is so) all his clearness of mind, M. de Lesseps knew the extent of his misfortune. In the hour which was tragic for his glory and his name, alone among his own in that rustic dwelling of La Chesnaie, where almost half a century before he had traced on a chart the little line which was to unite two worlds, feeble now, inert, afflicted, pulling up over his shivering knees his traveling rug, the great traveler was dying in silence. But one day on his dry cheeks they saw tears flowing.

Ferdinand de Lesseps finished dying December 7, 1894. I have been obliged to show him to you still laden with the faults which time will carry away. Such a man as I have made him appear to you, such as he was, imprudent, rash, too trustful in himself and his long good fortune, but generous, great, full of goodness, force, and courage, sympathizing with the human race, capable above all men of acting and inciting action, he worked on vast and peaceful tasks all his life, and won his place among the élite of useful men by hard toil. What he did is immense and good. He opened an outlet for the West, which was compressed in too tight limits. He blazed new ways for energy, he gave to the purposes of men causes for acting usefully in concord and harmony. Such a man has but one judge, the universe. He served the interests of humanity. Grateful humanity will keep for him the names of benefactor and friend. And his image, erected at Suez on the wall of the canal, will be saluted through the ages by the flags of the nations.

De Lesseps's Speech at the New York Dinner of March 1, 1880, as Reported in The Tribune

I should weaken the force of the eloquent words which your president has so kindly spoken in my favor, if I added a word to his admirable discourse. He has spoken like a true American, and has touched upon my project from a truly American point of view. I do not desire to enter upon a discussion of the questions he so gracefully and yet so forcibly touched upon, but as a Frenchman, I wish to add just one word. In our negotiations with reference to the opening of the new canal of Panama, for which I have the concession of the Government of Colombia, I formally declared that I had no political interest in the matter, and did not seek to further the particular interest of my own country. I frankly state this now, and I will say to the President of the United States, when I meet him in Washington on Thursday, that if ever any difficulty arises in regard to the control of this canal, I myself will carefully watch over the interests of the United States.

The United States ought to take a prominent part in this matter, and I sincerely trust they will. Science has pronounced this canal possible, and I am the servant of science. I will carry out this work, and make America Queen of the Seas.

I present my thanks to this assembly for its very gracious reception, and in the recollections of my visit to this great Republic this gathering will be one of the most prominent and pleasant features. I leave this city shortly and shall visit in turn Washington, Philadelphia, Boston, Chicago, and San Francisco, to lay before your people the merits of my project. I shall state frankly in those cities what I have stated here, and if it is as courteously received as in New York, the success of my undertaking will be assured. It is to the best interests of America and to her future prosperity that this enterprise will chiefly tend, and she ought, and I trust will, make her contributions toward the necessary outlay adequate to the immense advantages which are bound to accrue to her from its success. Gentlemen, I thank you.

BIBLIOGRAPHY

Recollections of Forty Years. Ferdinand de Lesseps. Translated by C. B. Pitman.

The Life and Enterprises of Ferdinand de Lesseps. G. Barnett Smith.

See also *Atlantic Monthly*, Vol. LXXVI, pp. 285 ff.; *The Chautauquan*, Vol. XVI, pp. 58 ff.

Date Due